ADVANCE PRAISE FOR THE BOOK

"An extremely well researched work on the evolution of Pakistan's Deep State, especially its new psy-war thrust under the Inter Services Public Relations, which makes it essential reading for Pakistan watchers."

Rana Banerji, Special Secretary (Retd),
Cabinet Secretariat

"A deep state is known to be a power centre; a state within a state which exercises authority beyond the ordinary and well in excess of the legally elected or appointed entity. In the case of Pakistan the deep state oversees the all-important domain of Indo Pak relations and determines the degree of hostility that it must invest in for the survival and enhancement of power of its own constituents. Jyoti M. Pathania unsheaths the shroud under which Pakistan's deep state has existed all these years and allows us a deep insight into its world of intrigue and subterfuge......"

Lt Gen **Syed Ata Hasnain**, PVSM, UYSM, AVSM, SM, VSM & BAR (Retd),
Former GOC 15 Corps (Kashmir)

"This timely volume deftly unpacks the concept of the 'Deep State' illustrating its manifestations and avatars in diverse historical and geographical contexts. Drawing on over two decades of intense research the author offers a fascinating account of its pervasive influence in the 'uniformed democracy' of Pakistan; how its ideological and propaganda tools, modes of coercion, intimidation and undermining of institutions conspire to persistently erode civilian authority in that country. The role of the ISI and its perceptions of National Security playing out to undermine prospects for peace on the subcontinent, is persuasively presented. An absolute must-read, for all interested in contemporary geopolitics and the continuing challenges to democracy in this century from the Praetorian weltanschauung."

Prof (Dr.) **Meenakshi Gopinath**, Padma Shri, Director, Women in Security
Conflict Management and Peace and Chair, Centre for Policy Research, New Delhi

"It is the most interesting and timely book that unravels the puzzle of the existence of state within a state as it exists not only in authoritarian but even in the so-called democratic regimes. The larger than life image of ISPR has been researched extensively for the first time by focussing on the deep state diktat in Pakistan. Their revisionist, strategic goals have resulted in the stalemate in the Indo-Pak relationship, which has been largely responsible for regional instability in South Asia. The book thought-provoking read especially for scholars, policymakers, the strategic community on South Asian and Pakistan watchers."

Professor **Swaran Singh** (Diplomacy and Disarmament Division)
Chairman, Center for International Politics, Organization & Disarmament,
School of International Studies, Jawaharlal Nehru University, New Delhi

"Pakistan as a nation state is difficult to be labelled in amongst the global comity of nations. Rising from the ashes of British colonial empire, saddling between liberal democracy and illiberal democracy, it has become a state rearing for an identity. Dr. Jyoti M. Pathania's work has endeavoured to decipher Pak and its identity crisis which has led it to undertake hybrid attitude towards her security. This has resulted into a major hurdle to attain peace & tranquillity in South Asia. India's policy options towards Pak has to operate within the complex mosaic of insecurity, political development and international security perspective."

Professor **Gautam Sen**
Adjunct Professor National Institute of Advance Studies, Bangalore

DEEP STATE CONTINUUM IN PAKISTAN

&

IMPLICATIONS FOR INDIA

"The jigsaw puzzle symbolises that behind the democratically elected parliament or 'majlis-e shura,' is the iron fist of the Army. The fire reflects the incessant problems which are created to enforce the Army control, but results into burning of the flames of democracy."

DEEP STATE CONTINUUM IN PAKISTAN
&
IMPLICATIONS FOR INDIA

Jyoti M. Pathania

KNOWLEDGE WORLD
KW Publishers Pvt Ltd
New Delhi

Centre for Land Warfare Studies
Delhi Cantt
New Delhi

The Centre for Land Warfare Studies (CLAWS), New Delhi, is an autonomous think tank dealing with contemporary issues of national security and conceptual aspects of land warfare, including conventional and sub-conventional conflicts and terrorism. CLAWS conducts research that is futuristic in outlook and policy-oriented in approach.

Centre for Land Warfare Studies
RPSO Complex, Parade Road, Delhi Cantt, New Delhi 110010
Tel: +91.11.25691308 **Fax:** +91.11.25692347
Email: landwarfare@gmail.com **Website:** www.claws.in
CLAWS Army No. 33098

ISBN 978-93-91490-62-1 Hardback
ISBN 978-93-91490-67-6 ebook

Published in India by Kalpana Shukla

KNOWLEDGE WORLD

KW Publishers Pvt Ltd
4676/21, First Floor, Ansari Road
Daryaganj, New Delhi 110002
Phone: +91 11 43528107
Marketing: kw@kwpub.in
Editorial: production@kwpub.in
Website: www.kwpub.in

Printed and Bound in India
Quiinkit Infotech Pvt. Ltd., Gurugram

Contents

Foreword

The renewal of the cease fire agreement between India and Pakistan in February 2021, was widely welcomed to bring peace and calm along the intensely active Line of Control (LoC). Following the withdrawal of US and NATO-backed forces from Afghanistan in August 2021, there has been an increase in cease-fire violations along the LoC, as well as Pakistan-backed proxy war against India using terrorists and non-state actors. As a result, several foreign terrorists, predominantly those who infiltrated from Pakistan across the LoC have been killed near the hinterland, during the counter-infiltration and counter terrorist (CI/CT) operations. Such actions have undoubtedly brought India-Pakistan relations to a new low.

It is indeed crucial to understand why Pakistan regards India as an existential threat and maintains a revisionist attitude towards it. Pakistan has not only multiple internal issues to address, it has continued to struggle with an under-developed and a fragile state of the economy. According to the UN Human Development Index 2019, Pakistan was ranked at 152nd amongst 189 countries. Not only this, Pakistan occupies 150th rank out of 163 countries, when it comes to the Global Peace Index (2021) evaluated by the Institute for Economics and Peace (IEP). Despite prevalence of such harsh conditions, the polity remains under the influence of the Pakistan Army, commonly referred to as the 'deep state.' Under the 'facade' of democracy, Pakistan Army holds the 'reins' of political, economic, foreign policy, and nuclear button control. This has contributed to the ongoing conflict between India and Pakistan, as well as regional instability in the South Asia, impeding progress and development.

Dr. Jyoti M. Pathania's research on the subject of 'deep state' and its contextualisation on Pakistan is first of its kind detailed and exhaustive academic exercise. She has traced the etymology of the term, its genesis and idea to as early as the 4th Century BC to an Indian political thinker and statesman Kautilya, and its modern conceptualisation from Turkey in the 20th century. Her work stands out as a thorough, lucid, incisive and an in-depth study into all contours of the subject. The book brings compelling findings and a fresh insight into the historical as well as contemporary writings on the evolution of the term deep state, different perspective and versions of its notion in different countries with major focus on Pak's deep state legacy and its current underpinnings. During her research and exploratory studies, she coined the term, '*Uniformed democracy*' and earned a *trademark* under application no: 5030906 in class 41 filed on 5th July 2021.

The author has articulated a new theory on deep state which can be attributed to her in-depth knowledge and astute understanding of the theoretical constructs of international relations coupled with her ingenious research on the topic. The book brings out that the deep state has had its moorings in Pakistan even before it existed as an independent state. Pakistan has always used the advantage of its strategic location to get aid from eternal donors which in turn have only facilitated the emboldening of the deep state regime.

The author has also explored various actors comprising the deep state in Pakistan. These have been individually studied and examined in great detail as separate chapters and she has lucidly presented her findings, with rationale, supported by diagrams, pictures, figures and tabulations. The book includes an interesting chapter on the Inter Services Public Relations (ISPR)wing of the Pakistan Army, examining its organisation, administration, and working mechanisms including the varied tools of social media for information warfare. This aspect has been researched in detail for the first time, leading to the understanding of ISPR sponsored '*virtual societal warfare*' or '*fifth generation warfare*'. The study also brings out the role of Inter-Services Intelligence Agency, which in cahoots with the Pak Army, has supported their '*extra-constitutional roles*' and used '*doctrine of necessity*' time and again to justify the multiple coups in the country. The concluding chapter throws light on the severe ramifications of Pakistan's deep state for India and how it is also the *raison d'etre* for the South Asian regional instability.

The book on "Deep State Continuum in Pakistan and Implications on India" makes a significant value addition in the field of security and strategic studies, international relations, and India-Pakistan relations. Dr. Jyoti M. Pathania has my appreciation and compliments for producing such a high-quality study, written in a logical, coherent, easy to read and comprehend form, which will immensely benefit students, scholars and academics alike as well as international security experts and policy makers, as a reference manual. It would be a gripping read for the members of the strategic and defence community worldwide.

New Delhi
January 2022

Lt. Gen (Dr.) VK Ahluwalia
PVSM, AVSM**, YSM, VSM (Retd.)
Director, Centre for Land Warfare Studies (CLAWS)
(*Former, Army Commander, Central Command;*
Former Member Armed Forces Tribunal, Jaipur)

Acknowledgements

I would like to convey my appreciation to the many people and organisations where I've studied and worked for more than two decades. Some are among the world's leading experts on South Asian security and international affairs. Few of them are my close friends, coworkers, and collaborators who have freely shared their ideas and perspectives serving as a steady source of guidance throughout this project.

I owe the deepest gratitude to (in alphabetical order) Dr Ashok Behuria, Prof. Ashwini Mohapatra, Mr Amber Sen, Prof. Christine Fair, Maj Gen Dipankar Banerjee (Retd.), Col. David. O. Smith, Prof. Deepsheekha Kotwal, Prof. Gautam Sen, Lt. Gen Gurmeet Singh (Retd.), Prof. Kanti Bajpai, Maj Gen Manoj Pandey, Brig Narender Singh (Retd.), Mr Rana Banerji, Lt. Gen Rakesh Sharma (Retd.), Prof. Surjit Mansingh, Mr Tilak Devasher, Maj Gen Vishwas Rao, Prof. Varun Sahni, and Late Prof. Veena Kukreja. I would also like to acknowledge a few Pakistani authors and academics like Prof Moonis Ahmar, Ayesha Siddiqa, Hussain Haqqani, Maria Rashid, Imad Zafar, Mohammad Waseem, Mazhar Aziz, Hasan Azkari Rizvi, Shuja Nawaz and Ayesha Jalal. Reading their literature enhanced my understanding and gave me an unbiased, holistic and organic perspective on the subject.

During the course of writing the book, I have greatly benefited from discussions, seminars, track two initiatives, and online conferences, held on the subject, especially the feedback and comments of the participants on my research and presentation. Also, my interactions with members of the defence services both serving as well as veterans provided me with a unique viewpoint on my research. All of this helped me have a deeper understanding of the subject and gave me a wide fresh perspective to incorporate into my writing.

I also want to convey my sincere gratitude to Mr Rana Banerjee for reading the complete manuscript and offering helpful ideas, suggestions, and edits. His constructive feedback assisted me in refining my arguments and fine-tuning the chapters.

I take this opportunity to thank Lt. Gen B.S. Nagal (Retd.), former Director of CLAWS for initiating me to start this project. I would also like to express my deep gratitude to Lt. Gen VK Ahluwalia (Retd.), Director, CLAWS for having shared his significant insights and views particularly on the subject of Pakistan Army as discussed in Chapter Three. I would like to thank Lt Gen Ranbir Singh (Director CLAWS from Feb 2022) for supporting me to complete this project.

I respectfully thank Ambassador Ajay Bisaria, Gen NC Vij (Retd.), Lt. Gen Syed Ata Hasnain (Retd.), Prof Gautam Sen, Prof Amitabh Mattoo, Dr. Meenakshi Gopinath, Mr Michael Kugelman, Mr Rana Banerji and Prof. Swaran Singh for their generous messages about the book.

Much of the data was collected courtesy the Pak defence literature, IDSA Pak Project team Publication, interactions and discussions at various defence training establishments, the MP-IDSA Library archives section, the JNU Library, the Nehru Museum Library, the Ministry of External Affairs website in India, and the findings of various reports and feedback from my questionnaire.

I thank the staff and faculty of CLAWS to include the Librarian Mr Nitesh, Office Assistant Mr Dharmender and the Deputy Directors for their institutional and administrative support. Grateful to Mr Sushanta Gayen, KW Publishers, and Shreya, Publication Manager, for ensuring timely publication. Without the combined support and assistance of all of my friends, colleagues, and institution, this project wouldn't have been accomplished.

Last but not the least, I am grateful to my family, especially my late father, mother, my sisters, Pitaji, and mother-in-law, for always encouraging me, especially my little daughter Devyani, who constantly pushed me to finish my assignment as soon as possible so that I could spend more time with her, my son Yuvraj, for cautioning me not to rush things, and, of course, my beloved husband Vishal, who has always been my pillar of support.

Finally, I thank God Almighty for giving me the strength to conquer all obstacles and successfully complete the study.

New Delhi **Jyoti M. Pathania**
January 2022

Abbreviations

AAP	Allah-o-Akbar Party
AICWA	All India Cine Workers Association
APNS	All Pakistan Newspaper Society
APHC	All Party Hurriyat Conference
ASF	Airport Security Force
BBC	British Broadcasting Corporation
CCP	Chinese Communist Party
CENTO	Central Treaty Organisation
CEO	Chief Executive Officer
CIA	Central Intelligence Agency
CMC	Central Military Commission
COAS	Chief of Army Staff
COMSAT	Commission on Science & Technology
CPAP	Civil Progressive Alliance Pakistan
CPECA	China-Pakistan Economic Corridor Authority
CRPF	Central Reserve Police Force
CSS	Committee for State Security
CUP	Committee of Union and Progress
DFR Lab	Digital Forensic Research Lab at the Atlantic Council
DG-C	Director General Counter Intelligence
ECP	Election Commission of Pakistan
EU EOM	European Union Election Observation Mission
FATA	Federally Administered Tribal Areas
FATF	Financial Action Task Force
FBI	Federal Bureau of Investigation
FIA	Federal Investigative Agency
FIU	Financial Intelligence Unit

FSF	Federal Security Force
FSS	Federal Security Service
GDP	Gross Domestic Production
GHQ	General Headquarters
IB	Intelligence Bureau
IED	Improvised Explosive Device
ISI	Inter-Services Intelligence
ISIS	Islamic State of Iraq and al-Sham
ISPR	Inter Service Public Relations
IHC	Islamabad High Court Judge
IJI	Islami Jamhoori Ittehad
IM	Indian Mujahideen
JeM	Jaish-e-Mohammed
JCIB	Joint Counter Intelligence Bureau
JI	Jamaat-e-Islami
JIB	Joint intelligence Bureau
JIH	Joint Intelligence Headquarters
JIN	Joint Intelligence North
JIM	Joint Intelligence of Middle East/Muslim
JIT	Joint Investigative Team
JuD	Jamat-ud-Dawa
KGB	Komitet Gosudarstvennoy Bezopasnosti
LeT	Lashkar-e-Taiba
LIC	Low Intensity Conflict
LoC	Line of Control
LWE	Left Wing Extremism
MFN	Most Favoured Nation
MI6	Military Intelligence, Section 6 of United Kingdom
MI	Military Intelligence
MoU	Memorandum of Understanding
MLO	Martial Law Order
MOSSAD	Chief Intelligence and Secret Service Agency of Israel
MP	Member of Parliament
MQM	Muhajir Quami Movement

MSR	Mir Shakil-ur-Rahman
MML	Milli Muslim League
NA	National Assembly
NAB	National Accountability Bureau
NDU	National Defence University
NSA	National Security Advisor
NSA	National Security Agency
NWFP	North West Frontier Province
PEMRA	Pakistan Electronic Media Regulatory Authority
PIA	Pakistan International Airlines
PMA	Pakistan Military Academy
PML-N	Pakistan Muslim League-Nawaz
POK	Pakistani Occupied Kashmir
POJK	Pakistan Occupied Jammu and Kashmir
PPP	Pakistan People's Party
PRO	Public Relations Officers
PSYWAR	Psychological Warfare
PSYOP	Psychological operations
PTI	Pakistan's Tehreek Insaaf
RAW	Research & Analysis Wing
RSF	Reporters Sans Frontiers
SAARC	South Asian Association for Regional Cooperation
SAFTA	South Asian Free Trade Area Agreement
SAPTA	South Asia Preferential Trading Agreement
SEATO	South-east Asia Treaty Organisation
SIMI	Students Islamic Movement of India
SIPRI	Stockholm International Peace Research Institute
SOCMINT	Social Media Intelligence
ST	Sunni Tehreek
TKN	Tehreek Khatm-i-Nabuwwat
TLP	Tehrik-e-Labbaik Pakistan
TLY	Tehreek-Labaik-ya-asool-Allah
TNW	Tactical Nuclear Weapons
USIS	United States Intelligence Community

USIC	United States Intelligence Community
ULFA	United Liberation Front of Assam
YeS	Youm-e-Shuhada
YeD	Youm-e-Difa

Introduction

Deep state terminology has always been a fascinating notion in international relations, a relatively new word that has not been well investigated by the strategic, defence, and academic communities. So I took it on to decode its theoretical underpinnings as part of the larger discourse on geopolitical and strategic studies, which helped me in filling the gaps on this under researched subject. In popular usage, the term carries a negative connotation as it is associated with authoritarianism, illiberal regimes signifying little more than tenuous military rule. But even in democracies it can function as a 'state within a state' to manipulate and control public opinion.

The book makes an in-depth study of the deep state apparatus in Pakistan to figure out the jigsaw conundrum depicted on the cover page. It symbolises that behind the democratically elected parliament or '*majlis-e shura*,' is the iron fist of the Army which wields real powers. The fire reflects the incessant problems which are created to enforce the Army's control, but results into burning of the flames of democracy. In the context of changing structure of '*geo-politics, geo-economics deep policy paralysis*' and the '*non-conforming neighbourhood states*', especially its implication for India's geo-strategic future, the significance and relevance of this study cannot be denied or understated.

The work serves as a timely reminder to scholars and policymakers alike to refocus attention on the deep state diktat in Pakistan. Its strategic goals have resulted in a stalemate in the Indo-Pak relationship, which is one of the main reasons of regional instability in South Asia. As a result, regional development remains in a limbo. This study is based on twenty years of research and familiarity with the subject, rather than on field work.

The definition of the deep state has different perspective and each country has its own version of the notion, for instance in the case of Pakistan and Syria it functions on the basis of ideological or religious dominance, regulating all sectors of governance, including national security, foreign policy, and nuclear strategy, denoting a complete erosion of civilian authority. Whereas in countries like Turkey and Russia, it functions by deceiving opponents and eliminating institutions that reject the deep state's ideas through fear, terror, and intimidation. In America, the deep state institutions, like the bureaucracy, FBI, CIA, and NSA, are the permanent arm of government asserting significant and independent power, which may not always toe the line of the ruling regimes.

The book is structured in six main chapters which delineate the seminal concepts in context of deep state continuum in Pakistan and investigates its ramifications for India.

Chapter One, discusses the deep state discourse in the world politics. What does the term mean, when did it come to be used in the field of International relations, how can we construct it theoretically? What are its drivers? This chapter tries to find answers to these intriguing questions. The geneses of the subject matter is traced to the 4th century BC Indian political thinker Kautliya, who had studied spies as a vital institution of statecraft in his book *Arthashatra*, but the concept in its modern avatar was triggered by the '*Susurluk incident*' in 1996, Turkey. The chapter introduces a new theoretical construct on the 'deep state' which is based on Kautilyan *Arthashastra* (institution of spies), Weberian theory (Power, domination and authoritarianism) and Conspiracy theory (covert activities).

In the next chapter, Pak's deep state intricacies have been deciphered by tracing the country's history and categorising its evolution into varying phases, culminating in the current regime. During my research and exploratory studies, I coined the term, *Uniformed democracy*™[1] to describe Pakistan's democratic system. It is a form of democracy in which the Pakistan military, or "men in uniform," are the main actors, relying on willing or forced cooperation from other state institutions to maintain control over national security, nuclear and foreign policy issues, as well as domestic politics, the economy, and civil society at large. Since independence the Army dominance continues, and it has no intention of relinquishing its control, ensuring that *Uniformed democracy*™ persists in one form or another. This system of democracy has been thoroughly researched both before and after independence, resulting in its own set of rules and precedents that have become so ingrained in governance structures that even when the civilian government rules, it inadvertently follows the earlier precedents, allowing the Army to rule by default.

Chapter Three, draws attention to the important attributes of the invincible and omnipotent Pak Army. Almost half of Pak's existence under direct Army rule and the other half under indirect Army rule, including the Imran Khan's regime, reveals a symbiotic cyclical pattern of military-political interactions. Pakistan may be termed the "Land of Coups" after the first coup attempt in 1951, which was followed by five successful coups, including a constitutional coup, and few unsuccessful coups. I conducted a thorough review of the several official defence literature and gleaned excellent insights that I have included in the chapter. In order to provide a sense of contemporary Pakistani politics, the 2018 elections have also been covered. The military dominance appears to be complete, as retired military officers are in charge of not just corporate institutions, but also heads of educational, public, private institutions and boards, as well as ambassadorial appointments, establishing the Army as a hegemon.

The fourth chapter makes as assessment of the most potent symbol of Pak deep state, the Inter-Services Intelligence Agency (ISI). Evaluating its role in domestic affairs under the guise of maintaining national security and understanding the working machinations. By employing extra-constitutional rules, they have become extremely powerful, virtually controlling and subverting domestic politics by funding, forming or breaking political alliances, supporting right wing extremists and radical sectarian Islamist political parties. These agencies have played a key role in establishing the reign of the military dictators which have also been tabulated by delineating few important functions and its effects.

For the first time, most up-to-date and comprehensive research has been conducted by understanding the 'virtual societal warfare' and 'social perception management' tools of the Army's social media wing, Inter-Services Public Relations (ISPR). A detailed information has been provided under Chapter Five. Its growth has been traced from a small non-existent work force to a Colossus. Till date, Indian strategic circles have greatly underestimated its impact on the geopolitics of our region. In order to gain a better grasp of the ISPR's mindset, I used primary sources like video games (including some mobile games), ISPR-produced films, and vernacular songs to determine who its target audience was.

The last chapter deduces information from data collected, analysed, and derived from the author's questionnaires and interviews. I must confess that in the middle of the pandemic and semi lockdowns, regular online sessions and telephonic conversations became a consistent tool of my research. This chapter demonstrates that the continuation of Pakistan's deep state will have far-reaching consequences for India in the geo-strategic, geo-economic, geo-political, and social-cultural arenas. Its ascension to superpower status is affected by Pak's revisionist strategic policies toward India. Consistent enmity between the two has been and will continue to be the norm until the Pakistani establishment moves away from *Uniformed democracy*™ towards rule of law and constitutional democracy, wherein the civilian government's writ overrides the military. Research suggests that deep state is here to stay for at least two decades or more.

The security perceptions of Pakistan Army, help to maintain the country's image as an unstable and incomplete state, surrounded on one side by Afghanistan and on the other by India. The Army has been indoctrinated with this mentality, which has spread across society. Deep state strategic policies like, using ideological instruments to instill nationalism, pursuing strategic depth in Afghanistan, and deploying proxy war fighters in the fight against India continues. Given Pak's fragile economy and polity, which affects well-being of society as a whole, the *Awaam*/people have a significant role to play by exercising their democratic right more efficiently.

NOTE

1. ™-Trade Mark, Uniformed democracy under Application No: 5030906 in class 41 filed on July 5, 2021 in the name of Dr. Jyoti M. Pathania.

Source: This Photo by Unknown is licensed under CC BY-NC-ND

1. Discourse on the Deep State in World Politics

> "*The idea of a deep state can be found as early as the 4th century BC in Kautilya's Arthasastra, but it's modern avatar comes from Turkey.*"

The term 'deep state' has resurfaced time and again as a subject of debate and discussion amongst the academic circles, policymakers and the media at large. Scholars of international relations have recognised the existence of this concept in recent geostrategic thinking in the west. Academics and practitioners are exploring and grappling with the conceptual technicalities of the term as it is in the nascent stage and definitely under researched. With respect to the precise scientific definition also there is disagreement amongst the experts. To begin with, it is worthwhile to study, the very term 'deep state', its etymology, genesis of the idea, definition, meaning and characteristics. It is a relatively new word, appearing in the dictionary for the first time in the 1990s.

ETYMOLOGY-DEEP STATE

Word-noun

noun: **deep state**; plural noun: **deep states**
A body of people, typically influential members of government agencies or the military, believed to be involved in the secret manipulation of control of government policy.

Origin

TURKISH

derin devlet → deep state
1990s

The 1990s: translation of Turkish word *derin devlet*, (the term was first used with reference to Turkey) Oxford Dictionary.[1]

The word is used in Merriam-Webster Dictionary for the first time in 2000s, and defined as "*an alleged secret network of especially non-elected government officials and sometimes private entities (as in the financial services and defence industries) operating extra legally to influence and enact government policy*".[2] The Cambridge Dictionary defines "*the deep state as the ruling elites from the military, judicial branch, business and media, which has long wielded tremendous power behind the scenes.*"[3]

Idea

The coinage of the term deep state is fairly a recent one but the notion certainly isn't. The idea of using covert activities by the state dates back to the 4th century BC, explicitly stated in the writings of famous Indian Political thinker Kautilya's *Arthashastra*, "Concerning Discipline", which contains a whole plethora of views on the espionage elements carefully crafted in the statecraft activities and suggesting mass participation in intelligence gathering through institution such as religion, with spies operating under various guises. Chapter 11, talks about the '*institution of spies*', assisted by the council of his ministers tried under espionage, the king shall proceed to create spies: spies under the guise of a fraudulent disciple (kāpaṭikachātra), a recluse (udāsthita), a householder (gṛhapatika), a merchant (vaidehaka), an ascetic practising austerities (tāpasa), a classmate or a colleague (satri), a fire-brand (tikṣṇa), a poisoner (rasada), and a mendicant woman (bhikṣuki). A skilful person capable of guessing the mind of others is a fraudulent disciple. Having encouraged such a spy with honour and money rewards, the minister shall tell him, "Sworn to the king and myself, thou shalt inform us of whatever wickedness thou findest in others."[4]

Chapter 12, elucidates on the '*creation of wandering spies*'. Those orphans (asambandhina) who are to be necessarily fed by the State and are put to study science, palmistry (aṅgavidyā), sorcery (māyāgata), the duties of the various orders of religious life, legerdemain (jambhakavidyā), and the reading of omens and augury (antara_cakra), are classmate spies, or spies learning by social intercourse (saṃsargavidyāsatriṇa). Such brave desperados of the country who, reckless of their own life, confront elephants or tigers in fight mainly for the purpose of earning money are termed fire-brands or fiery spies (tīkṣṇa). Those who have no trace of filial affection left in them and who are very cruel and indolent are poisoners (rasada).

Chapter 13, deals with '*the protection of parties*', having set up spies over his prime ministers (mahāmātra), the king shall proceed to spy on both citizens and country people. Classmate spies (satri) formed as opposing factions shall carry on disputations in places of pilgrimage (tīrtha), in assemblies, houses, corporations (pūga), and amid congregations of people. One spy may say: "This king is said to be endowed with all desirable qualities; he seems to be a stranger to such tendencies as would lead him to oppress citizens and country people by levying heavy fines and taxes." Against those who seem to commend this opinion, another spy may interrupt the speaker and say: the art and importance of espionage strategy. It talks about the covert agent's characteristic of having a ruthless passion, a strong hunger and infinite self-control for fighting against the enemy. This activity would also involve the pupils, monks, farmers, traders, mendicants and nuns; he believed they needed to be constantly scrutinised as well.[5]

Similar ideas can also be found in the Greek language κράτοςἐνκράτει, (*kratosenkratei*) which was later adopted into Latin as '*imperium in imperio*' or '*sattus in statu.*'[6]

The concept of the deep state was articulated in the sixteenth century by Niccolo Machiavelli's *Prince* (1513)—a political treatise and an instruction manual for future princes and royals, which uses means like 'deception', 'betrayal', 'criminality' and even violence to justify the rule of the Kings/Tyrants.[7] As a result, the classic adage "ends justify means" comes to mind. Political deceit, deviousness and real politik connote Machiavellian.

In the seventeenth and the eighteenth centuries, the idea finds mention in the writings of Francis Bacon (1624) who described the deepest of the deep states as, '*the government of God over the world is hidden*', '*the lord's reign over us,*' '*obscure and invisible*' as best way governments worked. Later reiterated by King James 1 in 1624, who believed that no one should "*meddle with anything concerning the government, or deep matters*".[8] It was felt that if the church was left unchecked it would turn into a kind of 'state within a state', hence the separation of church and the state became the maxim. At the beginning of the twentieth century, the deep state was also used to refer to government-owned corporations or private companies that acted independently of regulatory or government control.[9] The contemporary understanding of the term saw its roots in Turkey in the late twentieth century.

GENESIS

The term is derived from the secretive Turkish networks known as "derin devlet", which literally means 'deep state'. Ayşegül Sabutkay, from Turkey in her PhD thesis on the Susurluk incident, confesses that "to write and speak about the deep state means to handle an issue both well-known and unfamiliar at the same time. Using the metaphor of an iceberg, she writes that Turkey's deep state is an image almost everyone is familiar with and becomes visible from time to time. She argues that 2008 Ergenekon Trial for the first time brought and revealed a structure that defines itself as the 'deep state'. But it was the Susurluk incident (1996) which became the trigger for bringing the concept into the public domain. Deep state metaphor is used to describe the executive power that clandestinely operates as a part of the state to do illegal actions. If this secret operation somehow comes out in the open, no one assumes responsibility for it. In this sense, it usually has a legitimacy problem which is solved by remaining secret.[10]

According to historian Ryan Gingeras, the term (*derin devlet*) 'colloquially speaking' refers to 'criminal' or 'rogue' elements that have somehow muscled their way into power.[11] It generally refers to a kind of shadow or parallel system of government in which unofficial or publicly unacknowledged individuals play important roles in defining and implementing state policy. He traces its roots to the last days of the Ottoman Empire, where organised criminal gangs in both cities and provinces were useful to the young Turks, the Committee of Union and Progress (CUP), the party that dismantled the Empire and declared the Republic of Turkey in 1923.[12]

This clandestine force was operating in the first quarter of the century, encompassing the time span of the Balkan Wars (1912, 1913);[13] World War I, the Allied occupation of Istanbul (1918-1923); and the Turkish War of Independence (1919-1923).[14] A deep connection between state and underworld existed as seen in CUP, a case in point is of Sah Ismail, a bandit who became a CUP agent and then an enemy of the state. He goes on to say that the Turkish deep state is not a single institution that exists in the shadows of the bureaucracy, military, and civil society. Rather, it's an eclectic, ever-evolving political battleground, with components that are both expressly lawful and explicitly illegal. "Paramount [...] is the extreme emphasis placed upon state security, a need that places both law enforcement and clandestine agencies in the forefront of both the formulation and execution of state policies."[15] Traditionally, the United States Press has used this word to refer to governments of countries such as Russia and Turkey, but since the beginning of 2010, conspiracy theorists have also used deep state terminology to describe the United States government.[16]

DEFINITIONS

The following definitions will help to understand the different perspectives of this word. According to Robert Worth, the term 'deep state' is appropriate for networks in many countries other than Turkey,where governments have colluded with smugglers and jihadi (Syria), jihadi veterans of the Afghanistan war (Yemen), and other criminals working as irregular forces (Egypt, Algeria).[17] Few scholars, like Musgrave, believe the deep state originated in the Middle

East and North Africa, used to describe a "permanent national security structure that would function as a check on civilian governance."[18]

Jean-Pierre Filiu, a French historian, believes the autocracies of Syria, Egypt and Yemen suppressed the democratic uprisings of the "Arab Revolution" by relying on shadowy intelligence agencies and internal security arms of the so-called deep state-emulating strategies pioneered in Kemalist Turkey, which has long faced internal dissent, as well as Street Gangs (the Baltaguiyya in Egypt) or Death Squads (the Shabbiha in Syria). He blames the reconstituted deep state, security agencies, and authoritarian governments willing to maintain power at all costs for the upheaval in the Middle East.[19] Eminent Professor Moonis Ahmar of the University of Karachi, defines '*State within a State*' also a categorisation of the deep state in which power is wielded by invisible forces who bypass civilian government in the formulation and implementation of key foreign policy matters. As far as the domestic arena is concerned, the deep state wouldn't let a civilian government assert or strengthen its position.[20]

Another school of thought that sees the deep state governing from behind the scenes is termed as the Conspiracy theory. Michael Barkun, a member of this school believes that the universe is governed by design, based on three principles namely; nothing happens by accident, nothing is as it seems, and everything is connected.[21] In his book *The Open Societies and Their Enemies*, Karl Popper coined the term '*conspiracy theory of society*' to describe social phenomena like "war, unemployment, poverty, and shortages as the result of direct design by some powerful individuals and groups, arguing that totalitarianism was founded on this theory".[22] When 'entrenched unelected career civil servants,' act in a manner to further their own interests in areas like; job security, enhanced power and authority and pursuits of ideological goals, Methods like 'Obstructing', 'resisting', and 'subverting' are used to oppose the policies of the elected officials.[23] This phenomenon is common not only in developing countries but also evident in developed countries, like the United States when agencies like the Pentagon and the CIA along with other, act independently of Congress and the White House on matters of national interest and security. A former director of the Foreign Service Institute, Nancy McEldowney categorically rebuts this,

> "the term originated in the context of analysing the situations in Turkey and Egypt, where I served, usually to talk about propaganda, dirty tricks, and even

> violence to overthrow the government. To refer to career civil servants in the U.S. government as some form of deep state is a clear attempt to delegitimize voices of disagreement. Even worse, it carries with it the potential for fear-baiting and rumour-mongering, and is really a dark conspiratorial term that does not correspond to reality."[24]

Such diversity of opinion reflects the disagreement as to what exactly constitutes the deep state. But a common strain runs through various definitions, it is a body of influential people or a particular organisation in pursuit of their own agenda, having a determining influence on the functioning of the government. Broadly referred to institutions such as the military, bureaucracy, intelligence services, or any other private entities like a financial group, political group or even apolitical group that works secretly to preserve a particular interest and rule without being elected. This covert network has a long-lasting influence, difficult for any elected government to counter.

DRIVERS OF THE DEEP STATE

The motivation and the machinations of the deep state keep evolving and vary differently in different countries. A few of these have been enlisted:

Ideological Drivers

The deep state's ideology is the driving factor in countries like Egypt, Pakistan, and Turkey. As previously noted, the preservation of the secular-nationalist values of modern republic founder Ataturk led to frequent coups, assassinations, and repression of Kurds, leftists, and Islamists whenever this group gained too much popularity in Turkey. The deep state's goal in Egypt and Pakistan, on the other hand, was to secure the "perpetuation of the military-dominated political system"[25] through Islamist ideology.

Historical Roots

Pakistan's deep state roots can be traced back to its colonial past. The supremacy of the industrial elite and Army was supported throughout the British Raj and continued in the post-independence period, primarily due to a lack of middle-class leadership and a struggling national bourgeoisie, who were unable to exert in national affairs or even restrain the military and bureaucracy's authority.

The untimely death of Mohammad Ali Jinnah (Quaid-i-Azam) and the assassination of Pakistan's first Prime Minister, Liaquat Ali Khan (Quaid-i-Millet), less than a year after the country's formation, slowed the process of drafting a constitution. The Army stepped in to fill the void, bolstered by the perception that India posed an existential threat. This effectively ended the political leadership's feeble hold on the bureaucracy and the Army.[26]

Conspiratorial Theorists

The deep state is also driven by a climate of conspiracy and political polarisation, which encourages the people to question the pillars of civil society, from the judiciary to the press, and seek refuge in the shadow of a populist leader. The comparisons to American politics in the Trump era became all too real. Some scholars refer to this as a hybrid association of elements of government and top-level financial and industrial classes who are able to govern without the approval of the governed. On a psychological level, conspiracist ideation-belief in conspiracy theories can be harmful or pathological and is highly correlated with the paranoia and Machiavellianism.[27] The essence of conspiracy beliefs lies in an attempt to delineate and explain evil. At the broadest level, history is viewed as controlled by massive, demonic forces, an organization that is made up of individuals or groups which is acting covertly to achieve a malevolent end has conspiratorial belief.[28]

Weak and Fragile Polity

Some political systems are characterised by weak and fragile political parties, corruption, nepotism, abuse of power including irresponsible behaviour on the part of the current regime which jeopardises the functioning of the government institutions. They remain preoccupied with expanding their own interests and authority, rather than improving the quality of life of their populations or even meeting the basic ontological needs of the citizens. In such a scenario, the deep state emerges by confluence of the military, intelligence networks and the opposition parties and work together for undermining the authority of the elected government. In order to gain their hold on power, they attempt to destabilise the democratic process for instance by sponsoring political groups that are at odds with the ruling party or by starting a new party altogether.

Domination/Authoritarian Structure

In a Weberian sense, a political system represents a kind of domination that is both formal and informal or dual domination. The deep state occurs when the military lacks democratic control or when the executive body abuses its power, as in South American countries with presidential systems whereby military monitoring is inadequate or civil oversight is managed in undemocratic ways.[29] The military's autonomy, or decision-making capacity, can be utilised to statistically detect the deep state's presence. Military autonomy is a continuum that extends into the professional, political, and judicial sectors, with each domain becoming increasingly integrated, blurring the lines between them. When military autonomy is very high, constitutional institutions become Janus-faced. As a result of these Janus-faced official institutions, the threat of a coup, dictatorial cliques, mafia, organised crime, corruption, and extra judicial execution become effective. Dual dominance situations like this help to preserve the deep state.[30]

External Support and Assistance

Sometimes when the big powers or even a neighbouring country attempts to destabilise a particular country in order to keep it weak and tamed. They do so with the help of the deep state by making it a major player in the game. For instance, in 2012, external support from countries like Saudi Arabia and other Arab countries, including Israel, who did not want President of Egypt Morsi's rule to continue due to his staunch Islamist policies, prompted the Egyptian Army, led by General Sisi, to seize control and remove Morsi. In the case of Pakistan, when Prime Minister ZA Bhutto came to power, some analysts attributed it to American influence. Turkey and Egypt are examples of countries where non-elected state governments undercut civilian power by refusing to recognise it.

DEEP STATE NARRATIVE IN POLITICS

The study of international politics has benefited from various theories like realism, liberalism, neoliberalism, marxism, feminism and constructivism which focus on anarchy, power struggles, diplomacy, interdependence, survival, regime stability, and other aspects of international relations. The concept of deep state points to a 'special power configuration within a state' that has a significant influence on the running of the statecraft, determining national security, conduct of diplomacy and foreign relations. It can be found embedded in any of these theoretical paradigms as a critical determinant of state behaviour.

In certain states, the configuration of power is such that a section of the power elite consolidates its power base, irrespective of the political system operating in the state, and derives its legitimacy from substantive popular support gained out of popular disenchantment with repeated failure of the system to throw up a responsive government. It is also true that once such 'deep state' asserts its existence and power, its quest for its survival ensures perpetuation of a condition where the system finds it impossible to redress itself. Such a 'deep state' with its hold on the coercive machinery of the state tends to determine and dominate state craft policies in the realms of internal and international politics. The conceptual roots of 'deep state' can also be found in Kautilyan Arthashastra, Weberian system of dominance and Conspiracy theory as reflected in Figure 1.1.

Figure1.1: The Concept of Deep State

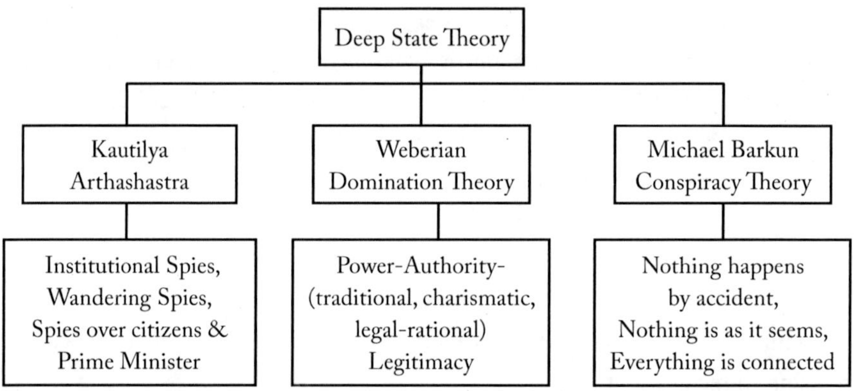

Source: Annotated by the Author.

By analysing the characteristics and tendencies through the ages, we can divide deep state narrative into two broad schools of thought:

- The deep state *supports* the current government (for instance, Pakistan under Imran Khan administration will continue till Army supports him)
- The deep state *opposes* the current government (for instance, previous dispensation as has occurred from time to time in America)

Some researchers contend that the deep state paradigm has limited relevance in countries like the United States, but are more visible in the study of developing countries like Egypt, Pakistan, and Turkey, Syria, Afghanistan "where shadowy elites in the military and government ministries have been known to countermand or simply defy democratic directives."[31] Others opine, when elected governments are incapable of exercising civilian control of the military, the function of strategic decision making is seized by the military. This absence of civilian control, results in the military managing national and foreign policies, leading to the creation of a '*state within a state*' or '*deep state*' as discussed by Samuel P. Huntington.[32]

DEEP STATE COMPOSITION

The deep state's composition is determined by the different actors that make up the country's political system. All analysts agree on one common aspect, namely the 'military and the intelligence community' play a critical role. Apart from these a few more actors or variables have been identified with respect to different countries where a deep state is thought to exist. The actors interface, intermingle and are interdependent, forming a strong nexus aiding the preservation and sustenance of their authority and rule. This is a recurrent phenomenon in the context of authoritarian regimes but it has now come to refer to other regimes across the world as shown in Figure 1.2.

Figure 1.2: Main Actors of the Deep State

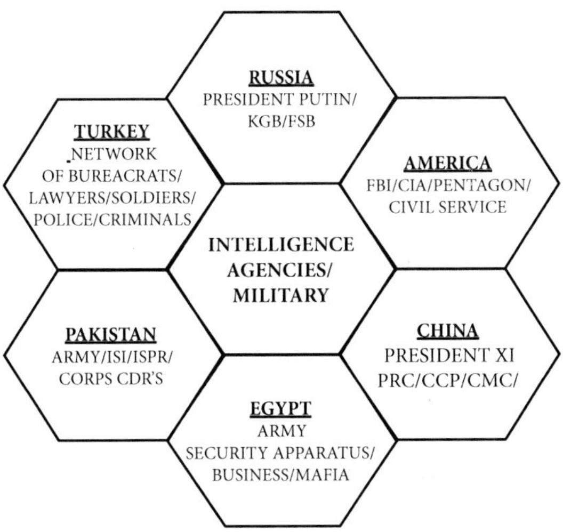

Source: Annotated by the Author.

Turkey

Turkey's covert state activities may be traced back to Sultan Selim III's reign from 1789 to 1807 when a secret committee was formed for his protection, which even his second-in-command didn't know about it. After the fall, Turkish field Marshall Mustafa Kemal Ataturk embedded several secret societies designed to further the republican cause. Such societies propelled deep states into further existence. Following the car crash or the 'Susurluk incident' in November 1996, everyone in Turkey and around the world acknowledged the presence of a deep state, as evidenced by the diverse group of passengers travelling together identified as "an MP, a high-ranking police chief (Istanbul's deputy chief of police), a beauty queen, and her lover, a prominent Turkish criminal and hitman named Abdullah Catli as proof of the deep state's complicated nexus between the state authorities and the criminal organisations including the grey wolves."[33]

Egypt

During President Mohamed Morsi term Egypt was subjected to recurrent blackouts and a dearth of foreign investment, where capriciousness, brutality and corruption become norm of the political system. Journalists routinely jailed, opponents of the governments imprisoned, security forces politicised, parliaments pliant and the news became another name for an elaborate information campaign under the auspices of the presidential palace. People believed in the existence of the deep state"[34]

Russia

In the Soviet Union, the KGB translated in English as the 'Committee for State Security' is a 'state within a state' as also endorsed by retired General Ion Mihai Pacepa in 2006, "Former KGB officers are now in charge of the Russian state. They are in charge of the country's 6,000 nuclear weapons, which were handed to the KGB in the 1950s, as well as the strategic oil business, which Putin renationalized." The Federal Security Service (FSB) KGB's successor, retains the ability to electronically monitor the populace, manage political parties, search homes and businesses, infiltrate the federal government, set up front companies, investigate cases, and run its own jail system. There was one KGB officer for every 428 persons in the Soviet

Union. For every FSB-ist in Putin's Russia, there is one FSB-ist for every 297 citizens.[35]

The current deep state consists of a group who have made their careers and profited from the twenty years of Putin's presidency, known as "*Putin's children*". Many are literally the children of the current elite, mostly long-term friends of Putin, and have now taken top jobs in government and business. All are billionaires and wield enormous influence at the highest echelon, benefitting hugely from Putin's patronage.[36]

United States

According to American researchers, the popularity of conspiracy theories demonstrates the deep State's clout in the country, as evidenced by Republican and Conservative political debates throughout the 2016 presidential election, to the point where Trump was dubbed "conspiracy candidate" due to his frequent use of the term. The "Pizzagate conspiracy theory",[37] the "Wiretapping" campaign[38], and "Russian intervention" are all instances of conspiracy theories that gained traction, Like fake news and corruption, Trump reverse-engineered deep state into a weapon against his enemies, real or perceived.[39]

Mike Lofgren, a former Republican Congressional staffer, believes it is a *hybrid organisation* made up of components of government and top-level finance and industry that can manage efficiently without the agreement of the governed.[40] According to a 2016 article in the Economist, the Central Intelligence Agency (CIA) was the centre of the US 'deep state,' which has grown to encompass 17 intelligence agencies known together as USIS, or the US Intelligence Community. Military, police, and other government officials who influence public policies are among the others. The conflict between the US and Russian "deep states" in the 2016 US presidential election was unprecedented.

American history is replete with instances wherein the former presidents have justified the existence of the deep state on several occasions. For example, in 1912, President Theodore Roosevelt warned: "Behind the ostensible government sits enthroned an invisible government paying no allegiance and acknowledging no obligation to the people."[41] President Dwight D. Eisenhower stated in 1961, "In the councils of government, we must guard against the acquisition of inappropriate power by the military-industrial complex, whether sought or unsought."[42]

Few scholars in the United States believe the deep state is "a collection of conspiring public employees with a secret-malevolent agenda" that spans ministries and political parties. The Russian Dossier, that looked into Russian connection to Trump's election victory, Edward Snowden, a former CIA employee, leaked classified documents (2013). "I am part of the resistance inside Trump's administration," an anonymous op-ed published by *The New York Times* in September 2018 read. "I work for current but like-minded co-workers, and I've promised to sabotage aspects of his agenda…"[43] Such statements signify the presence of civil servants who are not affiliated with the administration.

China

This country has been dominated for nearly a century by a single political party, whose charismatic leaders ruled with the help of the strong political party system and the military. Under the Chairman of Mao Zedong, the Chinese Communist Party (CCP) was always dictatorial, not only in theory but also in practise, during the first quarter-century of the people's republic. "Political power develops from the barrel of a handgun," he said, "and the party commands the gun, which must never be allowed to command the party." The massacre in Tiananmen Square in 1989, was a symbol of the communist regime's absolute power. Under President Xi Jinping's leadership, China's 'centralisation of political and economic life,' which includes government-run Catholic churches, has progressed to the point where top-down social control tactics are being used to bury a society of many millions of people in a mass grave of cultural amnesia.[44] This type of arbitrary power exercised by deep state actors, President Xi, CCP and Central Military Commission (CMC) is disturbing and reeks of Totalitarianism.

Pakistan

The military, the Inter-Services Intelligence (ISI), Inter-Services Public Relations (ISPR), and the corps commanders form the core of a deep and powerful nexus known as the deep state. When necessary, this collegiate leadership group has been responsible for forging and breaking political coalitions, as well as fostering animosity between civilians and military forces. This organisation is in charge of deconstructing or rather wiping out Quaid-i-Azam's liberal and secular intellectual framework by gradually transforming it into hardcore Islamic dogma. One example is Quaid-i-Azam's motto of Unity, Faith, and Discipline, which once was adopted as the Pakistan Army's motto but has been modified to Faith, Unity, and Discipline signalling priority given to faith of Islam. Even an icon like Fatima Ali Jinnah, the sister of Quaid-i-Azam, was not spared when she stood up to the deep state and opposed it; she was labelled a traitor to her nation. Under the regimes of both Pak Chief of Army Staff, Gen Raheel Sharif and Gen Qamar Javed Bajwa, the media wing of the army (ISPR) came into prominence as a formidable actor in the virtual domain.

IMPLICATIONS OF DEEP STATE

The deep state has far-reaching consequences that differ in each country. Broadly speaking, the privileged elite, align their interests in an authoritarian system and it aids both, the perpetrators as well as the benefactors in sustaining power. Diversity of politics and opinion are actively discouraged resulting in the marginalisation of democratic institutions including civil society. The deep state has a vast reach because it operates through ideological or religious supremacy, as seen in Pakistan and Syria, controlling all aspects of governance, including national security foreign policy and nuclear policy. In nations, such as Turkey, Russia, it operates through the deception of its opponents and the elimination of institutions that are opposed to the deep state's viewpoints through fear, terror, and intimidation. Institutions such as the Bureaucracy, FBI, CIA, and NSA ensure continuity in the administration of countries like America, even though at times they do not toe the line of the ruling government.

The scholarship on deep state establishes that it should not be seen in a negative sense always, but comprehended by understanding the complicated circumstances that necessitate its development. The chapter introduces a 'a new theoretical construct on the deep state' which is based on Kautilyan Arthashastra (institution of spies), Weberian theory (power, domination and authoritarianism) and Conspiracy theory (covert activities). This will undoubtedly be relevant in contemporary international discourse and studies.

NOTES

1. Definitions, Meanings, Synonyms, and Grammar by Oxford Dictionary on Lexico. com. Lexico Dictionaries | English. https://en.oxforddictionaries.com/definition/deep state. Accessed on June 23, 2019.
2. Deep State, *Merriam-Webster*, n.d. https://www.merriam-webster.com/dictionary/deep%20state#h1
3. "Deep State," *Cambridge Advanced Learner's Dictionary & Thesaurus,* Cambridge University Press.
4. Śukla Aśoka Kumāra. "Kauṭilya's Arthaśāstra: An Introduction, Sanskrit Text, English Translation & Notes". Delhi: Parimal Publications, 2019. https://www.wisdomlib.org/hinduism/book/kautilya-arthashastra/d/doc365589.html
5. Ibid.
6. Baruch Spinoza:, caput II, 6, "Tractatus Theologico-Politicus." Wikimedia Foundation, June 10, 2019. https://en.wikipedia.org/wiki/Tractatus_Theologico-Politicus.
7. Cassirer, Ernst. *Essay. In The Myth of the State, 141–45.* New Haven: Yale University Press, 1946.
8. Grandin, Greg. "What Is the Deep State?" *The Nation*, February 18, 2017. http://www.thenation.com/article/archive/what-is-the-deep-state/tnamp/.
9. Leon, Daniel De. "Imperium in Imperio", *Daily People.* New York: Marxists, June 4, 1903. https://www.marxists.org/archive/deleon/pdf/1903/jun04_1903.pdf.
10. Sabuktay, Aysegul. "Tracing the Deep State. Perspectives: Political Analysis and Commentary from Turkey Representation." The Heinrich Bőll Stiftung, n.d. https://www.boell.de/sites/default/files/Perspectives_1_eng.pdf.
11. Gingeras, Ryan. "In the Hunt for the 'Sultans of Smack:' Dope, Gangsters and the Construction of the Turkish Deep State." *The Middle East Journal* 65, no. 3 (2011): 426-41.
12. The Ottomans lost most of their European possessions. The Ottomans allied with the defeated Central Powers. Turkey fought on three fronts against Greek, French, and Armenian forces". Wills, M., 2021. The Turkish Origins of the "Deep State JSTOR Daily (online). https://daily.jstor.org/the-unacknowledged-origins-of-the-deep-state.
13. Tudury, Leila. "Deep State." Dictionary.com, January 19, 2021. http://www.dictionary.com/e/politics/deep-state.
14. Porter, Tom. "How the 'Deep State' Conspiracy Theory Went Mainstream." *Newsweek*, August 2, 2017. https://www.newsweek.com/deep-state-conspiracy-theory-trump-645376.
15. Jean-Pierre Filiu,. "From Deep State to Islamic State." *Sciences Po*, June 19, 2015. https://www.sciencespo.fr/recherche/en/content/deep-state-islamic-state.html. Accessed on March 3, 2019.
16. What Does Deep State Mean? Politics by Dictionary.comwww.dictionary.com/e/politics/deep-state.
17. Worth, Robert F., *A Rage for Order, the Middle east in turmoil from Tahrir Square to ISIS*, Macmillan Publishers, 2016, p. 139.
18. Tom Porter, "Deep State: How a conspiracy theory went from Political Fringe to Mainstream," *Newsweek*, September 12, 2018.

19. Jean-Pierre Filiu, n. 15.
20. Ahmar, Moonis. "Pakistan as a Deep State?", *Daily Times*, January 6, 2018. https://dailytimes.com.pk/174349/pakistan-deep-state/.
21. Barkun, Michael. *A Culture of Conspiracy: Apocalyptic Visions in Contemporary America*. Berkeley: University of California Press, 2013, pp. 3-4.
22. Popper, Karl Raimund. *The High Tide of Prophecy: Hegel, Marx, and the Aftermath*. Vol. 2. Princeton, NJ: Princeton University Press, 1971.
23. "What is State within a state", Audiopedia, YouTube, https://youtu.be/umFDvaq9RAA. Accessed on September 10, 2018.
24. Clark, Charles S. "Gov Exec: Deconstructing the Deep State. Government Executive", September 14, 2017. https://www.govexec.com/feature/gov-exec-deconstructing-deep-state/. Accessed on August 6, 2019.
25. Tharoor, Ishaan. "Analysis | What an Actual 'Deep State' Looks Like." *The Washington Post*, April 18, 2019. https://www.washingtonpost.com/news/worldviews/wp/2017/03/07/what-an-actual-deep-state-looks-like/.
26. Khān Muḥammad Aṣghar. *We've Learnt Nothing from History: Pakistan - Politics and Military Power*. Oxford: Oxford University Press, 2008.
27. Douglas, Karen M., and Robbie M. Sutton. "Does It Take One to Know One? Endorsement of Conspiracy Theories Is Influenced by Personal Willingness to Conspire." *British Journal of Social Psychology* 50, no. 3 (April 12, 2011): 544-52.
28. Barkun, Michael. *A Culture of Conspiracy: Apocalyptic Visions in Contemporary America*. Berkeley: University of California Press, 2013.
29. Weber, Max. *Essay. In Economy and Society* University of California Press, 1979, pp. 54-54.
30. I am expanding the analytical framework of Pion-Berlin from the professional-political arena to the judicial arena". Pion-Berlin, David. "Military Autonomy and Emerging Democracies in South America." *Comparative Politics* 25, no. 1 (1992): 83-102.
31. Michaels, Jon D. "Trump and the 'Deep State': The Government Strikes Back". *Foreign Affairs*, Sept./Oct. 2017. https://www.foreign affairs.com/articles/2017-08-15/trump-and-deep-state. 37. Glazov. Accessed on October 7, 2020.
32. Huntington Samuel P., "Political order in changing societies", Yale University, 1973. https://projects.iq.harvard.edu/gov2126/files/huntington_political_order_changing_soc.pdf. Accessed on July 7, 2019.
33. Park, Bill. "Turkey's Deep State." *The RUSI Journal* 153, no. 5 (2008): 54-59.
34. Cook, Steven A. "The Deep State Comes to America." *Foreign Policy*, February 24, 2017. https://foreignpolicy.com/2017/02/24/the-deep-state-comes-to-america/. Accessed on May 3, 2019.
35. Jamie. "When an Evil Empire Returns—The Cold War: It's back", interview with Ion Mihai Pacepa, R. James Woolsey, Jr., Yuri Yarim-Agaev, and Lt Gen Thomas McInerney. Free Republic.com, June 23, 2006.
36. Dobson, John. "Russia's deep sate changed Putin's Mind". *Sunday Guardian Live*, March 21, 2020. https://www.sundayguardianlive.com/opinion/russias-deep-state-changed-putins-mind. Accessed on October 7, 2020.

37. Pizza gate conspiracy theory involved allegations that Hillary Clinton and other prominent democrats held secret meetings in Washington D.C. Pizza restaurant. Greven, Thomas. "Deep State of Denial." Conspiracy theories: Deep state of denial - In focus 05/2017 | *IPS Journal*, June 24, 2021. https://www.ips-journal.eu/in-focus/conspiracy-theories/deep-state-of-denial-2071/.
38. Lofgren, Mike and Mike Lofgren. "Essay: Anatomy of the Deep State." BillMoyers.com, April 13, 2021. https://billmoyers.com/2014/02/21/anatomy-of-the-deep-state/.
39. "Origin and Evolution of the Term 'Deep State' in Political Discourse." English Language & Usage Stack Exchange, October 1, 1968. https://english.stackexchange.com/questions/527514/origin-and-evolution-of-the-term-deep-state-in-political-discourse.
40. Ibid.
41. Sound Recordings of Theodore Roosevelt's Voice, Articles and Essays, "Theodore Roosevelt: His Life and Times on Film", Digital Collections: Library of Congress. The Library of Congress, February 21, 2014. https://www.loc.gov/collections/theodore-roosevelt-films/articles-and-essays/sound-recordings-of-theodore-roosevelts-voice/.
42. "President Eisenhower Warns of Military-Industrial Complex." History.com. A&E Television Networks, November 16, 2009. Inside History Newsletter, January 17, 1961. https://www.history.com/this-day-in-history/eisenhower-warns-of-military-industrial-complex. Accessed on March 3, 2019.
43. "I Am Part of the Resistance Inside the Trump Administration." *The New York Times*, September 5, 2018. https://www.nytimes.com/2018/09/05/opinion/trump-white-house-anonymous-resistance.html.
44. Babones, Salvatore. "Yes, You can Use the Word T-Word to Describe China". *Foreign Policy*, April 10, 2021. https://foreignpolicy.com/2021/04/10/china-xi-jinping-totalitarian-authoritarian-debate/. Accessed on October 7, 2020.

Source: @samvadaworld.com

2. Deep State and 'Uniformed Democracy'

> "*Jinnah established a muslim country, Ayub Khan an Army's State, Zia-ul-Haq-an Islamic State, Musharraf re-defined the 'Martial Law State' and Imran Khan's puppet regime is the ultimate embodiment of 'Uniformed democracy'.*"

The Pakistan Army's deep integration into the state structure, including its involvement in politics is cause for concern, particularly when it interferes with the democratic system of governance as sanctioned by the constitution. This makes them inextricably intertwined to the extent that imperfect democratic experiments are tried and tested and 'Uniformed democracy™' functions unrestrained. It is a kind of democracy in which the '*men in uniform*', i.e., the Pakistan military is the main actor drawing its sustenance from the *willing or forced* collaboration from other state institutions such as the legislature, executive, judiciary, media, religious leaders and business entrepreneurs to maintain control over national security, nuclear, and foreign policy issues, as well as domestic politics, economy, and civil society. 'Uniformed' also because since independence the Army has ruled in an unyielding and persistent manner.

Even though it may not be in direct control all the time, it will never abandon its practice of maintaining domination, guaranteeing '*Uniformed democracy*' continues in some form or other.

In a four-page leaflet titled *Now or Never*, published in 1933, the word Pakistan was first used. Choudhary Rahmat Ali is credited for coining it, arguing that it is both a Persian and an Urdu word, made up of letters from parts of the Indian and Asian homelands, such as **P**unjab, **A**fghanistan (North-West Frontier Province), and **K**ashmir, **I**ran, **S**indh (including Kachch [also known as Kutch] and Kathiawar), **T**ukharistan, **A**fghanistan and **B**alochistan. "It means the 'land of the Pak'—the spiritually pure and clean symbolising the religious beliefs and the ethnical stocks of our people; and it stands for all the territorial constituents of our fatherland. It has no other origin and no other meaning; and it does not admit of any other interpretation."[1] In today's context, Ali's perception of pure and clean country is erroneous as proven by the historical and political events of the past few decades.

A succession of events before 1947, as well as Jinnah's unique role as president of the All-India Muslim League and Governor-General of Pakistan, laid the foundations on which nation's political structure was built. His speech to the Constituent Assembly on August 11, 1947, at the port city of Karachi. "You are free to go to your temples, you are free to go to your mosques or any other place of worship in this state of Pakistan. You may belong to any religion, caste or creed that has nothing to do with the business of state," he proposed that "in course of time Hindus would cease to be Hindus and Muslims would cease to be Muslims, not in the religious sense, because that is the personal faith of each individual, but in the political sense as citizens of the State,"[2] this concretises the image of Pakistan as a secular Muslim country, rather than a pure theocratic Islamic State. The difference between the two is that a Muslim state is one where Muslims are the majority, but an Islamic state is one where an Islamic-flavored version of totalitarianism is in place. Unfortunately, the vision of Pakistan's founding father, Quaid-i-Azam Muhammad Ali Jinnah is yet to be fulfilled.

The demand for an Islamic state goes back even before Pakistan became independent, as evidenced in Sir Muhammad Iqbal, Presidential Address, All-India Muslim League, Allahabad, 29 December 1930. "One lesson I have learnt from the history of Muslims. At critical moments in their history, it is Islam that has saved Muslims and not vice versa."[3] Who knew Iqbal's comments would be completely debunked, as we now see that Islam, the very foundation on which Pakistan was built, has been politicised and manipulated by nexus of terrorists, mullahs, and the military promoting their own interests at the expense of the pious religion of Islam. In words of a Pakistani analyst, "Islam in Pakistan has ceased to be a religion, it has become an obsession, a pathology. It has been drained of all ethics, and has become a mechanism for oppression and injustice".[4]

History is privy to the fact that Jinnah established a country for Muslims, Ayub Khan established a state for the Army; Zia wanted to establish an Islamic state; Musharraf started de-islamisation measures in Army training and other practices,[5] when he took over and redefined the veneer of Martial Law by coining the phrase 'Chief Executive'; Imran Khan's puppet regime is the ultimate embodiment of a 'Hybrid model' or 'Uniformed democracy'.

UNDERSTANDING DEEP STATE PAKISTAN

Perhaps it would not be wrong to assert that Pakistan's destiny has been guided by the deep state entity. The late Stephan Cohen, a well-known American academic and South Asian expert, defined Pakistan's deep state as "existing in the old and new social-economic order as the 'triad' of the Army, bureaucracy, and feudal landlords, known as the establishment, though the key role in this 'amorphous', 'unofficial', but 'powerful lobby' has shifted away from the bureaucrats towards the military."[6]

Prof. Moonis Ahmar alludes to the deep state having a 'deeper systemic failure' as the 'writ of the elected government is undermined repeatedly' by the military, bureaucracy, security establishment and the intelligence community. "One military intervention in fifty years could be seen as an incident; two as an aberration, but four military spells of military rule, and three more unsuccessful coups." Political parties unprofessional and corrupt actions also contribute to the formation of a deep state with repercussions on the parliament, civic society, and non-conformist media who get severely marginalised. It has a vast reach and operates through espionage on opponents, suppressing them by fear and intimidation. "The game of musical chair which is being played till today is a sad reflection of deep-rooted mistrust in civil-military relations."[7] Democracy is only on paper with power being held by a clique having connections with the rulers. Any civilian government which tries to override the deep state's red line on the national security and foreign policy matters relating to countries like the United States, India, Iran, Saudi Arabia, China and nuclear weapon's program is cursorily set aside. On the pretexts of 'national security' 'patriotism' and 'Islamic ideology' the Army maintains its power.

Echoing the same thought process, another Pakistani scholar, Imad Zafar elucidates on the deep state's 'corrosive character and affect' which has succeeded in weakening democracy and resistance by exerting its authority 'over all aspects of society'. Mullahs, property tycoons, businessmen; serving and retired officials; opportunistic politicians, all help these 'invisible forces' to keep the deep state running successfully.[8]

The Pakistan military elites aided and abetted by a 'ceremonial electoral process' and 'slavish media' that helps to strengthen their control of the nation. This has become a big propaganda success for the 'permanent governing elite', earning the title of a 'New Patron.'[9] The ex-Prime Minister Nawaz Sharif remarked, "we used to hear about 'a state within a state' but now things have gone to the extent that there's 'a state above the state' and we will have to change this."[10]

In the last 75 years, there's been a constant effort by the deep state to remove or to destabilise democratically elected Prime Ministers on some charge or other, like Prime Minister Zulfiqar Ali Bhutto was hanged, Benazir Bhutto assassinated, Nawaz Sharif pushed into exile, but military dictators like Ayub Khan, Yahya Khan, Zia and Musharraf,manipulated the constitution to their own advantage, imprisoned the judges too, yet remained scot-free just because they belonged to the 'Army lobby'.

HISTORICAL EXAMINATION

An examination of the military's pattern of dominance and intervention by historians and analysts can be comprehended better by understanding 'historical institutionalism,' as it gives one the opportunity to push beyond interpretations based purely on a historical or a cultural approach by examining the choices made early in the history of any polity which had subsequently developed into institutionalised commitments and determined subsequent decisions.[11] Therefore, it is necessary to examine historical antecedents in terms of both internal and external factors, wherein India looms large. This insecurity was exploited by the Pakistani military, helping them to legitimise its control and maintain dominance in the power structure of the deep state.

Internal Factors

- Religion as a separatist ideology
- Creation of Pakistan
- Sociological dynamics
- British Raj
- Muslim league
- Pakistan Army
- Provincialism vs. Centralism
- Jinnah's role play
- Leadership crisis

Religion as a Separatist Ideology

The foundations of Islamic separatist ideology crystallised in the 19th century among the Urdu-speaking Muslim elite of North India, with the establishment of the Anglo-Mohammedan Oriental College at Aligarh (1875) by Syed Ahmad Khan. As early as 1908, Sayyid Ali Imam spelt out civilisational differences in terms of socio-political interests and cultural factors between the Muslim elites and the Hindus, as a result, they were bound to be separatists and kept out of power.[12] Muslims argued, their faith qualified them to rule as 'ascriptive aristocratic elite' with Arab and Turkish forebears and legatees of the Mughal dynasty. In the early 20th century, The Aligarh movement shifted its focus to politics becoming the crucible of the Muslim League (1906), which was successful in attaining from the British Raj, first a separate electorate for Indian Muslims through the Morley & Minto Reforms (1909),[13] and then a separate state, Pakistan (1947).

This muslim separatism feeling born in pre-independence era continued in the post-independence times, preached and practiced by almost all the Pakistani leaders and the state institutions especially military, as it helped in forming a national identity based on religion. Developing a 'distinct Muslim identity' from that of 'Indian Muslims' was a powerful motivator for the formation of a separate state.[14] During the 1946 election campaigns, the public was encouraged to believe that once a muslim state was founded, everyone would become a better Muslim as Pakistan was supposed to be the Islamic laboratory and the citadel of Islam.[15]

In the post-independence era, the first step toward becoming an ideological Islamic state was taken in March 1949, when Liaquat Ali Khan presented the Objective Resolution in the Constituent Assembly, which stated that Allah Almighty alone has sovereignty over the entire universe, and the authority which he delegated to the state of Pakistan, with principles of democracy, socialism, and secularism, belonging to him alone. Hence religion became the cardinal principle for development of this new state, and a crucial tool for bolstering a distinct national identity and culture from India.[16] Article 2 of the constitution incorporated Islam as a state religion, but left Islam undefined and open-ended. In the fifties, the emphasis on Islam had started acting as a means for excommunicating a section of the population from the fold of Islam as seen in the anti-Ahmadiyya riots in Punjab. In the aftermath of these riots, a commission was set up, under Chief Justice Munir who brilliantly elucidated the different connotations within Islam. Justice Munir commission report gave a detailed explanation stating that even the Ulamas did not agree on one definition of Islam and if one attempts to accept the definition of each learned divine then the definition differs from that given by all others and it goes unanimously out of the fold of Islam. If one adopts the definition given by any one of the Ulama, we remain Muslims according to the view of that alim but Kafirs according to the definition of everyone else.[17]

The elite seeks legitimacy for its rule by citing 'Islam,' but this indirectly legitimises the extreme elements demand for the creation of an Islamic state. Since Pakistan's elite leaders have been unable to define the nation in non-religious geo-cultural terms, Islam has remained the most important symbol of Pakistani identity, if it is abandoned, a sense of identity crisis will emerge, and as long as it remains the most powerful referent, strong Islamist impulses will emerge, thereby legitimising the activity of extremist Islamic groups in Pakistan.[18]

After the Bangladesh War of 1971, this political commitment to an 'ideological state' morphed into a strategic commitment to Jihad ideology, the concept of holy war. As a result of this partnership between the mosque and the military, religious groups, both armed and unarmed, have gradually grown more influential.[19] Haqqani argues that Islam shifted from being a 'separatist ideology to becoming a religious nationalism' as state's policy. Since Islam was notional and could not play an effective role in binding the newly created nation, anti- India rhetoric was used to bind and this gave a head start to the Army as the core of the deep state. It was regarded as the only institution which could save the country from the onslaught of a bigger India, hence support for Army's supremacy and control. The alliance of the custodians of Islam, bureaucracy and intelligence apparatus, led to the emboldened deep state which played a new role as guardian of the state.[20]

Creation of Pakistan

The effects of the partition were unprecedented in South Asian history, as it resulted in the first extraordinary ethnic cleansing with unprecedented levels of violence and instability. A million Hindus and Muslims died, while ten million more fled to countries where their respective communities were the majority. India was seen as an 'existential threat' right from the birth of Pakistan, as argued by Mohammad Waseem, "The new nation was thus born with an image of India as a villain, a Satan and a monster next door, out to devour the New born state".[21] Most of the new state's institutions, be it the police, administration, banking sector, etc., were weak and thinly staffed, based in Karachi,the first capital. Moreover, many continued to believe that India does not accept Pakistan as a separate state and seeks to reabsorb it despite the fact that India has long recognised Pakistan.[22] This feeling is continually professed by the ruling establishment even today.

Another consequence of the newly created Pakistan was 'democratic hesitancy' among the Muslim elite of undivided India, who had migrated (from Muslim minority areas of India) and settled as migrants in the newly formed West Pakistan; they lacked indigenous roots and were hesitant to initiate a democratic process for fear of losing their elite status. Also, the worry that East Pakistan (which accounted for more than half of Pakistan's population) would dominate the elected legislature, taking power from West Pakistani politicians who considered it was their right to rule as they were part of the independence movement. Even the middle classes chose to become partners with the authoritarian and military rulers rather than seek political rights. Coupled with this was the low levels of industrialisation and capitalisation which made it difficult for many social groupings to accept democracy.[23]

Military control has been institutionalised through means such as constitutional reengineering, penetration of the public sector through the appointment of serving and retired military officers, and occupation of economic space through business activity, resulting in the formation of '*informal blocks*' that make it difficult for the political elite to roll back its influence, obstructing transition to a democratic form of government.[24] As a result of the lack of democratic foundations Army's control became easier; it was considered a key institution for binding the country together and defending from any external threats. Within weeks of independence, Muslim league newspaper Dawn called for "Guns rather than butter" urging a bigger and better-equipped Army to defend "the sacred soil of Pakistan."[25] Hence the defence of nationhood through military means took precedence over everything else, giving it a privileged position at the expense of political ideas and acts demanding ethnic rights, provincial autonomy and socio-economic-political growth, were all subverted. Insecurity against India created a culture of paranoia, aiding the deep state moorings wherein the Army played a significant role.

Sociological Dynamics

Upon investigating the sociological dimension amongst people, communities, and racial groups, it would be a truism to state that the 'Urdu-speaking upper-caste elite' or the 'aristocratic literati group' wanted to maintain its Mughal empire's legacy and were always concerned about their own societal decay. Their progenitors had prospered throughout the 16th and 17th centuries due to their administrative positions and land granted by the Mughal emperors, but the advent of colonialism in the 19th century brought these privileges into question. During the British Raj, the Hindus had established themselves in diverse roles of trade and industry, academic institutions and administration, which helped them boost and expand their political clout. The Muslims on the other hand, living in feudal past, felt isolated from the mainstream. In order to maintain their status, they used Islam as a ruse to propagate Muslim ideology to mobilise the masses not just for religious purposes but for their own survival.

Pakistan though was created as an Islamic nation but it has always been '*ethnically heterogeneous*', based on their origin, different attributes of ethnicity dominate people's identities. For the Bengalis of East Pakistan, for example, their ethnicity is rooted in cultural, linguistic and economic motivations. For the Pashtuns, it is racial and historic. The Baloch see tribal cultural and territory as the dominant factors of their ethnicity, while the Sindhi's prioritised their cultural and linguistic affiliations. The Mohajirs projected their linguistic identity.[26] This multi-ethnicity forced the Muslim League and the early Pakistani leadership to promote Islam and Urdu as the '*binding factors*' that would bring together the Muslim community of Pakistan.

The combination of tensions between socio-economic classes, interest groups, and ethnic communities created a crisis situation, as the Bengalis had a numerical advantage in the early years, but the Muhajirs held power since they controlled the administration, and Punjabis dominated the Army.[27] The response mechanism towards these sociologically ethnographically diverse identities was always repressive. The deep state's unwillingness to address the problems of these different ethnic groups, such as the Pashtuns, Balochs, Seraikias, and Mohajirs, resulted in frequent law and order crises.[28] The Army was frequently summoned by the local government to put a lid on Pandora's box of brewing ethnic and provincial rights, which resulted in the Army making inroads and strengthening its reach within civil administration.

British Raj

Strong centralising clauses were incorporated in constitutional measures such as the Government of India Act 1935 and the India Independence Act 1947 during British rule. For example, the Governor-General had emergency powers, including the ability to appoint and abolish ministers at his discretion. Pakistan's political elites are likely to have received and applied this expertise many times. Early federalism was subservient to centralised command and control, which had the authority to depose provincial governments and impose Governors' rule at any time even with the slightest of provocation. Such mechanisms resulted in bolstering of central bureaucratic authority in the North West Frontier Province (NWFP), Sindh and Punjab Assemblies, all suffered this fate early on.[29] This inclination towards a dictatorial and authoritarian pattern of governance possibly had an impact on the Pakistani political leaders, who got exposed and amenable to the easy acceptance of the despotic military rule.

To some extent, the military's importance to the state's existence, as well as its self-image as a guarantor of security, was perhaps imbibed from the Raj, as the Army had played a major role in extending and consolidating the East India Company's jurisdiction, serving as the supreme shield of British rule. It was involved in defence, internal security, and civilian authority support, as well as security operations against Pathan tribesmen in the northwest and participation in the empire's overseas military adventures. Despite the fact that the military and civilian governments in British India were frequently recognised as equal partners within the overarching framework of civilian dominance, the military remained the British Raj's bastion.

Muslim League

The Muslim League represented microcosm of elite group consisting of land owning and educated middle class, it became a mass-based party only by mid-1940s when a number of leaders from Muslim majority areas joined the party. Soon after Pakistan was created, Jinnah and Liaquat Ali Khan, took leadership of the party, refused to allow any Muslim league party cadre to become ministers, fearing that this would lead to schism within the party. They chose their ministers at their own discretion, asked the league volunteers to accept their choice only, hence effectively killing the party's grass-roots activism. Internal dissensions and conflicts arose as a result of frequent organisational issues both at the party and at the national/federal leadership level, as senior party leaders holding cabinet positions at the federal level came from Muslim minority provinces (that lacked a popular base) and had trust issues with the party's senior leaders. Rather than building the party apparatus from the ground up, the power structure encouraged the league's leaders to indulge in 'court politics' and 'factional battles.'[30]

The league failed to transform itself from a 'nationalist movement into a national party' as it couldn't serve as an effective political machine for aggregating the diverse interests and identities into a plural and participatory national framework.[31] The party's steering wheel was completely in the hands of Jinnah and once the main aim of establishing Pakistan was achieved, the party lost its zeal and momentum especially after his sudden death. Another reason for the weakening of the parliamentary politics and decline of the Muslim League was the direct fallout of the 'corruption within the league', its 'institutional weakness' and 'dominance of the rich landlord's interests over the party's interest.'[32] Weak party system sounded a death knell for the democratic aspirations of the newly created nation, giving way to the strong centralized military control.

The Pakistan Army

The Pakistan Army was made up of mostly Muslim soldiers of the British Indian Army which adapted to Islamic symbolism to give itself legitimacy within the society. Even the motto of the Pakistani Army was changed from the original (*ittehad, yaqeenaur tanzeem*) (unity, faith and discipline) to (*imaan, taqwa, jihad fisabilillah*) (faith, piety, holy war in the path of Allah) giving it a more Islamic connotation.

In the early years of independence, Army became an *'institution of prominence'* as it was the only professional, disciplined, cohesive and task-oriented organisation with a strong esprit de' corps. The manifold difficulties of partition including a larger chunk of military machinery going to India, border dispute and contested territorial dispute with regard to Kashmir provided the ideological legitimisation for the Army's resource capture in the early years. This 'early centrality of Army' allowed it to assume a place alongside the bureaucracy, and together they reinforced and benefited from the weakness of the young state's political sphere.[33]

Traditionally, the Army's image has been good primarily because of the respect it enjoys being from 'martial traditions of the Punjab and North West Frontier Province (NWFP)'; belief in the Islamic concept of Jihad (holy war), Ghazi (victorious) and Shaheed (martyr); and having strong ethnic and regional cohesion. A significant majority of the Army officers and other ranks hail from the Punjab, NWFP and the tribal areas. The Punjabis and Pathans/ Pakhtuns developed strong mutual ties and established links with the civilian bureaucratic elite. The Army's Punjabi±Pakhtun composition has been a source of strength which has inter alia contributed to enhancing the military's efficacy in politics, sealing fate of democratic aspirations early on. "Democratic±military elite pursued centralized and authoritarian governance, changed federal and provincial governments at will, and excluded those who questioned their political management."[34]

It was viewed as central to state's survival, as time and again when the civilian governments, were either incapable or were overwhelmed by the governance problems, they increasingly sought military's support for administering the state.

In the country's internal domestic politics, India also factored in as Prof. Christine Fair argues, Army used the India threat and believed in the strategic culture of restricting India's rise; restricting its presence and ability to harm Pakistan and overturning the territorial status quo at any cost."[35] The military almost always managed to co-opt one of the major political parties, so as to limit the possibilities of facing a united civilian opposition. The military's centrality in the polity can also be gauged by the 'large budgetary allocation of national resources for defence and security', as well as a common attitude among civilian and military elites to create strong defences and resources for the military. Defence expenditure was the single largest item in the national budget until the early 1990s, when debt servicing began to top the list, pushing defence expenditure to second position. Pakistan is a classic example of a country where the abundance of resources for defence and military programmes is in sharp contrast to resource-scarcity for human development.

Pakistan's military doctrine has an Islamic approach as Brigadier Askari Raza Malik of the Pakistan Army stated, "in a society that owes its existence to Islam, its adoption is inescapable, Any other system based on borrowed concepts will never appeal to the heart and soul of a Muslim soldier."[36] Hence, The 'mullah military alliance' is borne out of a symbiotic relationship that brought both the entities together. During the course of last seven decades, this relationship has become more complex with the Army using and dumping the clergy at will, depending on its requirements of legitimacy from time to time. The unintended consequences of this policy have been gradual political empowerment of the religious constituency which has acquired tremendous nuisance value in Pakistani society, so much so that at times this constituency has called the profession of the Army as un-Islamic. The Army's '*envy of the civilian political leaderships*', its '*own hunger for power*' and the '*Indian factor*' have resulted in its political assertiveness and its dominance over statecraft, leading commentators to characterise it as a deep state.

Jinnah's Role Play

Muhammad Ali Jinnah's political transmogrification from a secular nationalist to that of a peeved, vituperative and ambitious Muslim separatist, and eventually the creator and head of an Islamist nation, reflects that "he was a consummate tactician with little or no long-term strategy or vision and one who worked tirelessly to achieve his objective of creating Pakistan, but remained deliberately ambiguous about the nature of the projected state."[37] As a result of the tumultuous situation post-partition, Jinnah had to rely on the military both for internal and external subversive activities. This initial importance gave the Army a feel of significance within the political system.

Jinnah's title of *Quaid-i-Azam* and his powers were associated with a colonial-style governor-general which reinforced authoritarian centralising drift.[38] The staunch belief was that if Pakistan as a country had to survive it needed a strong central government which could impose its authority over provinces that for long had been governed from New Delhi.[39] The concept of 'strong personalisation of power' and 'powerful uniting force' was associated with him. For instance, he held two appointments, one as a Governor-General and the second as the president of the constituent assembly. As the Governor General, he was known to pre-decide himself the topics for discussions and debates held in the various meetings. The death of Pakistan's founder in 1948 set off a chain of events culminating in authoritarianism taking hold throughout the state, as the political elites were left without their leader. Simmering ethnic and sectarian violence started engulfing various provinces. The political leaders and the civilian administration including the police were unable to handle or quell the violence, resulting in instability and chaos. The military was called in to quell localised riots. This hands-on experience in crushing the anti-Ahmadiyya riots (1953) vetted its appetite for more civilian administrative power.

Many observers in Pakistan attribute the 'Army's obsession with power' to these early experiences in such anti-riot's operation in late 1940s and early 1950s. This allowed the state's strongest institutions—the Army and the bureaucracy to usurp power from the elites who were subsumed in the ethnic and regional rivalries.[40]

Provincialism vs. Centralism

M.A. Jinnah presented a federal future for Pakistan's constituent units mentioning provincial autonomy and sovereignty in the Lahore resolution in the 1940s, but shortly after Pakistan's independence, his approach to the federal plan changed dramatically, as can be judged by his speech, broadcasted from Radio Pakistan on 28 March 1948, "*I want you to be on your guard against this poison of provincialism that our enemies wish to inject into our state*".[41] He denounced federalism as a poison of provincialism, reviving tensions between national and regional leaders. During this period two diverging concepts emerged, centralism wherein the Muslim leaders were promoting not only Islam but also Urdu as a unifying factor in the lead to a unitary state as well as to contain the ethno-linguistic divisions, to help build a new home for Pakistanis; and Provincialism or federalism, wherein the ethnic groups would be able to use their own language and identity as their right. Such stark contradictory beliefs undermined the work of the constituent assembly for almost seven years when it tried to create an institutional framework satisfying both these school of thoughts. Even when a federal constitution was re-introduced, the provinces were never given the autonomy they demanded, whereas almost all of them-East Bengal, West Punjab, Sindh and the NWFP, had experienced some form of self-administration under the Raj, which coincided, by and large with an ethno-linguistic group.[42]

The 'constituent assembly, too, fell victim to the vigorous executive attack.' During Liaquat Ali Khan's tenure as Prime Minister (1947-51) the principle of cabinet government was followed, but after him, the prime minister's position was endangered by the governor general's overriding power. Following Jinnah's death, then-Governor-General Khwaja Nazimuddin become the Prime Minister, only to be dismissed in 1953 by the Governor-General, Ghulam Muhammad, for reasons like not meeting the law and order situation in Punjab, scuttled military budget, and cadre of West Pakistani bureaucrats who expressed their dislike of Bengali Nazimuddin's authoritarian rule.

Moreover, the Governor-General dismissed the Constituent Assembly itself in 1954, only three days before the county's first constitution was to be ratified. The assembly was dissolved as a result of this act by the speaker. Maulvi Tamizuddin Khan filed writs to have the dissolution statute overturned. Prior to the assembly's dissolution, the courts were granted writ authority.

Much to the dismay of Tamizuddin and the Sindh government High Court judgement, the court decided that the Governor General's permission is essential for enactment of the law.

In the Usif Patel vs The Crown case, 'state necessity doctrine' was used as the rule of law to increase the legislative power of the governor. This gave the Governor-General the kind of discretionary powers under his executive acts[43] which would otherwise have been illegal. This initial invocation of the 'doctrine of state necessity' gave impetus to its use in the service of validating military coups in Pakistan in subsequent decades.[44]

Leadership Crisis

The political instability in Pakistan can also be attributed to the leadership crisis as within four years, two great leaders died. Jinnah's untimely death on 11 September 1948, and the assassination of Liaquat Ali Khan on 16 October 1951. The lack of unity among politicians was evident as the constitution-making process dragged on for nearly seven years. The corrupt political system faltered and provided a window of opportunity to the Army to increase its role in the political sphere. Commander in Chief, General Ayub Khan, exploited this political vacuum and imposed first Martial Law in 1958, suspending the basic human rights. This set a precedent for military intervention into the political domain. Though, the nomination of serving Chief General Ayub Khan as Defense Minister by President Iskander Mirza in 1954 may be considered as one of the earliest military intrusions into the democratic government. Further more, the political system's failure to establish any norms of civilian supremacy; keeping the pre-independence military set up intact especially with regard to the ethnic composition; continuation of the British legacy (concept of martial race i.e. Pathans and Punjabis) in the Army recruitment increased the level of cohesion within the Army; which engendered political ambitions among the Army officers, increasing the possibility of success of military intervention.[45]

EXTERNAL FACTORS

- Geo-Strategic location
- India
- Kashmir

- Afghanistan
- United States

Geo-Strategic Location

Pakistan's strength is its geo-strategic location lying at the 'underbelly' of the Central Asian Republics, with proximity to West Asia and inroads into the Indian Sub-Continent. It has been the venue of the '*Great game*' of the bigger powers since the 1950s. With respect to India, it has suffered from the feeling of vulnerability and inferiority complex since partition. The initial war with India in 1948, the internal discord within the provinces and the mounting fear that partition will be undone by India compelled the founding father of Pakistan to invest heavily into defence at the cost of other institutions.[46] Both civilian and military leaders were convinced that Pakistan's tense relations with India (a stronger military power) and Afghanistan's irredentist territorial claims posed a serious threat to the country's national identity and territorial integrity, leading them to devote a significant portion of national resources to the military.

India factor

The belief in the often-cited text of *Ghazwa-e-Hind,* which mentions a prophesized war with India or Ghazwa (meaning war)-e-Hind (meaning 'of India'), purportedly mentioned by the Prophet, has been verified by Islamic Scholars as having weak authenticity. The mentions of war against India (Ghazwa-e-Hind) in a less authentic and single Hadith reference has been used by both Pakistani groups and jihadist organisations to legitimise their militant campaigns against India and to radicalise the impressionable and Islamically un-informed Muslims of Pakistan and India.[47] Since its creation, Pakistan seems to suffer from a small state syndrome in relation to India. Military has always regarded it as its principal adversary, an existential threat and this is taught throughout their military's study centres and training facilities.

Kashmir factor

In a detailed study carried out at New American Foundation, Stephan Tankel writes, Kashmir is not merely a territorial struggle but it was the latest chapter in a Hindu-Muslim struggle, existed ever since the time of the Prophet

Muhammad (with no regard for historical record). Once Kashmir was liberated, it would serve as a base of operations to conquer India and restore Muslim rule to the Indian subcontinent. Pakistan based Jihadi groups like Lashkar-e-Taiba and Jaish-e-Mohammed will continue attacking India believing in this narrative.[48] Pakistan is basically committed to taking a hostile stance toward India, as seen when its leadership made a number of assumptions contributing to the war on India in 1965. Until the surrender at Dhaka in 1971, its military policy was based on the mistaken notion that "East Pakistan's defence resides in the west." Throughout the 1980s, it used aggressive posturing to destabilise India by coveting support for Sikh separatists and its sponsorship of terrorist actions in the J&K region is well documented. Given Pakistan's size, position, and topography along its eastern border with India, the country has historically pursued an 'aggressive defence' strategy and has not shied away from using force to gain an early lead.

Afghanistan

In the 1940s, Pakistan suffered from an encirclement complex as the Kabul government desired that Britishers leave India with the option of allowing Pashtun tribes of the Raj to choose between asserting independence or becoming part of Afghanistan, joining Pakistan was not an option. Second, by not recognising the Durand Line as an international border in 1947, Pakistan did not have a distinct border as its territory was not clearly defined on the western side. Third, Pashtun nationalism was a cause of concern for the Pakistani founders, as the Pasthun nationalist had cultivated a good relationship with India, Khan Abdul Gaffar Kahn, also known as Frontier Gandhi, was a staunch supporter of Mahatma Gandhi.

In June 1947, Afghan Prime Minister Muhammad Hashim Khan declared, if an Independent Pukhtoonistan cannot be established, then the Frontier province should join Afghanistan.[49] Ayub Khan confided in his autobiography that Kabul and India tried to take his country in 'a pincer movement'.[50] Pakistan belief in and realisation of objective of 'strategic depth' through support to the Taliban seems to have borne fruit. Right from the inception of the word Talib, Pakistan has been like the Siamese twin to the Talibs. The strategic depth which wasn't provided by the geographical borders vis-à-vis India was brought through their support to the Taliban.

United States

Starting from the mid-1950s, America played an important role in shaping Pakistan's military's professional and political profile. This strengthened the Army's position in domestic context and gave them the confidence to withstand India's military superiority. The acquisition of modern technology and the support of alliances strengthened the military further. Former Army Chief General Mirza Aslam Beg, known for his penchant for manipulating the political system when he was in power, identified three 'power brokers' that emerged after Pakistan's first martial law government of 1958, namely 'the Military, the Judiciary, and the United States' ... [which] have since manipulated power in Pakistan to their advantage. The 'military has acted as the catalyst'; the 'judiciary as the facilitator' under the cover of the 'Law of Necessity', and the 'United States as the manipulator', using the political parties and the vested interest groups to bring military dictators to power to accomplish the agenda of 'regime change'.[51]

United States has been lending a helping hand to the military rulers right from the very first military dictator, Gen Ayub Khan, Prime Minister Zulfikar Ali Bhotto Bhutto's martial law in the aftermath of the March 1977 general elections, wouldn't have been possible without their support. The endorsement of the first coup (1958) by the American President Eisenhower, in a letter dated 11th October of the same year, stated that the military deemed pro-western would take the lead in ensuring political stability, economic development and ironically, perhaps, creating conditions for a constitutional and democratic rule.[52]

During Gen Zia-ul-Haq's time, Pakistan was eulogised as a front line state, President Bush cozied up to Pervez Musharraf by saying he could do business with him. Four mutual security arrangements, starting with the signing of the mutual defence assistance agreement in 1954, SEATO, a year later, the Bagdad pact, CENTO made it America's most trusted ally in Asia. Most of their relationships were related to military and intelligence cooperation. The US gave its 'strategic and frequently short-term foreign policy goals preference over defending democracy in Pakistan', by partnering with the Army and the military dictators who were at the helm of power at various times.

THE EVOLVING STAGES IN THE MAKING OF DEEP STATE

Pakistani scholars of repute like Ayesha Jalal, Hussain Haqqani, Hassan Abbas, Shahid Shafqat, Mazhar Aziz argue that the military has brought under its ambit multiple roles, in a very manipulative manner making the state and the political system weak at the same time. There remains a deep sense of distrust between the political class and citizens; the deep state takes advantage of this mistrust, periodically obstructing the growth of healthy democracy; using tools like politics and propaganda for deeper in roads into the political system.

The propagandist overtures of the deep states have obliterated Jinnah's ideology; Islam's genuine meaning has been perverted to include Jihad as an essential component; security concerns have taken precedence even at the expense of socio-economic progress. The deep state has evolved with diverse stakeholders who have played their roles in a seamless manner. This evolutionary process has been classified into eight stages based on the general traits that prevailed during a span of time, as illustrated below:

Figure 2.1: Eight Stages of the Deep State

Stage	Duration	Key Characteristics
First Stage	1947-57	The Military Gathers Confidence; Military-Bureaucratic Alliance Develops
Second Stage	1958-71	Landlord-Military-Bureaucratic Capitalist Alliance (TROIKA) (Military Dictatorship Starts)
Third Stage	1972-77	Military Bounces Back, Civilian Failure, Nuclear Project Takes Shape
Fourth Stage	1978-88	Military-Mujahideen Alliance (Islamic Army-ISI Nexus)
Fifth Stage	1989-98	Effort to Control the Democratic Experiment
Sixth Stage	1999-08	Military-Led National Discourse (Military Backed-Uber-Patriotism) Uniformed democracy
Seventh Stage	2009-18	Army Re-assertion and Spoiler's Role vis-à-vis the Coalition Governments
Eight Stage	Post-2018	Back to Uniformed democracy

Source: Annotated by the Author.

First Stage–During this stage, the military was used to start a guerrilla war (1947-48) vis-à-vis India; to bring normalcy to the State of Punjab in the wake of the Anti-Ahmadiyya riots in the early 1950s; dominance of the Army in the decision making processes; weak divided political forces and institutions; the bureaucratic elite acquired an advantage as far as policymaking was concerned. The appointment of Ghulam Muhammad, a former bureaucrat from the Indian Audit and Accounts Service, as Governor-General in October 1951, to be succeeded by another bureaucrat-cum-military man, Iskander Mirza, in August 1955, laid the groundwork for the 'bureaucracy's ascendancy aided by the military'. Since the task of running the government needed trained personnel, it was imperative that the base of the civil services was enlarged, as a result, a number of military officers were appointed.[53] To top it all the 'first Constitutional Coup dealt a fatal blow to political leaders' democratic aspirations', and this apathy for democracy persists to this day. The cabinet-style government increasingly gave way to a more authoritarian system of control represented by the 'bureaucracy-military alliance', strengthened by the first military coup in 1958.

Second Stage–The deep state comprised of the civil bureaucracy and the military as partners, with large landowners and feudal landlords, mainly from Punjab, willing to support this ruling combine. These powerful feudal classes had benefited from the green revolution started by President, General Ayub Khan under his 'controlled democracy' and their backing of the military-bureaucratic elite led to strengthening of the deep state. Ayub's 1962 constitution saw disengagement of the military from politics and this new political and constitutional arrangement reflected the Army's ethos of hierarchy, order and discipline. The civilian rule reflected a 'Patron-Client relationship but not partnership', which meant that the major institutions and political forces drew their power from their proximity to the chief.

Third Stage–Due to external factors like Indo-Pak War 1971, the deep state suffered a legitimacy crisis. However, soon afterwards, the United States bonhomie with the military rulers, support of external military alliances and weak civilian rule, made the deep state bounce back during this stage.

Fourth Stage–The deep state gathered momentum again, making a strong authoritarian system possible when General Zia-ul-Haq grabbed power in a coup in 1977 by ousting Prime Minister Zulfikar Ali Bhutto, who was sentenced to death and executed in 1979. Zia promoted Islamisation, turned against minorities like Ahmadis and the Shias, supported the Mujaheddin fighters in Afghanistan with the help of the ISI against the Soviet Troops. The 'military ruled directly'.

Fifth Stage–Hasan-Askari Rizvi, one of Pakistan's foremost scholars of civil-military relations, has described the Pakistani political system after the death of Zia ul-Haq, post-1988 power structure as the Army Chief being a pivot, together with the President and the Prime Minister, constituting the 'Troika'—an extra-constitutional arrangement for civilian-military consensus-building on key domestic, foreign policy and security issues.

Sixth Stage–The military and the civilian leaders constantly engaged in interaction and bargaining on major policy issues. The balance tilted in one direction or another, depending on the stakes of the military, the issue in question and the context of the interaction. General Pervez Musharraf overturned the elected government of Prime Minister Nawaz Sharif in a coup in 1999, after he was fired by Sharif, when he was on a visit abroad. This stage witnessed 'Uniformed democracy' as the military leader himself stood for election to hold on to power for the second term.

Seventh Stage–President Musharraf's control began to ebb in 2007, when he was challenged by Justice Choudhary, and it got further accentuated with the assassination of Benazir Bhutto in an election rally campaign in 2007. Pakistan People's Party (PPP) nominee, Yusuf Gilani became the Prime Minister and President Musharraf was forced to resign later, as two main political parties decided an impeachment motion against him. A coalition government of sorts emerged and continued, through constitutional measures including transfer of power from President to the Prime minister, tension between the govt and the military over 'Memogate scandal', etc., until Nawaz Sharif became the Prime Minister in 2013, but forced to leave the country as the court held him guilty on corruption charges. Hence upstaging of democratically elected prime minister was a key characteristic of this stage.

Eighth Stage–Following Imran Khan's victory in the 2018 elections, purportedly with the Army's help, the military is contributing significantly to policymaking arena as well and also enjoying sufficient autonomy in its professional affairs. This '*hybrid way of working*' ensures that the overall democratic dispensation is maintained, with political leaders managing the affairs of the state but with the consent of the military. Another institution of some sort that has gained prominence is the Corps Commander conference presided over by the Army Chief, includes top commanders, principal staff officers at the Army headquarters and other senior officers holding strategic appointments.[54] Smooth interaction among the Troika or the collegiate group consisting of ISI Chief, Corps Commanders, and Principal Staff Officers, operate as a peer pressure group in guiding the Army Chief but if serious differences develop among these key players, the military remains well-placed to exert pressure.[55]

The evolution of the Pakistani state and the way leadership ran the state have enabled the Army to gradually evolve as a powerful stakeholder in the overall power architecture. Without a doubt, the military remains an integral component of the state, or rather 'Army is the state'.

THE PARADOXICAL PUZZLE

While constitutional democracy has never truly blossomed, authoritarianism too has also not garnered widespread legitimacy. This Paradoxical puzzle has hobbled Pakistan's political development most of the time. The Army grows in strength and size and at the same time, it stunts the growth of the political system. No attempt is made to redress this power imbalance between the various institutions of governance and Army. In fact, by calling the Army to settle political differences amongst themselves, the country's power remains diffused among three broad centres, creating political instability.[56] In moral and spiritual matters, the 'ulama and the 'mashaikh' [religious scholars and leaders] still command the undivided loyalty of the bulk of the people. In temporal matters, the coercive authority is seen to reside clearly with the 'military and civil bureaucracy'. Political leadership, therefore motivated mainly by the power of patronage, is burdened with a constant struggle for legitimacy; unlike European countries, in the popular perception [among Pakistanis] no moral legitimacy is conferred by-elections, with the result that politicians seldom have been able to control the bureaucracy."[57]

The deep state has always attributed failures to elected authorities, democracy and those who questioned the deep state's narrative, like Fatima Jinnah, Sheikh Mujib, Zulfikar Bhutto, Nawaz Sharif who were labelled as traitors/non-Muslim. Dictatorships were imposed, and wars funded by the United States and Saudi Arabia were waged in the guise of patriotism and religious freedom. Benazir

Bhutto was appointed Prime Minister on the condition that she would not meddle in internal security or foreign policy matters. After Pervez Musharraf's departure, the invisible forces shifted their strategy, and instead of intervening directly, they managed matters from behind closed doors.[58]

Despite being ousted by the deep state, again and again, it did not take long for Prime Minister Nawaz Sharif to counter it (deep State) as a serious challenge. In the end, it was the judiciary which stifled his image. Pakistani judiciary kowtows to the '*doctrine of necessity*', including the superior courts helped to legitimise the illegitimate. Coup d'etat's in the history of Pakistan have been validated by the superior courts by the misinterpretation of three maxims of Roman Law: '*Id quod alias non est, licitum, necessitas licitum facit*' (that which otherwise is not lawful, necessity makes lawful), '*Salus populi est suprema lex*' (the public welfare is the highest law), and '*Salus republicae est suprema lex*' (Safety of the State is the supreme law). The Army has completely disregarded civilian institutions and ironically the judiciary has legalised it by invoking the doctrine of necessity.

The prominent belief is, the Pakistani Army serves as a pre-eminent guardian not only of Pakistan's foreign and domestic interests but also of the nation's ideology, variously construed by the military dictators.[59] The question remains why the military alone is viewed as the state's guardian and not the constitution? First perspective is that Pakistan's political parties, whether in power or opposition that did not commit to the concepts of accountability, transparency, and rule of law created a political vacuum that was filled by the deep state. Second, Pakistan's national security problem stemmed from the fear of a much larger India at the time of partition, therefore military strength and domination were present from the very outset. Third, the state itself induced military into the political domain which laid the foundation for erosion of civilian authority and dominance of the Army into decision making processes as happened in the fifties, this had a long-term impact on the country's political trajectory. Another factor is the policy pursued by neighbouring countries or great powers with the connivance of the deep state. For instance was it not in the United States' interest to depose then Prime Minister ZA Bhutto's rule in the aftermath of the March 1977 general elections, because martial law would not have been implemented in Pakistan without Washington's support.

COMPOSITION

The actors or rather variables, which are part of the deep state have no fixed composition. For the sake of clear understanding, these have been labelled in concentric circles. Their importance and position keep changing depending on which particular actor has a powerful lobby among the core actors. The inner core actors, namely, the Army and intelligence institutions remain constant as their importance and authority is a consistent factor in the deep state continuum.

The actors/variables in the peripheral circles change according to their importance and influence in the conduct of state affairs. The farther a variable is from the centre, the less influence it has on the core; and alternately, the closer an actor is to the core, its relation is stronger via-à-vis the core. As seen in the diagram, the concentric circles reflect the dynamics of the working of the actors/variables that constitute the deep state.

Figure 2.2: Composition of the Pakistan's Deep State

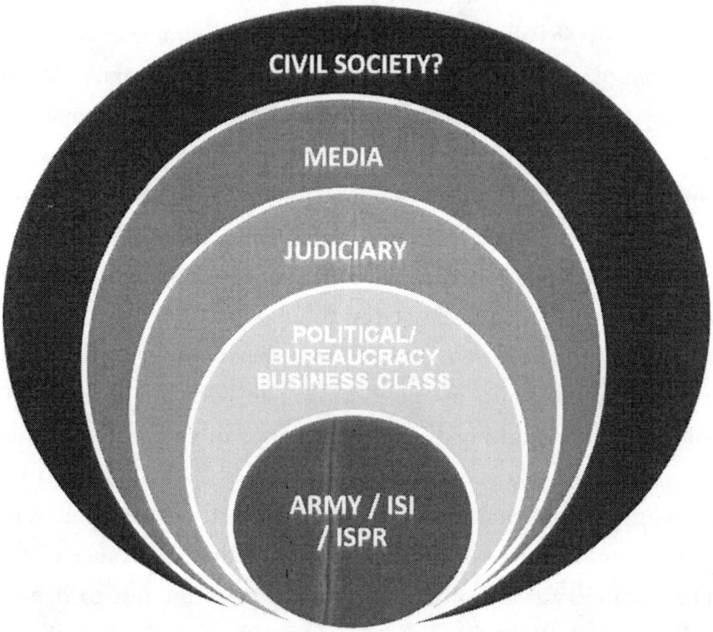

Source: Annotated by the Author.

IMPLICATIONS

Pakistan has been under direct military rule for more than three decades. Even when the Army is not in power, it has used its clout to keep a solid hold on politics and national security. Establishing democratic institutions, including civilian control of the military, has thus been a difficult process marked by ambiguity, reversal, and backsliding.[60] The continuation of military as a constant feature in Pakistan's deep state has the following ramifications:

- Creates a privileged class composed of defence forces, bureaucracy and their business partners, which is elitist and authoritarian in character, this leads to marginalisation of the parliament and civil society
- Prevents political plurality and obstructs organic democratic process by robbing people of their right to choose their government, and even if they are allowed to exercise their franchise, at times, the election processes are manipulated against or in favour of certain political groups to serve the interests of the deep state.
- The deep state operates with all means at its command such as espionage of its opponents, suppression of dissent through fear and terror to perpetuate its hold on power.
- It plots perennially to keep the legitimate government weak and even destabilise if it becomes too assertive. It adopts a strategy of putting its own trusted people as members of political parties and if any government seeks to shackle it, it engineers political agitations, judicial and extra-constitutional interventions to oust such government.[61]
- According to Stephan Cohen, "in the foreseeable future, the Pakistan Army's vision of itself, its domestic role, and its strategic environment will be the most important factors shaping Pakistan's identity. The Army will continue to set the limits on what is and what is not possible in the state."[62]
- Castigating the Army leadership in no uncertain terms, outspoken Pakistani Police officer Tariq Khosa has observed that frequent military rule has resulted in '*erosion of democratic institutions*', leading to '*constant tension*' and an '*undercurrent of mistrust between the military and civilian leadership*'. While the military projects itself as defender of national interests, leaders of political parties, feudal barons and business tycoons are perceived (only) as defenders of special interests.[63]

- Deep state ensures that the civilian politicians manipulate laws to accommodate the Army and stabilise the government; even when they realise that by so doing they undermine the trust of the people and damage the long-term prospects for democracy, enhancing their own power.
- Because of overweening power of the deep state, other tools of governance like education, civic administration, free press, independent judiciary etc. have not flourished the way they should have, in a democracy. The four pillars of democracy have not grown and developed appreciably.
- The dominance of the defence and security machinery on the statecraft has led the security concerns of the state to always prevail over developmental concerns leading to the abysmal state of the economy today.
- 'Institutionalisation of the military control, through means like 'constitutional reengineering', penetration of public sector by 'appointing serving and retired military officers' and 'occupying economic space' through business activity, makes it difficult for the political elite to roll back deep state's influence creating 'informal blocks' to stall processes of transition to a democratic form of government in Pakistan,' points out Mazhar Aziz.[64]

Looking at the arguments enumerated in the chapter one can conclude, Pakistan has been filled with deep state DNA since its inception, and it now appears to have reached its apex. With each new government, it gets stronger, infiltrating more and more aspects of public life. The progress and development of a modern liberal and progressive democracy are at odds with the deep state. Is there any hope? A strong judiciary, a diversely educated and inclusive society and a true constitutional democracy, where successive elected civilian government rules for at least three terms. However, on the ground, the deep state continue to be labelled as a '*Praetorian state*,' '*Garrison state*,' '*Controlled democracy*,' '*Hybrid state*,' '*Coupless coup*,' '*non-coup Coup*,' or '*Uniformed democracy*'.

NOTES

1. Choudhary Rahmat Ali, "Pakistan the Fatherland of the Pak Nation", London; The Pak National Liberation Movement, 1947, p. 225.
2. G. Allana, *Pakistan Movement Historical Documents* (Karachi: Department of International Relations, University of Karachi, n.d. [1969]), pp. 407-411. Paragraph numbers in double brackets have been added by FWP for classroom use; punctuation has been slightly adjusted for clarity. Editorial comments in square brackets have

been added by FWP. http://www.columbia.edu/itc/mealac/pritchett/00islamlinks/txt_jinnah_assembly_1947.html. Accessed on September 8, 2019.
3. Khalid Sayeed, Pakistan the formative phase, 1857-1928, p. 105, no. 1.
4. Special report on the news on Sunday, August 29, 2010. http://jang.com.pk/the news/aug2010-weekly/nos-29-08-2010/spr.htm, Interview with Ziauddin Sardar. Accessed on July 4, 2020.
5. Such changes had been initiated earlier, in tenures of Chiefs—Asif Nawaz, Waheed & Karamat as well.
6. Stephen Philip Cohen, *The idea of Pakistan*, New Delhi: Oxford University Press 2004, p. 93.
7. Dr Moonis Ahmar, "Pakistan as a deep state?". *Daily Times* Op-ed, January 5, 2001. https://dailytimes.com.pk/174349/Pakistan-deep-state/.
8. Imad Zafar, "The corrosive influence of Pakistan's 'deep state'," *Asia Times*, March 28, 2018. https://asiatimes.com/2018/03/red-line-needs-redefined-power-corridors/. Accessed on August 4, 2020.
9. Walter Russel Mead, "Pakistan's Deep state Seeks a New Patron", Global view July 30, 2018 *Wall Street Journal.*
10. Zilquernain Tahir, "Nawaz says he will rid Pakistan of state above state", July 12, 2018, *Dawn* https://www.dawn.com/news/1419533
11. Mazhar Aziz, *Military control in Pakistan, the Parallel State*, Routledge, 2008, p. 26.
12. Frazana Shaikh, "Community and Consensus in Islam", op. cit., p. 153.
13. Also known as India Council Act of 1909. The number of members of legislative council of Governor General and the Governors of various provinces was increased along with the provision for separate electorates for Muslims.
14. Husain Haqqani, *Pakistan Between Mosque and Military*. Gurugram: Penguin Viking publishers, 2016, p. 2.
15. Khalid Bin Sayeed. *Pakistan: The Formative Phase, 1857-1948*. London: Oxford University Press, 1968, pp. 198-199.
16. Yasmin Khan, *The Great Partition. The Making of India and Pakistan*, New Haven: Yale University Press, 2007.
17. Munir commission report of the court of Inquiry on the Punjab disturbance of 1953. http://www.thepersecution.org/archive/munir/p212.html
18. Ashok Behuria, "The Islamist Impulse Haunting Pakistan", *Strategic Analysis*, 2010, Vol. 35, Issue 1, pp. 12-16.
19. Hussain Haqqani, n. 14.
20. Ibid., p. 16.
21. Mohammad Waseem, "Politics and the State in Pakistan", Islamabad, National Institute of Historical and Cultural Research, 1994, p. 99.
22. Christine Fair, "Why Pakistan Army is here to Stay: Prospects for civilian governance", *International Affairs*, Vol. 87, No. 3 (May 2011), p. 571.
23. S. Akbar Zaidi, "State, Military and Social Transition: Improbable Future of Democracy in Pakistan", *Economic and Political Weekly*, Vol. 40, No. 49 (Dec. 3-9, 2005), pp. 5173-5181, https://www.jstor.org/stable/4417489
24. n. 9, p. 45.

25. Bourke-White, Margaret. *Halfway to Freedom*. New York: Simon and Schuster 1949, p. 103.
26. Umbreen Javaid and Rehana Saeed Hashmi, "Contending Ethnic Identities: An Issue to Pakistan's Internal Security (The case of Karachi)," *Journal of Political Studies* 19 no. 1, 2012, p. 60.
27. Christophe Jaffrelot, *The Pakistan Paradox: Instability and Resilience*, Gurugram: Random Penguin Books, 2015.
28. Kirti Shah and Sushant Sareen, "The Mohajir Identity and Politics in Multi-ethnic Pakistan". ORF Occasional Paper, November 6, 2019. https://www.orfonline.org/research/the-mohajir-identity-and-politics-in-multiethnic-pakistan-57322/. Accessed on May 3, 2020.
29. Sadaf Aziz, *The Constitution of Pakistan: A contextual Analysis*, UK: Bloomsbury, 2018.
30. S. Mahmood, "Decline of the Pakistan Muslim League and its Implications (1947-54)", *Pakistan Journal of History and Culture*, 15(2), July-December 1994, pp. 63-84.
31. Military, State and Society in Pakistan by Hasan-Askari Rizvi(auth.) (z-lib.org).pdf
32. *Hasan Askari Rizvi, Military, State and Society in Pakistan (New York: St. Martin's Press, 2000)* p. 4.
33. n. 4, p. 30.
34. Military, State and Society in Pakistan by Hasan-Askari Rizvi (auth.) (z-lib.org).pdf
35. C. Christine Fair, *Fighting to the end. The Pakistan Army's way of War*, New York: Oxford University Press, 2014, p. 6.
36. Pakistan Army Green Book, Pakistan Army General Headquarters, Rawalpindi, Ferozsons (Pvt.) Ltd. 13.
37. Ishtiaq Ahmed, *Jinnah: His success, Failures and Role in History*, Gurugram: Penguin Viking, 2020.
38. Ibid., p. 29.
39. Hamza Rizvi, *The Military and Politics in Pakistan,1947-1997*, 3rd ed. Lahore: Progressive Publishers,1986.
40. Paul E. Lenze Jr. *Civil-Military relations In the Islamic World*, London: Lexington Books, 2016, p. 77.
41. Excerpt from a speech made by Jinnah broadcast from radio Pakistan, Dhaka, 28 March 1948.
    M.A. Jinnah, "Farewell message to East Pakistan", *Jinnah. Speeches and statements, 1947-48*, Karachi, Oxford University Press, 2009, p. 174.
42. Christopher Jaffrelot, *The Pakistan Paradox, Instability and Resilience*, Gurugram: Random House India Pvt Ltd, 2015. p. 9.
43. Brigadier A.R. Siddiqui, The: 1996.
44. Nusrat Bhutto v Chief of Army Staff PLD, 1977 SC 657; Zafar Alu Shah v general Pervez Musharraf PLD 2000 SC 869.
45. Veena Kukreja, "Military Intervention in Politics", First Published July 1, 1982. "Contrasting cases of Pakistan and India", *India Quarterly*, https://journals.sagepub.com/doi/abs/10.1177/097492848203800303
46. Zhao Shurong and Saif Ur Rahman, "Rethinking Civil-Military relations in a Pakistan: Some Lessons from Turkey", *Journal of Social Omics*, Vol. 6, Issue 3, 2017.

47. Adil Rasheed, *Countering the Radical Narrative*, New Delhi: KW Publishers Pvt Ltd, 2020.
48. Jyoti M. Pathania, "An Insight into the narrative creation of Pakistan Based Groups", January 31, 2021. https://www.claws.in/an-insight-into-the-narrative-creation-of-pakistan-based-groups/. Accessed on January 31, 2021.
49. Abdul Sattar, *Pakistan Foreign Policy, 1947-2009*, Karachi: oxford University Press, 2010, p. 21.
50. Muhammad Ayub Khan President of Pakistan, *Friends not Masters: A Political Autobiography*, Karachi: Oxford University Press, 1967.
51. General (retd.) Mirza Aslam Beg, "The Powerbrokers of Democracy", *The Nation*, Lahore, 6 April 2007.
52. Ibid., p. 83.
53. Chaudhri Muhammad Ali, *The emergence of Pakistan*, Lahore: University of Punjab, 1983, p. 57.
54. It meets periodically and discusses issues like security, organizational and professional matters, law and order, and general political conditions.
55. Hussain Haqqani, *Pakistan between Mosque and Military*, UK: Penguin, 2005.
56. Shuja Nawaz, *Crossed Swords, Pakistan Army and the wars within*, Karachi: Oxford University Press, 2008.
57. Arshad Zaman, former chief economist, planning commission, "National Security and Development Strategy in Pakistan." Paper presented at the National Defence College, 26 September 1998.
58. Imad Zafar, "The corrosive influence of Pakistan's 'deep state'" March 28, 2018.
59. C. Christine Fair, "Why Pakistan Army is here to stay: prospects for civilian governance?" *International Affairs*, Vol. 87, No. 3 (May 2011), pp. 571-588.
60. By Aqil Shah, "How Pakistan's Politicians Help the Military", *The New York Times*, January 23, 2020. https://www.nytimes.com/2020/01/23/opinion/pakistan-politicians-military.html
61. Moonis Ahmar argues that despite seventy years of its existence as a state, Pakistan has not been able to transform its political culture which is still overshadowed by those elements who wield the real power and are able to strike back when they realise that an elected government has crossed the limit. *Hence, the 'culture of Pakistan conforms to the reality of deep state'.*
62. Brookings institution press Washington, D.C. 2004.
63. Criticising the extension given to Gen Bajwa, Khosa had written, "if they (the political leadership) think that by giving extension in service to army chiefs, they can attain stability of tenure and promote the mantra of civilian and military on same page, they are sadly mistaken" 'A reform agenda', *Dawn* May 20, 2021: www.dawn.com;
64. Mazhar Aziz, "The military control in Pakistan", London ; New York : Routledge, 2008.

Source: www.cartoonistsatish.com

3. An Omnipotent, Omnipresent & Omnificent Army

> "*The first constitutional coup d'etat marked the end of Jinnah's Muslim League and the beginning of a history of military coups in Pakistan, thereafter bringing King's Party as façade of democracy.*"

Pakistan Army is the single most dominant and the largest service institution that has ruled the country for much of the state's existence either through covert or overt means. As a result, the country has a national discourse influenced by the Army. Despite the fact that the Air Force, Navy and other paramilitary organisations also exist, but their participation in the domain of governance remains comparatively less. Based on the premise of their duty to the nation and its citizens, the Army Generals, primarily the Army Chief, Director of Inter-Services Intelligence (ISI) and the Corps Commanders, step in when they believe that the civilian order is failing or when their interest is being compromised by the ruling government. The military autonomy has strengthened over time with the top brass resenting any interference from the civilian government as they consider it to be their professional and internal service affair.

To be precise, thirty-four years of military rule under four serving generals i.e., almost half of Pakistan's existence as an independent nation has been under direct Army rule, the rest half under indirect Army rule, signifying military's control as 'complete and comprehensive', including the virtual surrender of mainstream political forces; the only change is that the Military leadership now prefers to control from behind a '*malleable civilian façade*'.[1] In the past it has been observed, politicians like Zulfikar Ali Bhutto, Nawaz Sharif, Imran Khan have tried to align their views with the military as an easy and successful route to power, allowing the Army to be powerful and all-pervasive institution. The uniqueness of the Pakistan Army has been summed up by South Asian expert, late Stephen P. Cohen who believed that generally countries have armies but the Pakistan Army has a country. The Army has been integral to state survival and state-building right from its earliest days. Its role was a carryover from the British rule, shaped by the developments of both pre- and post-Independence eras.[2]

UNDERPINNINGS OF THE DEEP STATE: POST-INDEPENDENCE

The pre-Independence deep state moorings discussed in the preceding chapter continue to dominate the post-Independence era due to several interrelated reasons. *First* and foremost, the '*incompetence of the political class*' prevented civilian ascendancy, creating a vacuum that the military inadvertently filled. This led to the development of the Army into an '*overgrown institution*' which helped in sustaining its own institutional (business) interests, at the cost of growth of other democratic institutions. *Second*, the Armys' characteristics of '*organisational coherence with professionalism*' have elevated it above other institutions, providing it with a competitive advantage. Likewise, Shuja Nawaz argues, "the military ... pays ritualistic obeisance to the concept of civilian supremacy … but the actual decision making on defence matters tends to be largely in the hands of men in uniform …".[3] *Third*, in some general sense, the Army has succeeded in enabling its own existence, making appropriate adjustments along the way to ensure that its policies and preferences do not in fact destroy the state.[4] *Fourth*, Army's psyche is based on the '*narrow state ideology* as *protector of country's ideology, unity and sovereignty*,' using the crutch of conservative Islam-Imam (belief), Taqwa (fear of Islam), jihad-fi-sabilillah (fight in the cause of Allah), as a binding factor for a nation which had not tasted nationalism.[5]

Fifth, the Army crafts out ways and means to ensure that civilian institutions remain weak and kept at bay. Beginning with the first war to resist India, restricting its presence was made a '*core strategic culture*' passed on by every government including the ordinary citizens who shared same strategic concerns. *Sixth*, Army is uniquely positioned to protect not just territorial integrity but the '*Islamic ideology of Pakistan*', which believes in protecting Pakistan Muslim identity from India's supposed Hindu identity.[6] Every Army Chief served as a '*protector and beholder of Islam*', the most important symbol for unifying the country. *Seventh*, due to the '*weak parliamentary politics*'; '*corruption within Muslim league Party*'; its '*institutional weakness*' and '*dominance of the rich landlords interests over the party's interest*', led the Army to always stand intact to lead in any crisis situation. *Eighth*, '*constitutional re-engineering*' has been used to gain parliamentary legitimacy. The first indication of this was when Prime Minister Khwaja Nazimuddin tried to initiate an amendment to curtail the power of the Governor-General. Fearing this, Governor-General Ghulam Muhammad dismissed him in April 1953 and subsequently, the Constituent Assembly on October 24, 1954. In a way, this maiden "*Constitutional Coup d'état marked the end of Jinnah's Muslim League and the beginning of a history of military coups in Pakistan.*"[7] Hobnobbing between Islamism and secularism, provincialism and centralism, parliamentary and presidential systems demonstrated the ambivalence and dilemma of the elite leadership throughout the *seven-year period of constitution-making*.

Another example of tweaking the constitution at will was under Gen Zia ul-Haq, after he usurped power in 1977. Article 58 (2) (b) of the 1973 constitution was inserted vide the eighth amendment, allowing the President to dismiss the Prime Minister, provincial Chief Ministers, dissolve the national and provincial assemblies, nominate Judges of the superior judiciary, and appoint the chief of armed services. The after-effects of this amendment was that no government lasted its full tenure, including the governments of Benazir Bhutto (1990) and Nawaz Sharif (1993). It was only in the year 1997, with the return to a parliamentary form of democracy, this was repealed with a two-thirds majority by Nawaz Sharif's government, though it lasted only for a brief period. As soon as General Musharraf seized power in October 1999, he restored 58(2) (b) and set up a National Security Council, which further empowered the President to appoint the chief of the armed forces and dissolve the National Assembly. The eighteenth amendment restored many provisions that seek to endorse parliamentary supremacy under Prime minister Yousaf Raza Gilani in April 2010. The subsequent developments have proved that such constitutional revisions do not automatically reinstate civilian supremacy. The deep state continues to hold its sway.

Ninth, the progressive subordination of Pakistan's *'national Identity and interests to the growing power of the military's image'*. Brigadier (retd.) Abdurrahman Siddiqi has asserted "*in controlling instruments of violence, Army's predominance and power has led to the birth of a 'sort of Prussianism' to produce an 'Army with a nation in place of nation with an Army"*.[8] In the same vein, Pakistani scholar Mazhar Aziz calls the Pakistan Army a "*Parallel State*".

Tenth, military's projection of itself as a 'key player in power politics' has continued unabated, and Aqil Shah blames this on the founding father Muhammad Ali Jinnah's bad habit of not disciplining the Army Chief's insubordination during the 1947/48 war, therefore failing to build a '*positive patron-client relationship*.'[9] *Eleventh*, conflict with India is always seen in '*existential terms*,' i.e., simply having the ability to fight and threaten India is its success. Moreover, Pak Armys revisionism persists in regards to its efforts not only to undermine the territorial status quo in Kashmir but also to undermine India's position in the region and beyond.[10] This attitude has not changed.

Stephen Cohen has rightly remarked, "For the foreseeable future, the Army's vision of itself, its domestic role, and Pakistan's strategic environment will be the most important factors shaping Pakistan's identity."[11] Therefore, the ideology cultivated by the Army has deep resonance for the Pakistan polity as well as for civilian politicians and bureaucrats; and even if the

Army were to one day suffer a loss of power, change in strategy would be unlikely.[12]

SYMBIOTIC RELATIONSHIP BETWEEN MILITARY AND THE POLITY

Studying the pattern of relationship between the Army and the political process across seven decades, it is possible to conclude that the two are interdependent, with the relationship generally following a cyclic pattern showcasing the military's embedded influence in the polity as seen in the self-explanatory diagram Figure 3.1.

Figure 3.1: Symbiotic Cyclical Pattern

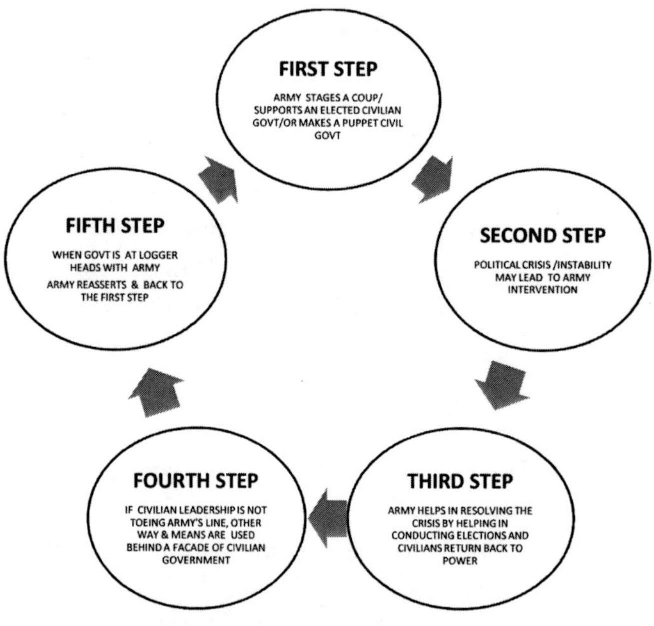

Source: Annotated by the Author.

Note: This diagram is generic in nature as steps do overlap and are drawn in a pattern that might not be the same all the time as there are cumulative factors involved.

Studies on the civil-military interaction, as well as the Army's internal deliberations on ideology, philosophy, and a prospective doctrine are mostly culled from the *National Defence University (NDU) Journals*, '*Margalla papers*', '*Monographs*', '*Hilal*' magazine and the '*Green Book*'[13] As a result of serious introspection by military minds, who tried to reason out the Pakistani loss in the 1971 war, there was a move to produce a written document which shaped and represented the thinking of the military. In the early 1990s, General Aslam Beg published the first '*Green Book*', which was originally intended for internal circulation only.[14]

A road map for the '*new model army*' was proposed by Lieutenant General Tariq Majid, Chief of the Joint Chiefs of Staff Committee (2007-2010), in the *Green Book* in its 1991 edition. He wrote that as an "Islamic state, apart from the standing forces", Pakistan should [keep] a volunteer force of the people and [employ] the other lot of able-bodied manpower to strengthen the other elements of the military system during war. The volunteer force of the people would, in time, evolve into ISI-backed jihadist networks which Pakistan now sponsors."[15]

The *Green Book* (1994) acknowledging Brigadier Saifi Ahmad Naqvi's statement, argued that "*Pakistan is an ideological state based on the ideology of Islam,* [and] *its existence and survival depends upon complete implementation of Islamic ideology in true sense. If the ideology is not preserved then the very existence of Pakistan becomes doubtful*". In his view, it was the Army's duty to be "responsible for the defence of the country, to safeguard [its] integrity [and] territorial boundaries, and the ideological frontiers, to which the country owes its existence."[16]

The need to patronise jihadist groups was cited in the *Green Book* (2002), by Brig. Muneer Mahmood, who wrote that Pakistan was being projected as a '*torch-bearer of the Muslim ummah [country] by the biased western media and Jewish lobby*'. It was 'likely to be the target of these forces' at some point, and while a 'conventional war' between India and Pakistan is unlikely, the situation appears perfect for a LIC [low-intensity conflict] battle."[17] General Pervez Musharraf, recording the deliberations of Brigadier Zia and his brother officers, said that this edition of the *Green Book* (2002) was a "valuable document for posterity." The tactical patronage of jihadist groups operating against Afghanistan, India and the West is derived from the system of ideas outlined in these *Green Books.*[18]

The *Green Book* (2008) highlighted the misgivings of the officers as then ongoing counter-insurgency operations in the north-west after 2002 raised an issue of legitimacy. Brigadier Waqar Hassan Khan,wrote in it: "The superpower's foray into Middle East and West Asia was not feasible without a Pearl Harbour; 9/11 was either created or branded as the second Pearl Harbour," "Now it has come out in the open that people have been mistaking the jungle for a tree; the so-called Pakistani Taliban was a bogey created by RAW, MOSSAD, and most likely the US-led coalition to keep the Durand Line burning and de-stabilise Pakistan internally in order to achieve the ultimate goal of undermining the only nuclear Islamic state on the planet." He claimed that Pakistan's counter-insurgency efforts were beset with a "legitimacy concern." "If a segment of society is not convinced about the task's moral standing, and a broad view along these lines exists among the masses," he said, "it gravely erodes the military's performance, which is affected by societal pressures." Military actions within one's own country necessitate that the troops feel just and fair about the operations being carried out, and that popular support exists. No amount of training, drive, or technological advantage will make a difference unless it happens. Pakistan's Army simply could not, engage in a war against jihadist militia that it had fathered without undermining the foundations of its own legitimacy. [19]

The *Green Book* (2013), mentions the adoption of new doctrine of war-fighting termed sub-conventional warfare & home grown militancy "as the biggest threat to national security, making a clear shift from the past where the threats from India were tagged as most serious."[20] This form of low-intensity warfare continues to give Army a prominent role in the statecraft. The *Green Book* (2020 edition) was India-centric, with issues like J&K remaining the focal point of its propaganda. There were concerns about US-India growing ties, nuclear deterrence, and '*false historical narrative building*' by mentioning that India 'surreptitiously occupied the vacant area north of NJ 9842' in 1984, but Pakistan was blamed sans evidence for the 'engineered' October 1, 2001, and December 13, 2001 attacks in J&K and Delhi, respectively. The book clearly mentions future wars to be driven by '*propaganda and mind-games*' promoting alternate and counter-narratives with an emotional appeal.[21] The Green Book (2021) focuses on Kashmir; naming India as a rogue state with hindutva rightist ideology; Post Balakot regional strategic matrix is trilateral as limited wars between India & Pak or India & Chiana can escalate into bigger regional conflict and cyber warfare will be the new big war.[22]

PAKISTAN MILITARY DOCTRINE

A military doctrine is the fundamental set of principles that guides military forces as they pursue national security objectives. These principles could range from the policies and procedures put in place by a particular military branch to the tactics and techniques taught to new members during training.[23] Hence, doctrines are a *set of guidelines based on the strategy, war-fighting plans, threats and challenges that nation faces representing military's institutional belief systems.*[24] A majority of organised military forces of the world operate under the shadow of some form of military doctrine, contained or unspoken.

Pakistan's military doctrine is not stated in black and white as they have not come out with it. But its' possible moorings, based on the past historical experience, ethos and institutional beliefs are documented in its security policies & strategies. One can only cull out certain traits which can be considered as the foundation of its military doctrine. Each successive generation of the military is taught this and is also required to abide by them. It is necessary to understand the military doctrine in order to truly comprehend the subtleties of the deep state. The security strategy and war fighting doctrine are centred around two real security concerns, i.e., military & geography whereby the absence of strategic depth affects it's insecurity dilemma, stripping it of this classic defence strategy and two, the extent and availability of resources for the conduct of conventional military operations.[25]

In order to understand Pak military philosophy, it is essential to study the fundamental roots of the doctrine. The Figure 3.2 below represents the main influencers on the fundamental military outlook.

Figure 3.2: The Military Outlook/Doctrine-Main Philosophy

Source: Annotated by the Author.

Roots of Pakistan Fundamental Military Doctrine

- India
- Islam
- Jihad & Terrorism
- Kashmir
- Nuclear issues

India

Since independence, Pakistan has suffered from a small state syndrome vis-à-vis India considering it as the main enemy. Army's axiomatic distrust of India is followed as a legacy traced during the partition that any insult or slight must be avenged, not only to punish the aggressor but to honour the sacrifices of the earlier generations. Hence its threat perception, and therefore its security policy, security strategy and war fighting doctrine, is driven almost entirely by its understanding of India's strategic thought.[26] It is fair to say that Pakistan is essentially committed to an aggressive posture towards India. From the start of the first Indo-Pak conflict, through the proxy war of Op Gulmarg (1947-48), the Indo-Pak war of 1965, the Indo-Pak war of 1971, and the limited war Op Koi Paima in Kargil in 1999. Throughout the 1980s, this aggressive posture was obvious in its attempt to destabilise India by providing covert support to insurgents in the North East and the Sikh separatist in Panjab, including the sponsoring of terrorist activities in the J&K region since the late 1980s is a well-known fact.

Pak Army's mentality and behaviour are strongly imbued with Indian-centric discourse, accusing it of aiding Baloch, Pashtun, and Sindh ethnic insurgencies in Pakistan. Many also believe that India has never really accepted the subcontinent's division, which was mostly based on sectarian lines, and that it is constantly looking for ways to exploit vulnerabilities. Despite the fact that India recognises Pakistan as a sovereign and independent state. Shuja Nawaz cautions that "Pakistan's military doctrine, such as it is, is caught between the rock of India and the hard place of its internal threats and economic difficulties. It is not clear if there is a coherent and consensual view on how to proceed next."[27]

Islam

From the first Pakistani Army Chief to the present, the belief of military as the *'guardian of the state'* and *'protector of Islamic democracy'* continues to be advocated. The nexus of the serving as well as retired Army officers with the religious Islamist groups is growing stronger and bigger as the military and its leadership have remained Islamic, followed as a code of conduct in all spheres of life including military.[28]

The Islamic concept of military leadership has a firm belief in basic tenets of Islam i.e. '*Tauheed*' (belief in oneness of Allah), '*Risalat*', (belief that Allah has been sending his messages of divine guidance through various prophet, '*Akhirat*', (the belief that all human beings and jinn's will have to render an account of their deeds on the Day of Judgement); firm adherence to the mission assigned by Allah, through the Holy Prophet (Peace be upon him). The Islamic concept of Leadership is required to be adopted both at the individual and the collective level.

At the Individual level, each officer is expected to study the Quran and understand the Islamic concept of leadership; read the Islamic history of great leaders like Khulfa-e-Rashideen; Tariq, Khalid bin Waleed and Abu Obaida. At the Collective level, the officers should make all possible efforts to create a clean and healthy environment; strive to remove the dichotomy between thought and action; help subordinates to become true Muslims; prepare for war in accordance with the Quranic injunctions and the life of Holy Prophet; the Military academy curriculum includes the "*Islamic dimension of strategy*" namely *'fighting for the honour and memory of previous generation, as well as the larger Muslim community'*.[29] Zia-ul-Haq was the first military ruler who translated military doctrines & strategy in terms of Islamic ideology.

Pakistan's fundamental military doctrine's Islamic character is recapped by Brigadier Askari Raza Malik of the Pakistan Army, "in a society that owes its existence to Islam, its adoption is inescapable, any other system based on borrowed concepts will never appeal to the heart and soul of a Muslim soldier and with regard to modernisation and transformation, also, all modern techniques which are not foreign to this concept can be accommodated."[30]

Jihad, terrorism and Islamic militancy as an unofficial policy continue unabated. In the words of Ayres, "the multiple players who make up the deep state in Pakistan have constructed an ideological environment in which Jihadi has been accepted, flourished, conceived the contours of and formalised the employment of terror as an extension of state policy." The use of terror as a means of warfare has helped justify covert Pakistani support for militant groups operating in Indian administered Kashmir and other parts of India. *If terror is sanctioned by Quran, then it is legitimate instrument of power.* The Quranic notion of Jihad has been reinterpreted to signify 'holy battle' rather than what it originally intended. This position is widely held in the Pakistan Military. Therefore the justification for the belief in jihad and terrorism. In the words of Hussain Haqqani, "*Pakistan sees jihad as a low-cost option to bleed India viewing terrorism as irregular warfare as Islamabad feels this is the only way to ensure some form of military parity.*"[31] Examples of state-sponsored terrorism have surfaced time and again as Pakistan's Army DNA;[32] the Pathankot attack (January 2, 2016), Uri attack (September 18, 2016), Pulwama terror attack (February 14, 2019), Attack on the Indian Parliament (December 13, 2001). These attacks were carried out by militant groups such as Lashkar-e-Taiba (LeT) and Jaish-e-Muhammad (JeM), both Pakistan-based terrorist organisations. Army's strategic ideology based on Islam will continue to employ jihad and terrorism as a strategic tool for the foreseeable future.

Kashmir

Since the partition of the Indian subcontinent, military and political leaders have seen Kashmir as the "*jugular vein,*" as characterised by Mohammed Ali Jinnah, which remains partition's unfinished agenda and the source of all troubles. To reclaim Kashmir from India, it has launched four full-scale wars, innumerable border skirmishes, and a number of small-scale proxy conflicts, 1947-48, 1965, 1971 and 1999, which remain intractable. The Kashmir issue is frequently brought up not just in political debates, but also by Army Chief Gen. Qamar Javed Bajwa, who confirms support for Jammu and Kashmir's "right to self-determination" and believes that the development of nuclear weapons has rendered the country's defence impregnable.[33] The Pakistani military is unlikely to change its mind about Kashmir, its active support for militants, their nurturing, use as tools to further their own goals of fuelling the Kashmir conflict will continue unabated; providing direct assistance to the Kashmiri resistance; supporting jihad and terrorism on religious and moral grounds remains the doctrine's core. This does not seem to be changing anytime soon.

Nuclear Issues

The cornerstone of war fighting doctrine is its nuclear weapons and policy, which are well-designed to counter and match India's conventional and nuclear superiority. The logic is to balance the scales by acquiring nuclear weapons and establishing a first-use doctrine. General Mirza Aslam Beg revealed that after the defeat in the 1971 war, nuclear capability was achieved in 1987. Following that, nuclear deterrence became an important part of the military doctrine rhetoric employed repeatedly against India.

This attitude was reaffirmed by Brig. (retd.) Ahmad, who told Paula Cotta-Ramusino and M. Martellini[34] that he initially disagreed with the nuclear programme, but later felt that nuclear testing was a necessary step to show India and the rest of the world that Pakistan was capable of matching India's nuclear capabilities. According to Gen Kidwai, it does not have a "*No First Use Policy*," which is only employed "*if the very life of Pakistan as a state is at peril*," and has been detailed as follows:[35]

"*Nuclear weapons are aimed solely at India. In case that deterrence fails, they will* be used if

1. India attacks Pakistan and conquers a large part of its territory (space threshold)
2. India destroys a large part either of its land or air forces (military threshold)
3. India proceeds to the economic strangling of Pakistan (economic strangling)[36]
4. India pushes Pakistan into political destabilization or creates a large scale internal subversion in Pakistan (domestic destabilisation)"[37]

Though there have been several reviews of military doctrine due to changes in environmental conditions but the fundamentals have remained unchanged. The Army's official publications indicate that there has been a shift in threat perception, as the top most danger for internal security is the rise of '*non-state actors*' and '*sub-conventional warfare capability*'. Even though India is considered a lesser threat, its idea as an existential enemy persists.

The Pakistan Army's attitudes and values have remained the same for the past 37 years, and there is no reason to expect them to change now.[38] The radical strategic transformation is most unlikely to happen because it would sacrifice Pakistan's vital national interests.[39] And no nation ever will let its national interest be at stake. The Army's ascension to pre-eminence in the Pakistani state is captured in the quotation "There are many Armies that guard their nation's borders, there are those that are concerned with protecting their own position in society, and then there are those that defend a cause or an idea. The Pakistan Army does all three."[40]

SUBSTANTIATION OF THE 'TRIAD' BY PAK ANALYSTS

Seasoned Pakistani academicians and analysts support the view of Pak Army as a 'TRIAD'—'*Omnipotent, Omnipresent* and *Omnificent institution*' in their writings:

Hussain Haqqani, the former advisor to three Pakistan Prime Ministers, writes in his book, 'Reimagining Pakistan, Transforming a Dysfunctional Nuclear State,' about how a warm and hospitable people have paid the price for their leaders' "*magnificent mistakes*," described around the world today as "*dangerous*" and "*unstable*," a "*terrorist incubator*," and the "*land of the intolerant*," He further argues, "*Pakistan's military-led national discourse is also used by every Pakistani politician from Zulfikar Ali Bhutto to Nawaz Sharif and now Imran Khan, to hew their views close to the military as an easy route to power*".[41] It can also be regarded as a '*praetorian state*' where the military has acquired the 'capability, will, and sufficient experience' to dominate the main political institutions and processes, argues a notable military analyst Hasan Askari Rizvi. The military's disposition has a considerable impact on the course of political change, particularly the transfer of power from one set of elites to another, as the political forces are fragmented and weak. *Such an expanded role is at variance with the traditions and temperament of the military at the time of independence in 1947*."[42]

The first military takeover in 1958 removed the political leaders and the so-called democratic institutions from the scene, giving a free hand to the civil servants and the Army to run the country: "The Army served as the brain and the civil servants as the hand of the new regime."[43] General Ayub Khan also established a pattern for keeping '*political parties in check*.' Article

173 of the 1962 constitution made it illegal for anyone to run for office as a member of a political party unless an act of the central legislature allowed it. Only little political activity was permitted under the Political Parties Act, which was passed in July 1962. These and other harsh tactics against political parties were maintained by successive military rulers, who adopted a slew of laws and regulations restricting or prohibiting political parties and political activities that threatened their control. When the Army rule is not direct, the Army searches for a state and society, ensuring the installation of a civilian government which acts like its puppet.[44] The Imran Khan regime is the best example till the time he toes the Army's line. The Army has perfected the art of 'non-coup coup' and because of its diverse traits, it has been able to influence political, social-cultural, economic domains, earning the adage of '*Omnipresent institution*'.

The Army capitalises on its creative potential by employing a pool of intellectually and creatively talented young people in military public relations wing, the ISPR, establishing an intellectual and creative hegemon, adding credibility to the concept of an '*Omnificent*' organisation over and above political dominance, the age of military hegemon includes possessing '*economic clout and intellectual influence over society*.[45] In October 2014, the Pakistan student union at Oxford University provided one illustration of Army's intellectual dominance. Ever Since 2011, the Pakistani students union at Oxford University conducts an annual, three-day Young Pakistan Leadership Conference to bring together Pakistani students to debate about their country. The student union was persuaded to reject Hamid Mir's invitation, a journalist critical of the military leadership, and instead extended invitations to other pro-Pak Army writers, highlighting its strong penetration even amongst the international student community, hence intervening in the intellectual narrative building processes of the youth. A detailed explanation on societal perception management is given in Chapter Five.

The '*Omnipotent Army*' is the foremost decision making entity creating its own sets of precedents and institutions which enables it to perform like an invincible shadow government. Sadaf Aziz outlines three factors responsible for the oscillation between militarism and democracy in Pakistan; first was the empowerment of the military-bureaucratic elite in the early years of executive rule which by passed constitutional rigidities very conveniently. The second factor was the regional demands, provincialism or local inequality and the third one was the espousal of a state religion i.e., Islam within the structure of liberal Constitutionalism.[46] Pakistan passed its three Constitution in 1956, 1962, 1973 which reflects the changes in the form of militarism and democracy. The military's ceaseless pursuit of an imagined image of itself shows how triviality rather than greatness, accident rather than design, fiction rather than fact have often been the quintessence of Pakistan's military history.[47]

Governmental instability emerging from the 2018 elections makes the role of the Army even more powerful, given the general perception; if the new government falters or fails, there is the perennial spectre of the much-discussed soft coup of the military being followed by a hard coup to establish what Shuja Nawaz, a distinguished fellow at the South Asian Centre, Atlantic Council calls an "*Egypt of the Indus*".[48] Hasan Askari Rizvi contends, the institutional constructs designed by the military for retaining influence in the political domain through executive orders and decrees, constitutional and legal changes, manipulation of political forces helped to entrench themselves in promoting leadership that moved in accordance with their game plan.[49]

The military coups of 1958, 1969, 1977 and 1999 resulted in the '*swift civilianisation of military regimes*'—this military governance by co-opting civilianising sharing of office is evidence of the military's confidence in its ability to control political mechanisms and political space, and to achieve internal and international legitimacy as coups d'état's are an illegal method of deposing governments.[50]

ANALYSIS OF THE 2018 ELECTION PROCESS

The 2018 elections were the third consecutive electoral exercise without the intervening period of any military coup or military rule; speaks volumes about the democratic aspirations of the people, but the system remains mired under the complexities of '*military rule*', '*patronage politics*', '*religious* and *bourgeoisie dictatorship.*' Military rule is exercised through indirect intervention in day-today governance; its policy of forging alliances with the political elites has resulted in the military infiltrating virtually every political party.

This election saw the '*mainstreaming of the radical groups*' such as the militant groups, terrorist outfits, far-right religious groups, banned militant organisations, etc. all were successful in entering the electoral arena. Senate

Chairman and senior PPP leader Raza Rabbani brought this to the notice of the interim set-up much before the elections, but to no avail.[51] The stupendous increase in their numbers has become the new norm and a cause of concern for the democratic stakeholders. Distinct examples include the exponential and sudden rise of *Tehreek-i-Labbaik Pakistan*, an Islamic far-right political party; *Milli Muslim League (MML)*—an Islamic political party launched by Jamat-ud-Dawaa which openly works as LeT. Though the Election Commission of Pakistan (ECP) does not recognize MML and the US Dept. of State too regards it as a terrorist organization, but it continues to operate unabated; *Allah-o-Akbar Tehreek*, the latest incarnation of the LeT's political wing; the *Ahle Sunnat Wal Jamaat*, initially known as Sipah-e-Sahaba Pakistan was banned by Pervez Musharraf in 2002 as a terrorist organisation but was removed from the terror list by the establishment in June 2018, along with their party chief Muhammad Ahmed Ludhianvi, to facilitate their participation in these elections. Hafiz Saeed, a UN-designated terrorist, carried out rallies and campaigned without any disruptions, only because he had the blessing of the Army. This further adds on to the vagaries of the democratic system.

Pakistan continues to remain under Financial Action Task Force (FATF) Grey list for failing to comply with the international commitments to prevent its financial system from being used by radical groups designated by the United Nations as terrorist entities. The election results showed that the people's verdict was against these ultra-right religious and militant groups, but their entry in the electoral fora proves backing of the military which will continue to remain in Pakistan's political circle.[52] It is obvious that the Army was able to select a Prime Minister rather than electing one as the entire campaign was designed to bring one party (Tehreek-e-Insaaf) to power.

The election engineering exercise conducted under the tacit supervision of the deep state thus indicates a new form of '*Quasi—military censorship*' where the '*weapon of mass destruction*' was both '*threat and coercion*', as noted by journalist, Hameed Haroon. For instance, the Army played its card safely and timely by removing Mr Nawaz Sharif, a popular leader from the electoral scene altogether, implicating him on charges of corruption;the political leaders in Baluchistan claimed they were threatened by the Army establishment to switch parties. The electorate felt increasingly abused and cheated as the military was successful in quashing the media both online and offline, freedom of Press and any prospective political opponents. Vetting his angst against the military inroad in the electoral process, editor of Dawn, Zaffar Abbas wrote that the restrictions on media were suffocating and worse than the martial law, Army played '*twin strategy*' of '*culling the political leadership*' and '*curtailing the electorates access to information.*'[53]

The ECP had registered 122 political parties, far more than in the past but its working reflected the diktat of the Military brass. When citizens were exercising their basic political rights, more than 80,000 military personnel were stationed inside as well as outside the polling booths. The judiciary too failed in asserting its voice on the electoral malpractices and election related violence, which saw a rise in the suicide attacks in Peshawar, Bannu and Mastang. The turn out was average and results were far from representative.

The Chief of European Union Election Observation Mission (EU EOM) to Pakistan, Mr. Michael Gahler, with his team of more than 100 election observers in Islamabad, Punjab, Sindh and Khyber Pankhtunkhwa; felt that these elections were not as good as in 2013. The preliminary statement of the Report stated—"*Positive changes to the legal framework were overshadowed by restrictions on freedom of expression and unequal campaign opportunities*", thereby suggesting that more transparency measures were required to make these elections truly democratic.[54]

On the other hand, International Observers from the Commonwealth and the European Union countries had differing opinions about the conduct of elections. Mr SY Quraishi, former Chief Election Commissioner of India, observed that the elections were free and fair; based on his analysis of monitoring the polls in the twin cities of Islamabad and Rawalpindi only.[55]

The election process also had first-time franchisees, the Transgender community, known as "*Khawajasiras*" (denoting transsexuals, transvestites and eunuchs), as the Pak Election Commission removed gender as criteria for a candidate to contest. Led by Nadeem Kashish, who believed that votes of the people gave them an identity. This certainly was an '*icing on the cake of the 2018 process.*'

Christopher Jaffrelot, pointed out, throughout his campaigning "Khan's nationalism made him deeply hostile towards India"[56] but in his victory speech in July 2018, Khan offered to take two steps if India responded positively.[57] His close links with the Jihadist Islamic networks has earned him the sobriquet of *Taliban Khan* and he acted true to his name by describing Osama Bin Laden as a *Martyr*; and also removing the renowned Ahmadian economist Atif Mian from the economic advisory board because of his faith. In the first two years of his administration, 31 members of the religious minorities were killed, 58 were injured and 25 were targeted by blasphemy cases.[58]

The Trajectory of 2018 elections was mired with controversies, violence, rigging and corruption. The concept of free and fair elections continues to be a distant mirage as the results seemingly were not genuine. To realise the people's right to representation, voters require not just accurate information to help make informed decisions, but also a safe environment to vote. Rule of law based on constitutional democracy would remain an illusion until and unless the military and political roles are clearly defined.

MILITARY USURPS BUREAUCRATIC TURF

Imran Khan regime, under the tutelage of the Army, has enlarged the intake of both serving and retired military officials in a number of important government portfolios, which were traditionally given to the civilian bureaucrats. Tauseef Ahmed Khan, a Karachi-based political analyst, argues that previous governments tried to resist military's dominance in policy making, but Khan's government has no issue with it. Few instances can be cited to substantiate this point, The replacement of civilian Firdous Ashiq Awan with retired General Asim Bajwa as special advisor for communication and broadcasting; appointment of Air Marshall Arshad Malik as the head of Pakistan's state-owned airline within two months rule. However, the crash of a Pakistan International Airlines (PIA) plane in a heavily populated colony on May 22, 2020, sparked citizens demand his resignation as the plane was reportedly in poor condition and yet was allowed to carry a hundred passengers taking a huge risk," Noreen Haider, a Pakistani columnist and rights activist, has also commented on the increasingly taking over of all important civilian posts, practically running the government.[59]

The *diplomatic positions* which are largely held by civilians are also taken over by the generals. The Khan's government-appointed General Bilal Akbar to the post of Pakistan's Saudi Arabia envoy. "Besides the mission in Riyadh going back to a general, Ambassadors in Brunei, Jordan, Syria, Sri Lanka, Ukraine, the

Maldives, Nigeria and Libya are all with retired armed forces officers," Analysing all these, one can state that '*Imran Khan is the civilian face of a military state*' and is just trying to appease the military establishment to stay in power. The '*military considers itself above the law and is not answerable to anyone*'.

Michael Kugelman states, the military has been scaling up its role in policy, directly and indirectly as the "members of the powerful military have grabbed many civilian posts in the past two years, raising concerns that PM Imran Khan 's civilian government is ceding most of its power to general."[60]

A list of few high-level civilian posts, occupied by the Pakistani military (serving & retired) in his regime is shown below (private corporations and defence industries are not included) see Table 3.1 below.

Table 3.1: Military Officers as Heads of Organisations/Departments/Institutions

S. No.	Organisation/ Department/Ministry	Chief Executive	Headed by/Led by/Presided by
1.	Anti-Narcotics Force	Director-General	**Major General** Ghulam Shabbir Narejo
2.	Space & Upper Atmosphere Research Commission (SUPARCO)	Director	**Major General** Amer Nadeem
3.	Pakistan International Airlines (PIA)	CEO	**Air Marshal** Arshad Malik
4.	National Development Council (NDC)	Board Member	**General** Qamar JavedBajwa
5.	Economic Advisory Committee	Board Member	Umar Asad S/O **Major General** Ghulam Umar
6.	National logistics cell	Director-General	**Major General** Imtiaz Ahmed
7.	Water And Power Development Authority (WAPDA)	Chairman	**Lieutenant General** Muzammil Hussain
8.	China Pakistan Economic Corridor	SAPM Chairman	Current: Khalid Mansoor Previous: **Lieutenant General** Aseem Bajwa
9.	National development Council	Member	**General** Qamar Javed Bajwa

10.	Pakistan Broadcasting Corporation	Member	**Major General** Babar Iftikhar
11.	Civil Aviation Authority	Director General	**Flight Lieutenant** (Retd.) Khaqan Murtaza
12.	Airport Security Force	Director-General	**Major General** Sohail Ahmad Khan
13.	Secretary of Defence	Secretary	**Lieutenant General** (Retd.) Mian Hilal Hussain
15.	National Disaster Management	Chairman	**Lieutenant General** Akhtar Nawaz Satti
16.	Federal Public Service Commission	Chairman	**Captain** (Retd.) Zahid Saeed
17.	Pakistan Shipping Corporation	Chairman, CEO	Nadir Mumtaz Warraich **(Naval family)**
18.	Karachi Port	Board member	**Captain** Anwar Shah
19.	Frontier Works Organization	Director General	**Major General** Kamal Azfar
20.	National Medical University	Vice-Chancellor	**Lieutenant General** Syed Muhammad
21.	National Command and Operation Centre	National Coordinator	**Lieutenant General** Hamooduz Zaman
22.	Pakistan Steel Mills	Chairman	**Brigadier** Shujah Hassan Khurazmi
23.	Ministry of Defence Production	Federal secretary	**Lieutenant General** (Retd.) Tanvir Tahir
24.	Special Communications Organisation	Director General	**Major General** Muhammad Shahid Siddeeq
25	Minister of Interior	Minister	**Brigadier** Ijaz Shah

Source: Data collected by the Author from various open source materials including Twitter.

Findings from the above-mentioned data suggests, the Imran Khan government has engaged the aids and friends of the military brass for example, the appointment of former IB Chief Brig Ijaz Shah as a full fledged interior minister was in order to solidify Army's control over the internal security. Brig Shah's main claim to 'fame' was refuge given to Omar Sheikh, to obfuscate his role in kidnapping of Daniel Pearl. He was close to Musharraf and Imran appointed him, thinking current Army leaders would be pleased. They were not really delighted, as he was very infirm & incapable. Former Prime Minister late Benazir Bhutto, had named him as one of the masterminds to assassinate her, and accused him of orchestrating the formation of the Pakistan Muslim League-Q as the "King's party" before the general elections of 2002, by gaining the loyalty of PML-Nawaz supporters. He is said to have deep ties with a variety of despicable jihadists, including Al Qaeda and Omar Sayeed, killer of American Journalist, Daniel Pearl.[61] Ironically, Dr. Abdul Hafeez Sheikh, replaced Asad Umar,[62] whom apparently Khan, had never met before appointing him as his finance adviser (de facto finance minister). The appointments of Lt. Gen. (retd.) Aseem Saleem Bajwa as the first chairman of the newly-established China-Pakistan Economic Corridor Authority (CPECA), and Brigadier Khurazmi as the director or CEO of Pakistan Steel Mills, one of the largest public sector enterprises, was aimed to ensure timely completion of the multi-billion dollars projects.[63]

Illuminating on Imran Khan's political setup as a '*hybrid martial law*', Ayesha Siddiqa says, "I think the military wants to directly get involved in governance because it feels that Khan's Pakistan Tehreek-e-Insaaf party can't run the country without its support." The generals prefer a government with a civilian façade in reality, they want to control everything, including the economy.[64] More ministries appear to be taken over by military authorities in the coming years. In October 1998, Jamaat Islami (JI) Amir Qazi Husain Ahmed referred to the Pak Army as "*crore commanders*," and his remarks still ring true two decades later. CPEC Chairman Lt. Gen. Asim Bajwa's undisclosed wealth, went viral on social media, the 'deep state,' did everything it could to shut down his social media accounts and websites. As Pakistani journalist Ahmad Noorni pointed out, it's not surprising that his monetary assets expanded in proportion to his rank structure. The 'Bajwa Group' family's businesses in the United States spent $52.2 million on company development and $14.5 million on real estate purchases.[65]

The Army is the richest institution and has institutionalised its power thriving on its entrepreneurial ventures, which have continued to flourish even in times of economic meltdown. The generals never retire and are among Pakistan's wealthiest people. Islamabad's exorbitant defence spending (2.86 per cent of GDP) and failing to account for the country's already overburdened healthcare infrastructure aren't just mistakes. The military's control over the government and the weak administration's reluctance to push back is reflected in the fact that 40 million Pakistanis are food insecure, and hospitals across the country are buckling as they deal with an influx of coronavirus patients.[66]

Amjad Shoaib, a retired general and defence analyst dismisses criticism that the military is power-hungry and the civilian appointments are made solely on the basis of merit. Many government agencies began to work better once military authorities seized command. Citing examples, "PIA becoming a prosperous organisation under Air Marshall Noor Khan's leadership. General Qayyum performed the same thing with Pakistan Steel Mills, which was in trouble.[67]

As per the report of the European Foundation of South Asian Studies, the military dominance in Pakistan has increased manifold since the Imran Khan Govt took over. "It is not just that military interference in matters of governance continues to be a reality, rather the military has gone far beyond the traditional realms of national security and foreign policy and strengthened its hold over other aspects of state rule, including finance, commerce, interior, railways, China-Pakistan Economic Corridor (CPEC) and even media management."[68] Expressing concerns over the Army inroads the governance, renowned Pakistani physicist, Pervez Hoodboy says '*retired Generals shouldn't head civilian organisations, Military is only for war*.' Pakistani institutions are desperately short of competence and sorely need the right people in the right places. Retired officers when put at the head of organisations can make cosmetic changes and may superficially improve institutional discipline but not much else. Soldiers should stick to what they are good at and paid for—fighting wars rather than running businesses or making movies.[69]

First cabinet reshuffle in April 2019, just eight months after forming the government on August 20, 2018, saw Imran Khan appointing more *classic establishment puppets*, on April 16, 2021, more than halfway through his five-year mandate, it is the sixth time significant overhaul was done. This is evidenced of his chaotic governance, which is also ascertained in the worsening economic situation, declining growth, rising indebtedness, rising unemployment, and increased inflation. This misgovernance led to a novel situation wherein civilians gathered in huge numbers in Azadi Protest march (October 28, 2019) led by Maulana Fazl-ur-Rehman of Jamiat-e-Islam, demanding Khan's resignation and fresh elections, the rallies highlight being—first time a serving Chief of the Army and the military were criticised. The Khan government neither has the majority in parliament to push important legislation nor the political capital to pursue all major parties on board. The cabinet reshuffle smacks of a soft coup, in which the military is inserting directly into running the country through proxies, using Imran Khan as the civilian political face of the government. By granting bail to the opposition leader Shahbaz Sharif, and Nawaz Sharif on medical grounds the military establishment is trying to ease things for the opposition.[70]

Despite the fanfare of "*Naya Pakistan*," Imran Khan's rule has been entirely governed by the Army. This has further weakened democratic standards slowing down political and economic development. With several coups, including a constitutional coup, four successful military coups, and few failed military coups, Pakistan may be dubbed the "*land of coups*" and the "*Army as a Hegemon*" (Figure 3.3).

Figure 3.3: Army as a Hegemon

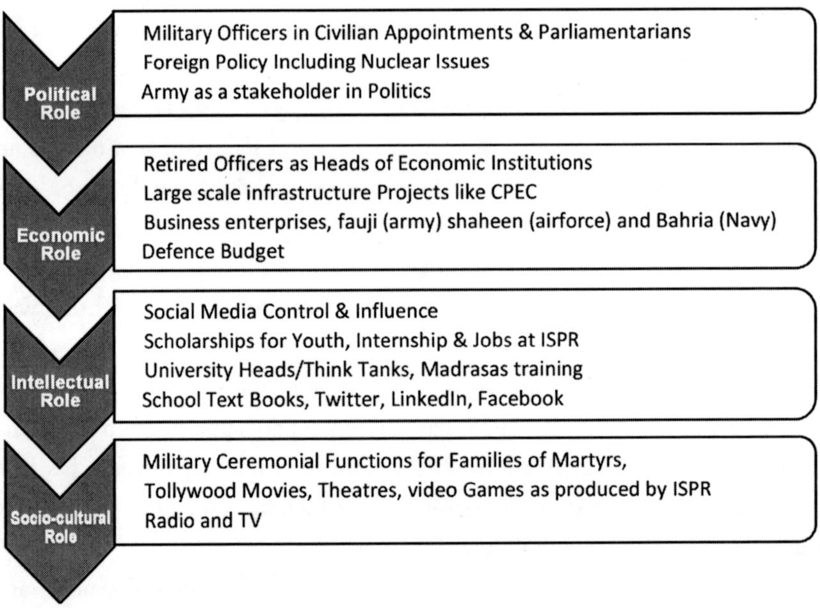

Source: Annotated by the Author.

The nexus of military and the state is bound to continue. With each round of military intervention, the political and bureaucratic institutions become even more ineffective and consensus around the modalities of government (prime minister versus president, presidential versus parliamentary) becomes ever more elusive.[71] The serving military official is presumably answerable only to the (GHQ), and this raises questions of accountability.[72] Usman Kakar, an opposition lawmaker was quoted as saying—"When we summon civilian bureaucrats, they show up and pay heed to our recommendations. When we call upon the military officials, who are heading civilian departments, they don't care to respond," The military-run institutions see more malpractices than the civilian ones. "The department responsible for dealing with the coronavirus pandemic told us that it spent rupees 2.5 million (€13,000, $16,000) on a single COVID patient. When we called the military officials working in that department to come to our parliamentary committee and explain why such a huge amount was spent, they didn't care to respond," he alleged.[73]

Eminent Pakistani authors and journalists like Hussain Haqqani, Ayesha Siddiqa, Nazir Naji, Najam Sethi, Cyril Almedia, Kashir Abbasi, Shahid Masood Ejaz Haider, believe that national, social, political, and economic policies should not be defined by the military including the ISI/ISPR but should be under complete civilian control. The fact is that Army is the largest and most powerful political party in Pakistan, the de facto government, the biggest and most diverse business conglomerate, (that owns everything from factories and bakeries to farmland and golf courses)[74] and the biggest landowner.

The Army derives its strength from the people. The populace sees military as the only institution standing tall amongst the corrupt political system, ineffective judiciary, unconcerned bureaucrats. It is the only organisation in the country that is not reserved for elites, rather it makes elites out of everyday people. Small town officers can rise to eminence if they do well in Army. Hence to that extent, it is seen as a level player. '*Army's faith in the populace and vice versa is very important for sustaining the deep state regime.*' As also reiterated in the statement, '*Time and time again the Army's way has been the Pakistan's Way*'.[75] The Army's hegemony on political, socio-economic, cultural and intellectual spheres is complete, justifying the statement, Pakistan Army is the '*Omnipotent, Omnipresent and Omnificent institution*'.

NOTES

1. Rana Banerji, former Special Secretary, Cabinet Secretariat, Government of India: Paper read at National Seminar on Pakistan: The Changing Security dimension,' Organised by Centre For Land Warfare Studies, February, 07-03-2020.
2. Stephen Philip Cohen, *The idea of Pakistan*, Brookings Institution Press, Washington D.C., 2004.
3. Shuja Nawaz, *Crossed Swords: Pakistan, Its Army and the wars within*, Oxford University Press, Pakistan 2010.
4. Christine Fair, *Fighting to the end. The Pakistan Army's Way of war*. Oxford University Press, New York, 2014.
5. Christofer Jaffrelot, *Paradox of Pakistan*, Random House India, Noida, 2015, p. 13.
6. Ibid., p. 21.
7. Dr. Jyoti M. Pathania, April 25, 2019, "Constitutional Coup d'état: Pakistan", Claws Focus, Centre for Land Warfare Studies, New Delhi.
8. Siddiqi, Brig. Abdurrahman, (Retd.) *The Military in Pakistan: Image and Reality*, Vanguard, Lahore, 1996.
9. Peter D. Feaver, *Armed Servants: Agency, Oversight and Civil-Military Relations.* Harvard University Press, Cambridge, 2005.
10. C. Christine Fair, *Fighting to the End: The Pakistan Army's Way of War*, Oxford University Press, 2014
11. Stephan Cohen, n. 2.
12. C. Christine Fair, n. 4.
13. Pakistan Army Green Book which records the Army's internal deliberations is issued every two year by the Army's Training and Evaluation Command, bearing the authoritative approval of the Army Chief himself.
14. Author conducted interview with Brig. Narender Kumar SM, VSM, United Service Institute fellow, New Delhi.
15. General Headquater, GHQ_Pakistan Army Green Book1991, Year of Commanding Officer, call NO-954.9/355 GHQ, 375 pages, Ist edition.
16. General Headquater, GHQ_Pakistan Army Green Book 1994, Training in Pakistan, Call No-954.9/355 GHQ, 292 pages, Ist edition.
17. Praveen Swami, "God's soldiers: Pakistan army's ideology", *The Hindu*, August 4, 2016.
18. https://mea.gov.in/articles-in-indian-media.htm?dtl/13152/Gods+soldiers+Pakistan+armys+ideology
19. Praveen Swami, n. 17.
20. MONITORS, "Examining Pakistan Army's new doctrine", January 4, 2013, Observer Research Foundation, https://www.orfonline.org/research/examining-pakistan-armys-new-doctrine/
21. *Green Book* 2020, National Defence University, Kakul (Abbottabad), 6 February 2020, p. 73, http://ndu.edu.pk/downloads/Green-Book-2020-Final-06-Feb-2020.pdf, accessed on May 22, 2021.
22. Pakistan Army Green Book 2021, General Headquarters, Rawalpindi, Pakistan.
23. https://www.rand.org/topics/military-doctrine.html

24. Aaron P. Jackson, "The Roots of Military Doctrine, Change and Continuity in Understanding the Practice of Warfare," Real Clear Defense, https://www.realcleardefense.com/articles/2017/11/15/the_nature_of_military_doctrine_a_decade_of_study_in_1500_ words_112638.html. Accessed on April 4, 2019.
25. Kanishkan Sathasivam, *Uneasy neighbours, India, Pakistan and US Foreign Policy*, Ashgate Publishing Company, 2005, p. 153.
26. Ibid., p. 149.
27. Shuja Nawaz, *The Battle For Pakistan: The Bitter US Friendship and a Tough Neighbourhood*, Vintage (Penguin), 2019.
28. Malik, Lt. Gen Ghulam Muhammad, Chapter on "Islamic Concept of Leadership, Pakistan Army Green Book", 1990, p. 2, Ferozsons Pvt. Ltd., Lahore.
29. Ibid., p. 10.
30. Ibid., p. 13.
31. Hussain Haqqani, "Pakistan diplomat in 2016", via *Business Standard*, Indo-Asia News Service.
32. Kapila, Subhash, "Pakistan imposes conflict escalation template on India", Paper no. 6403, March 3, 2019, Saag.org.
33. Read more at: Pakistan supports "self-determination in Kashmir", *Economic Times*, September 7, 2018, https://economictimes.indiatimes.com/articleshow/65721768.cms?from=mdr&utm_source=contentofinterest&utm_medium=text&utm_campaign=cppst. Accessed on April 26, 2019.
34. P. Cotta-Ramusino and M. Martellini Landau Network-Centro Volta, Como, Italy Como, January 14, 2002, Landau network Kidwai Pak nuclear doctrine.pdf—Report on Nuclear safety, nuclear stability and nuclear strategy in Pakistan January 14, 2002 / February 16, 2018/South Asia
35. Ibid., https://pugwash.org/2002/01/14/report-on-nuclear-safety-nuclear-stability-and-nuclear-strategy-in-pakistan/
36. Examples of economic strangling of Pakistan included a naval blockade and the stopping of the waters of the Indus river.
37. The political destabilisation and the internal subversion scenarios are considered as distinct possibilities.
38. Smith O. David, "The Quetta Experience: A study of Attitudes and Values within the Pakistan Army", Woodrow Wilson Centre, Asia Program, 2018.
39. Dr. Robert G. Wirsing, "Pakistan's Transformation: Why it will not (and Need Not) Happen", Asia-Pacific Security Studies, 2005.
40. Stephen P. Cohen, *The Pakistan Army*. Oxford University Press, Karachi, 1984, p. 105.
41. Neena Gopala, "Praetorian Pakistan: What the future holds", *Deccan Chronicle*, May 4, 2018, https://www.deccanchronicle.com/lifestyle/books-and-art/040518/a-praetorian-pakistan-what-the-future-holds.html
42. Ahmad Ali Khalid, "The supreme praetorian state of Pakistan", *Daily Times*, June 28, 2011.
43. Hasan Askari Rizvi, *The Military and Politics in Pakistan 1947–86*, Sang-e-Meel Publications, Lahore, 2000, pp. 91-92.

44. YouTube, "The University of Chicago", August 29, 2015. Military Inc: Inside Pakistan's Military Economy-Ayesha Siddiqa.
45. http://india-seminar.com/2014/664/664_ayesha_siddiqa.htm
46. Sadaf Aziz, The Constitution of Pakistan, A Contextual Analysis, Bloomsbury, 2018.
47. Brig AR Sidiqqi, The Military In Pakistan, Image and Reality, Vanguard Book, 1996.
48. Shuja Nawaz, Crossed Swords: Pakistan, its Army and the Wars Within, Oxford University Press, Pakistan 2010.
49. Hasan Aksari Rizvi, Military, state and society in Pakistan, Basingstoke: Macmillan, 2000, p. 1.
50. Barry R.Weingast, "The political foundations of democracy and the rule of law", *The American Political Science Review*, Vol. 91, issue 2, June 1997, fn 1, p. 247.
51. www.dawn.com/news, July 21, 2018.
52. Dr. Jyoti M. Pathania, Commentary on Pakistan Elections 2018: Verdict is Out & the Winner is—"Uniform-Ed Democracy" August 17, 2018, https://archive.claws.in/1924/commentary-on-pakistan-elections-2018-verdict-is-out-the-winner-is-"uniform-ed-democracy"-dr-jyoti-m-pathania.html. Accessed on April 23, 2021.
53. Ibid.
54. www.dawn.com/new, July 25, 2018.
55. http://timesofindia.indiatimes.com/ July 29, 2018.
56. Imran Khan, "The Army's Choice", Christopher Jaffrelot, *The Nation*, September 4, 2018.
57. Imran Khan's Speech in Full. Al Jazeera, 26th July 2018, www.aljazeera.com/news2018/07/Imran-khan-speech-full-180726124850706.html
58. FarahnazIspahani, "Imran Khan has Normalized Prejudice in Pakistan", *The Diplomatist*, June 30, 2021.
59. https://www.dw.com/en/pakistan-why-is-the-military-taking-over-civilian-posts/a-56473442
60. @ Michael Kugelman, 27, April, 2020, Tweet.
61. Ibid.
62. https://www.dawn.com/news/1477072/imran-shuffles-cabinet-without-completing-one-year-in-govt
63. www.the hindu-com.cdn.ampproject.org
64. https://www.globalsecurity.org/military/world/pakistan/army-politics.htm
65. "Bajwa family business empire grew in four countries in sync with AsimBajwa's risein military", Ahmad Noorani, August 27, 2020, https://factfocus.com/politics/1756/
66. Zuha Siddiqui, "In Pakistan, the army Tightens Its Grip", July 8, 2020, https://foreignpolicy.com/2020/07/08/in-pakistan-the-army-tightens-its-grip/.
67. https://www.dw.com/en/why-are-pakistans-generals-taking-uptop-civilian-posts/a-53605774
68. www,dw.com, "Why are Pakistani's generals taking up top civilian posts?", amp-dw-com.cdn.ampproject.org, Accessed on May 28, 2020.
69. https://theprint.in/opinion/pakistan-retd-officers-shouldnt-head-organisations-military-is-only-for-war/520900/

70. Sushant Sareen, Soft Coup, Hard Fall In Pakistan: Imran Khan is in total crisis, Facing economic and political ruin, Can India exploit the situation? April 27, 2019, https://www.dailyo.in/politics/imran-khan-pakistan-pakistan-military-parvez-musharraf-pakistan-cabinet-reshuffle-asad-umar-pak-terrorists-imf-reforms-pakistan-economic-collapse/story/1/30461.html
71. C. Christine Fair, "Why the Pakistan army is here to stay: prospects for civilian governance" *International Affairs (Royal Institute of International Affairs 1944-87*, no. 3 (2011): 571-88. http://www.jstor.org/stable/20869714.
72. *Dawn*, October 4, 2003.
73. https://www.dw.com/en/pakistan-why-is-the-military-taking-over-civilian-posts/a-56473442
74. https://www.spectator.co.uk/article/the-military-millionaires-who-control-pakistan-inc
75. Cohen Philip Stephan, *The idea of Pakistan,* Oxford University Press, New Delhi, 2005.

Source: ISI Headquarter Inner Outer View—Pak Army ISI 2018 Pfree

4. Inter-Services Intelligence (ISI) Control over Domestic Politics

> "*Meddling and Muddling in domestic affairs under the guise of National Security gave ISI extra-constitutional powers and enhanced its core role in the deep state.*"

The journey of Inter-Services Intelligence (ISI) from a small and limited task agency with almost no counter-intelligence apparatus in the late 1940s, to its current status as a mammoth espionage institution, dubbed as the "*Invisible Government*," "*State Within the State*," and "*Khalai Makhlooq*" (means Celestial Beings in Urdu) is worth examining. With ever-increasing responsibilities in domestic, political, national security, and foreign policy matters, it is without a doubt a great intelligence organisation. Pakistani newspaper reports reveal, there are 33 intelligence agencies having 600,000 personnel and still there are 56,000 more vacancies available.[1] This chapter delves into the role of the ISI in domestic politics.

Tyrants, politicians and military leaders have used Pakistan's intelligence organisations to safeguard not only their own political supporters, but also to spy on individuals who disagree with their thought process. As a result, it has deviated from its original professional objective and morphed into a '*necessary evil*' for the deep state's seamless operation. A senior Pakistani journalist, Abbas Nasir writes, "*this intelligence set up is one of the best organised in the business, functioning like a well-oiled, super-efficient machine, for over the last two decades.*"[2] The intelligence agencies scope has expanded far beyond their mandated tasks, to the point where their operations are frequently covert and at odds with one another.

The Intelligence Bureau (IB), a quasi-police organisation, was once the only intelligence agency, but its poor performance during the India-Pakistan war (1947-48) led to the creation of the Bureau of National Research and Reconstruction, or ISI agency. Initially the overseeing of domestic role was looked after by the IB, but as the first signs of secessionism surfaced in late 1950's East Pakistan, the politico-bureaucratic leadership suspecting the Bengali IB officers directed the ISI to operate.[3] The Generals relied on this agency with a military character rather than a quasi-police organisation. Other key institutions providing intelligence from the provinces include Military Intelligence (MI) and the State Police Special Branch.

The ISI was led by Maj. Gen. Cawthorne, the first and last British commander to leave Pakistan, until 1956. Brig. Riaz Hussain, the second Chief of ISI till 1966, enlarged the mandate and institutional design by creating a '*covert operations section*' to support militant groups in the North East India in the 1950s and a *Sikh militant* 'division' to aid Sikh militants in Punjab in the 1970s. For the first three decades of its existence, it focused on internal intelligence issues with a limited India focus, but that changed in the 1980s when it became involved in the guerrilla battle in Afghanistan against Soviet forces. Long periods of military rule also increased the military's involvement in domestic matters, including tracking down and pursuing political figures who might pose a danger to the military's power.

The ISI Headquarters is located on Khayaban-e-Suhrawardy Street in Islamabad. The entrance according to the journalist Declan Walsh, "is suitably discreet, no sign, just plainclothes officer packing a pistol who directs visitors through a chicane of barriers, soldiers and sniffer dogs", with a sliding giant electric gate, revealing a sleek grey building, with one difference that nothing is signposted. Powerful and notorious in equal measures this premier spy agency, which for decades has operated behind a dense veil of secrecy, impervious to allegations of election rigging, terrorist training, abductions and assassinations.[4]

The ISI operatives dressed in plain clothes can be found in towns and cities across Pakistan, low-key but ubiquitous, like pigeons on a power line. With experience, it is easy to spot them, with their tinted-window jeeps, handheld radio sets and air of unspoken menace. In Urdu, Pakistanis call them '*farishtay*', or '*angels*'—a double-edged euphemism that refers both to the traditional white long shirts typically worn by ISI men and to the vast uncircumscribed powers at their disposal. *The angels, as everyone knows, can knock on any door, flout any law, question or harass or even abduct any citizen.*[5]

WORKING MACHINATIONS OF THE ISI

The organisational structure of the ISI was designed as an '*adjunct of the Army*'. The earliest known organisational format was structured in Joint Intelligence terms, along with Military Intelligence as shown in (Figure 4.1). The Headquarters was referred to as Joint Intelligence Headquarters (JIX), whereas field deployments were the Joint Intelligence North(JIN). Other sections designated as Joint Intelligence for Middle East/Muslim countries (JIM), Joint Counter Intelligence Bureau (JCIB) and Joint Intelligence Bureau included the technical and signals (JIB).[6] The location of the Filed Intelligence Units (FIU) of the Army is mainly near border areas.

The main aim and responsibilities include coordinating with the Army, Navy, and Air Force intelligence networks; collecting foreign and domestic intelligence reports; conducting covert offensive operations, primarily in Kashmir and Afghanistan; spying on foreigners, domestic media (print and online), foreign diplomats, and even Pakistani diplomats serving abroad. It has become a catalyst for bolstering domestic political activity, whether it is assisting in the execution of a successful coup or thwarting one. Meddling and muddling in domestic issues is now part of their charter of duty under the authority of the Chief of Army Staff (COAS).

Figure 4.1: ISI/JIB (Joint Intelligence Bureau)

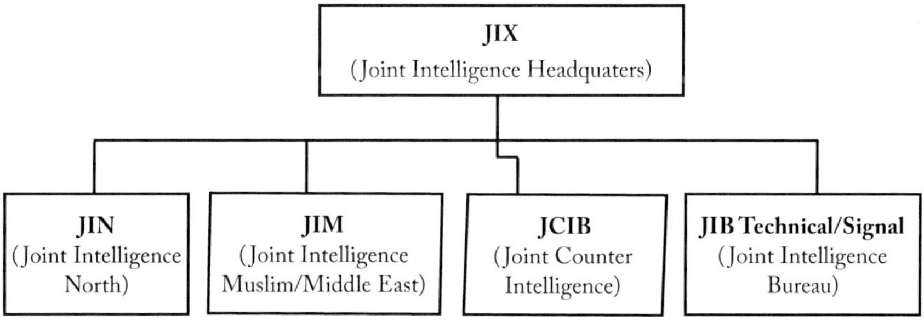

Source: IDSA Defence Journal October 2011.

The core functions are maintaining social control; protecting the regime against all sources of disturbance, and promoting acceptance of regime policies by the population.[7] To fulfil these they have gone beyond their prescribed role, even violating the constitution at times to preserve their rule. As the editor of Pakistani national newspaper *Dawn*, late Mazhar Ali Khan wrote:

> "The ISI is seen by many people to be an unwanted legacy of the military rule. While under martial law regimes, the agency's expanding constitutional role was at least understandable, because with the constitution suspended, the will of the military dictators took precedence over every rule, law and tradition, but after the end of military rule and restoration of the Constitution, for ISI's functioning to go beyond its parameters was violative of the Constitution. It also defied the regulations that govern the network of agencies and the institutions that serve the armed forces."[8]

The political role of such agencies is a mix of '*militarisation*,' '*political surveillance*,' and '*state terror*,' with the intensity and relative importance of each component varying over time and situation, but all three are always present, subverting the political system to their advantage by making civilian governments victims of their manipulations (Figure 4.2).

Figure 4.2: ISI Work Expanse

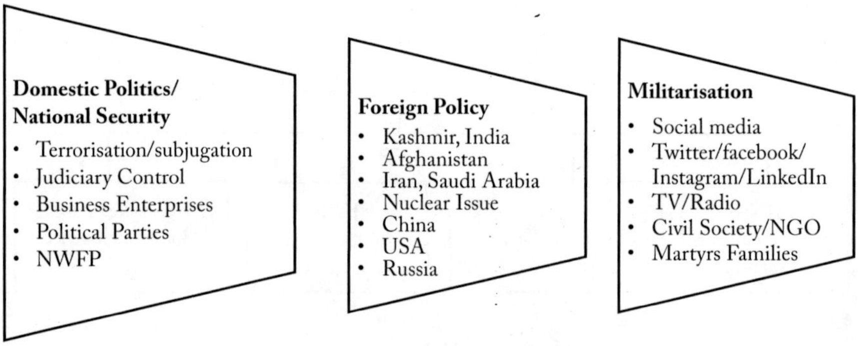

Funding political parties; providing assistance to religious groups; forming or dissolving political party alliances to suit its objectives; influencing social media; manipulating political violence; and even democratic control through constitutional and legislative amendments are some of the methods used. The reason intelligence agencies get directly involved in political matters is with an assumed logic i.e., to play divide and rule as, well-known defence analyst Hasan-Aksari Rizvi states, "their interests in these matters stem from the assumption that a polity in turmoil cannot sustain a professional military, and a weak and divided polity can be instrumental in preserving the position of the military, hence the necessity of involving ISI."[9] By retaining civilian intelligence agencies in the background, the Army including the ISI, manipulate politics and indirectly rule the country, as these services may one day become powerful with the support of an elected government.

ISI INROADS IN DOMESTIC POLITY

Numerous instances of ISI participation in the internal political affairs can be traced throughout the country's history. As previously noted, ISI's political activities began in the early 1950s and peaked with the coup d'etat staged by General Ayub Khan in 1958, when a '*distinct clandestine division*' was established within the agency, to monitor politicians, oversee the media, track civil society activists/organisations, trader organisations and students groups. All three intelligence agencies together became the '*bulwark for consolidation of his reign*'. Under the excuse of jeopardising national security, any dissent to his rule was suppressed, and in the 1964 presidential elections, ISI assured his re-election.

The intelligence agencies enlarged their role to include '*monitoring ethnic minorities and separatists activities*' under the military ruler General Yahya Khan. This was done primarily to monitor the political activities of East Pakistan's premier nationalist party, the Awami League. To cite an example, a nationalist security team to infiltrate Awami League circles was set up in order to ensure that no political party won the 1970 elections. Razakar and Al Badr organisations were created in response to the League's proposal for a separate Bengali country. The ISI was instrumental in unleashing genocide in East Pakistan, which is now Bangladesh.

The civilian leaders did not hesitate in using intelligence agencies for their '*personal political motives*' as Prime Minister Zulfikar Ali Bhutto created, an internal security wing cell primarily for monitoring his political opponents by bugging the ministers phones and offices, including monitoring of his own cabinet ministers, rigging of the 1977 elections and even suppression of the Baloch Nationalists.[10] A big achievement of this cell was the foiling of the Attock conspiracy (1973), wherein a group of disgruntled young Army officers unhappy with Bhutto's dictatorial style wanted to overthrow him. The trial was overseen by then Major General Zia-ul-Haq, who awarded the conspirators heavy punishment in exchange for Prime Minister Bhutto's loyalty. The '*system of personalised reporting*' under a '*parallel system of intelligence reporting*', comprised of Bhutto's known loyalists from police, federal investigative agency (FIA), airport security force (ASF), federal security force (FSF) also started. He also embarked on a nuclear programme, which resulted in the agency receiving an increasing amount of funds and discretion.

This '*surveillance agency*' propelled to higher-profile operation, feared by the people under General Zia-al-Haq's Martial law regime. Midnight knocks, arrests, extorted confessions and phone taps became the order of the day. All political and religious organisation's opposing Zia's regime came under the ISI scanner. Maj Gen Ghulam Jilani Khan, Director General of the ISI, directly assisted Gen Zia in quelling initial dissent against his martial law takeover; informed him of Bhutto's plans, particularly after the July 1977 election; and assisted in the selection of amenable politicians such as Junejo and the Sharif family to sugar coat Zia's gradual revival of political activities in the mid/late

1980s. Zia rewarded him by promoting him to the positions of the Defence Secretary and Punjab Governor.[11]

Tasks like gathering intelligence on the '*operations of Sindhi Nationalists*'; '*activities of Shia organisations*'; '*monitoring the actions and leadership of Bhutto's Pakistan People's Party (PPP*) became the norm. Brigadier Imtiaz Ahmad, better known in the Army circles as '*Billa*' (the cat), for his crafty nature and the colour of his eyes as a young colonel was in charge of the ISI Karachi Det (detachment) when Bhutto was overthrown. He led the famous raid on Bhutto's 70 Clifton residence, to discover some "important and incriminating" documents, which soon earned Zia's admiration and trust, which elevated him to the influential position of assistant director-general (internal security) at the ISI. He headed the dreaded political cell for many years, and at times even bypassed his own Director General (DG) to report directly to Zia.[12]

The democratically elected leaders like former Prime Ministers Benazir Bhutto and Nawaz Sharif questioned the strong nexus of ISI and the Army under the '*Charter of Democracy*,'[13] signed in London (2006), in the hope to make the intelligence agencies accountable to the ruling government. According to Article 32 of the charter, "the ISI, MI, and other security agencies shall be accountable to the elected government through the Prime Minister Secretariat, Ministry of Defence and cabinet division respectively."[14] Also to note, the 2008 election manifesto of the Pakistan People's Party mentioned that "all security agencies, including ISI and MI, will be answerable to the elected Prime Minister."[15]

Benazir Bhutto took the bold step of '*reforming the intelligence agencies*' under a commission headed by Air Chief Marshal Zulfiqar Ali Khan, but it was of no consequence. The ISI's strength was on display during Indian Prime Minister Rajiv Gandhi's visit to Pakistan in December 1988, when both leaders were advised to be cautious in their conversations as the office was bugged. A senior RAW officer, late B. Raman wrote, "ISI's internal political division was suspected of assassinating through poisoning Shah Nawaz Bhutto, one of Benazir Bhutto's two brothers, in the French Riviera in the middle of 1985, in an attempt to intimidate her not returning to Pakistan for directing the movement against Zia".[16]

'*ISI in-roads into the party activities*' was evident when the Deputy of DG ISI, Brig Imitiaz Ahmed led the '*Operation midnight Jackal*', a political scandal to assist the vote of no confidence motion against the PPP to pave for elections. Also, the ISI political wing in Sindh tried to destabilise the fragile alliance of PPP and Muhajir Quami Movement (MQM).

A '*complete latitude was given to ISI to meddle in political parties,*' during General Pervez Musharraf military rule, with the liberty to finance and weaken the major political parties in order to ensure his party continues to remain in power. DG ISI, Gen Kiyani was involved in *political rapprochement* between Benazir and Musharraf, with his frequent trip to Dubai, where Benazir was staying in exile. The Imran Khan government too has supported the Army's and ISI's engagement in domestic politics for sheer survival, servility and longevity.

SUBVERSION OF THE DOMESTIC POLITICAL SYSTEM

Apart from the military dictators under whose leadership ISI manipulated domestic politics, on its own too, it has successfully subverted the political system ensuring an unchallenged Army rule. After 1989, there was manifold increase in its political activity, be it funding of parties, dismissal of civilian governments or helping sectarian organisations. Such meddling became so common that narratives on social media emerged about, "intelligence agencies being above the law and beholden to neither the administration nor the court."

ISI employed a few techniques to sabotage the political system, which are listed below:

'*Setting up alliances and factions within political parties*' for example, under the patronage of DG ISI Lt. General Hameed Gul, the ISI formed and supported the Islami-Jamhori Ittehad party (IJI), an alliance of mostly nine right-wing parties that brought together right-wing politicians like Nawaz Sharif with religious leaders in 1988. This was done to prevent Benazir Bhutto's Pakistan People's Party (PPP) from sweeping the polls. As proved in the statement of former ISI director General Hamid Gul's, "the decision to hold onto or relinquish power rests squarely with the Army", even creating rifts within political parties if a particular party becomes too powerful or non-compliant.[17]

Pakistan's political system's powerlessness in the face of the Army and intelligence services was once again revealed, when Benazir appointed Lt Gen Shamsur Rehman Kallu as the new Director General of the ISI in

May 1989,the intelligence agencies were outraged. Army Chief Gen Aslam Beg used '*internal political wing*' of ISI to destabilise her party PPP without Gen Kallu's knowledge. It is a well-known fact that they were involved in the removal of Prime Minister Benazir Bhutto from office in August 1990, based on charges of corruption, refusal to engage with the provinces, and questioning of the military's authority. As the military's eyes and ears,[18] the ISI had the power to persuade President Ghulam Ishaq Khan to intervene in Benazir's case.

The '*funding of political parties*' is another way to undermine the party system. In a study conducted by Pakistani analyst Zafarullah Khan of the Liberal Forum of Pakistan,[19]—the 1990's elections divulged that ISI had distributed over Rs 140 million among its favourite politicians. The '*Mehran Bank Scandal*' established ISI involvement during this period. The intelligence agencies prevailed upon politicians from different parties to trade their loyalties for a price with the objective to destabilise a hostile government and put in place a friendly regime. This scandal comprised of the entire gamut of financial crimes, like fake loans, kickbacks, illegal transactions, bribes involving several high profile names of politicians and a serving Army chief.[20] Pakistani newspaper Nation wrote, "the case has refocused public attention on what is widely perceived to be a government within a government- the intelligence agencies and their virtually autonomous role in the political affairs of the country. The baneful influence of the intelligence agencies has spread its malign shadow over the political destiny of the country."[21] The Supreme Court Chief Justice, Sajjad Ali Shah, during the hearing on the ISI's role in domestic politics in the year 1997, recorded Gen (retd.) Mirza Aslam Beg statement admitted to the practice of ISI supporting candidates and using secret service accounts for the disposal of money during the election season, mentioning that Lt General Asad Durrani had received Rs 60 million for funding certain candidates.

The intelligence agencies have been supportive of the '*right-wing extremists and radical sectarian Islamist political parties*'. Military ruler Zia-ul-Haq, led the country to the Islamisation process that included enacting new Islamic laws, establishing a federal Sharia court, mandating Islamic education in schools, promoting religious schools or madrassas, and incorporating Islamic teachings into military training.[22] Support to religious parties like the Islami Jamhoori Ittehad (IJI), creation of party like Mohajir Quami Movement (MQM) in 1984, creating a rift within MQM to split the party into three dissidents' factions, MQM,—Afaq Ahmad, Aamir Khan, and Badar Iqbal and manipulation of elections were notably ISI's doing. The ISI underwent tremendous enhancement of covert capabilities during the Afghanistan war under Gen Zia ul Haq dictatorial rule with Director General, Lt Gen Muhammad Riaz Khan and Lt Gen Akhtar Abdur Rahman Khan. Zia also promulgated the Martial Law Order (MLO) in June 1978, setting up disqualification tribunals to inquire into charges of misconduct against those who had contested the 1977 elections. Even as the US & NATO forces left Afghanistan after two decades, On September 4, 2021, three days after the visit of ISI Chief Lt Gen Faiz Hameed to Kabul, the Taliban which was struggling to form an inclusive Government, finalised and annonced an interim government. This speaks of the ISI & Taliban nexus.

Support to the '*armed religious parties*' between 1982 and 1990 became manifest with the Central Intelligence Agency (CIA), ISI and Saudi Arabia's intelligence service together funded the training, arrival, and arming of some thirty-five thousand Islamic militants from forty-three Muslim countries in Pakistani madrassas. Pakistani journalist, Ahmed Rashid warned, "this will sow the seeds of al-Qaeda and turn Pakistan into the world centre of jihadism for the next two decades."[23] Such linkages and close connections with the Islamic fundamentalist groups, like the Harkat ul Ansar, Lashkar-e-Taiba continue till date fostering anti- India stand. Prime Minister Imran Khan himself admitted that the Pakistani Army and ISI trained al-Qaida and other terrorists' groups to fight in the Afghanistan war.[24] Therefore, the intelligence agencies are to be blamed for '*instigating political violence*,' be it with jihadi or sectarian groups or the MQM. This has created a series of Frankenstein's whose powers they had to limit at times by pitting them against each other, not to eliminate them, but to ensure that they remained compliant enough for whatever task they were assigned.[25]

Another method used for destabilising the political system was by '*creating schisms within parties*' if they became too dominant and non-complaint. During the constitution of the PML-Q, ISI openly twisted politicians arms for joining newly formed "King's party."[26] Primarily done in order to shift the support base from the PPP towards the opposition. In 2018 elections, DG ISI General

Hameed was accused of instrumenting defections from Sharif's Pakistan Muslim League (Nawaz) party to Khan's PTI.[27]

"My case is politically contrived," Maryam Nawaz, vice president of MLN, said "The ISI had ordered the Islamabad High Court's Justice Shaukat Siddiqui to ensure that she and Nawaz Sharif did not walk out of jail before the July 25, 2018 elections." "Not only that, but ISI's head General Faiz Hameed, pursued them and brought the London Aven field apartments case against them, and found guilty in Judge Bashir's court." Shaukat Aziz Siddiqui, a former IHC judge, claimed that the DG-C (Director-General Counter Intelligence), General Faiz Hameed, went to him [Siddiqui] and instructed him not to give bail to Nawaz Sharif and Maryam Nawaz. If you give them bail, it will waste two years of my hard work".[28]

To further elucidate on the '*intelligence agencies*' nexus with the right wing political parties and their use in the electoral process, the 2018 elections can also be highlighted when the military launched two far-right religious parties namely Tehrik-e-Labbaik Pakistan (TLP) and Allah-o-Akbar-Party (AAP). Although neither party won any seats in the National Assembly (NA), they made a significant dent in the Barelvi-Sunni and Wahabi (religious sects) vote bank of the PML-N.

By using '*extra-constitutional means*,' the intelligence agencies along with the Army have '*sabotaged the constitution*', '*statutory laws and remedies*' to an extent. For instance, articles like Article 4,[29] Article 8[30] and Article 90[31] have provided a check on the extra-constitutional power of the political executive which includes these agencies as well. But the military rulers in cahoots with the intelligence agencies have amended these laws to tighten their ire on those political outfits which are recalcitrant. Successive dictators perpetuated tough measures by introducing various laws and regulations to restrict or ban those political parties and activities that threatened Army's rule.

The ISI underwent tremendous enhancement of covert capabilities during the Afghanistan war under Gen Zia ul Haq dictatorial rule with Director General, Lt Gen Muhammad Riaz Khan and Lt Gen Akhtar Abdur Rahman Khan. Zia also promulgated the Martial Law Order (MLO) in June 1978, setting up disqualification tribunals to inquire into charges of misconduct against those who had contested the 1977 elections.

The intelligence agencies played a key part in *maligning the political system* by marginalising provincial and ethnic nationalist sentiments within the country, "The military in unison with the ISI maintained power for almost nine long years of General Pervez Musharraf coup d'état rule. He consolidated his power primarily through the passage of the 17th amendment to the constitution (2003)transferred several powers from the prime minister to the president, including the authority to dismiss the prime minister and the 'national assembly.'[32] In search of political legitimacy, Musharraf regenerated the Mohajir Qaumi Movement (MQM) in an attempt to make it a national organization but subsequently made it an ally of pro-Musharraf PML (Q). The MQM benefited in particular from the rigging of the 2002 election, which gave it de facto control of most of urban Sindh.

This period was also an era of relative normalisation of the MQM, whose terror tactics were temporarily kept in check. The organisation was reactivated in 2007 following a demonstration in favour of the deposed Chief Justice Iftikhar Muhammad Chaudhry, the MQM organised a counter demonstration in Karachi on May 12, attacking and killing PPP workers.[33] The killing of the American Journalist Daniel Pearl unravelled the deadly cocktail of radical Islamic groups and intelligence agencies as it was believed that some rogue element of the ISI known to have patronised Taliban were involved in this gory episode.

The conflict between the 'ISI vs the political executive clash' was glaring when Prime Minister Benazir Bhutto, wanting to reorganise and downsize the intelligence agencies, issued a memorandum placing administrative, financial, and long-term management of both the ISI and the IB under the interior ministry (July 26, 2008). The DG ISI, Lt. Gen Hamid Gul, wielded so much power that this order was revoked within an hour. Another case in point, when Prime Minister Nawaz Sharif sought to create a new Federal Investigative Agency (FIA) to investigate overseas accounts of opposition leaders, his efforts were thwarted by the ISI and MI. He was in a similar situation as the former President Asif Zardari, who was threatened by the country's secret services. He was informed that an ambulance was on its way to transport him to the hospital.[34] The former ISI Chief Zahir-ul-Islam tried to topple Sharif in 2014 with the tacit blessings of Army Chief General Raheel Sharif, exposes the hybrid setup revealing the uncontrollable ISI.

Soon after becoming the Prime Minister Imran Khan's first visit to the ISI headquarters in September 2018, demonstrated his close association with the DG ISI. Lt. Gen Faiz Hameed's organisation.[35] The Army's position in national security decision-making intensified with ISI assuming a major role in defining a national security discourse. Imran Khan's administration has essentially handed over control of several critical policy concerns to the Army and the ISI.

It is a well-known fact that political engineering efforts of the ISI and the Army manoeuvred Tehreek-e-Labbaik (TLP), a hard line religious party into mainstream politics. It was feared that separating the far right from the PML-N conservative support base would hurt the party in the 2018 general election. And, to some extent, the damage was done; indeed, three ticket-holders were elected to the Sindh Assembly, and the party finished fourth with about 2.5 million votes cast across the country. This was one facet of the Army's excellent effort to bring the extremists into the mainstream. The TLP raised to prominence in the Asia Bibi blasphemy case in the first year of the Imran-Bajwa hybrid rule. Once banned, the TLP will not be able to take part in elections, but the ban will not prevent its use in power games on the streets. The tragic part is, the Pakistani Army never learns.[36]

On the contrary, most of the leaders have endorsed the role of the intelligence agencies in domestic politics to such an extent that they seem to be the '*real power wielders*'. Though constitutionally, the ISI is responsible for dealing with external security threats, but in practice this organisation has been deeply involved in the country's domestic politics.[37] Imran Khan gave in to the demands of the radical outfit, Tehreek-e-Labaaik-Pakistan (TLP), which the country had designated as a terrorist group and banned, to pass a resolution in its national assembly to remove the French ambassador. It is obvious they have given decision with Army's approval, as foreign policy matters are looked after by the Army and ousting an ambassador will certainly need their approval.

In all successful democracies, the notion of civilian primacy in the intelligence community is widely accepted; but in Pakistan, disregarding this principle has sown the seeds of the current state of things.[38] ISI has evolved into a shadow state that is not always accountable to either the military or the civilian administration. As a result, there is no true check and balance in place to oversee the money circulation mechanism, further complicating the country's democratic process. The Army chief, along with the ISI, remains at the heart of the political structure and are responsible for not just security but also professional, organisational, domestic and foreign policy matters. This proves that the Hawk-eyed ISI enjoys complete dominance in domestic politics.

Table: 4.1: Tabulation of Inter Services Intelligence Service (ISI) Most Important Functions and its Effect

Head of state	Year	Director General ISI	ISI Functions	Effect/Result
Gen Ayub Khan Martial Law	1958-62	Maj General Shahid Hamid 1948-50 Major General Robert Cawthorne (1950-59) Brig Riaz Hussain (1959-66)	Monitoring of media, political parties & civil society activists	All intelligence agencies directly under Gen Ayub
Gen Yahya Khan Martial Law	1962-71	Brig Mohammad Akbar Khan (1966-71)	Entrenched in domestic politics- crushed sectarian & ethnic movements in East Bengal	Idea and inception of National Security Council
Zulfiqar Ali Bhutto Prime Minster	1972-77	Maj Gen Ghulam Jilani Khan (1971-78)	New Political cell New Federal Security force (FSF)	Rigging of 1977 elections & Increase in ISI budget Assumption of power by the Army.
Gen Zia-ul Haq Martial law	1978-88	Lt. Gen Muhammad Riaz Khan (1978-79) Lt. Gen Akhtar Abdur Rahman Khan (1979-87)	Collect Domestic intel on Political & Religious organizations that opposed him	Atrocities on Sindhi Nationalist activists, PPP dissidents' political leaders & Shii organisations

Benazir Bhutto Prime Minister	1988-1990	Lt. Gen Hamid Gul (1987-89) Lt Gen Shamsur Rahman Kallu (1989-1990)	Gen Gul's had a direct say in the Afghan policy even after retiring. Lt Gen Kallu, a PPP loyalist, led Benazir down by helping the Army to topple her govt in the horse-trading drama, Operation Midnight Jackal	Re-energise ISI control over Mujahideen in & as a backyard for strategic depth.
Nawaz Sharif Prime Minister	1990-1993	Lt. Gen Ahmed Durrani (1990-1992) Lt. Gen Javed Nasir (1992-1993)	President Leghari uses Art 58 (2)b in conjunction with the Army to dislodge the elected government.	The PPP and PML-N camps danced like puppets in ISI hands and succeeded in toppling each other's governments once each.
Benazir Bhutto Prime Minister	1993-1996	Lt. Gen Javed Ashraf Qazi (1993-1995) Lt. Gen Naseem Rana (1995-1998)	Reform ISI directorate under (civilian control)	ISI's role in Benazir's removal in 1990 & 1996, assassination attempts in 2007
Nawaz Sharif Prime Minster	1997-1999	Lt. Gen Ziauddin Butt (1998-1999)	Dawn Leaks...	ISI Pressurising The Civilian Government & Media
Gen Pervez Musharraf Military rule	1999-2008	Mahmud Ahmed (1999-2001) Ehsan ul Haq (2001-2004) Lt. Gen Pervez Ashfaq Kiyani (2004-2007) Lt. Gen Nadeem Taj (2007-2008)	Most visible ISI meddling in political affairs	Legal framework Order No. 2002

Yousaf Raza Gilani Prime Minister	2008-2012	Lt. Gen Ahmad Shuja Pasha (2008-12)	DG ISI named as Time Magazine 100 most influential people	Close ally to Chief, CIA and support anti-Taliban viewpoints
Nawaz Sharif Prime Minister	2013-2016	Lt. Gen Zaheerul Islam (2012-14) Lt Gen Rizwan Akhtar (2014-16)	Consolidation of the Hybrid State System	PM forced out of office on corruption charges
Imran Khan Prime Minister	2018-	Lt. Gen Naveed Mukhtar (2016-2018) Lt. Gen Asim Munir Ahmad Shah (2018-2019) Lt. Gen Faiz Hameed (2019-2021) Lt. Gen Nadeem Anjum (2021 onwards)	Propagate and sustain anti-India sentiments. Enable Taliban	Once again imposition of the Army over the civilian government in the selection of the new DG ISI, Gen Nadeem

Source: Annotated by the Author.
Note: All the DG's after 1978 have been of Lt. Gen rank.

NOTES

1. Musa Khan Jalalzai, "Pakistan: reorganisation of the intelligence structure", *Daily Times*, March 24, 2014, https://dailytimes.com.pk/105378/pakistan-reorganisation-of-intelligence-infrastructure/
2. Abbas Nassir, "Pakistan Intelligence Stories: The Inside Story", September 14, 2017, https://herald.dawn.com/news/1153827
3. Dr. Bidana M. Chengappa, "The ISI role in Domestic politics", *Strategic Analysis*, Vol. XXIII, No. 11, Feb 2020.
4. Declan Walsh, "The ISI, Pakistan's notorious and feared spy agency, comes in from the cold", *The Guardian*, August 5, 2009, https://www.theguardian.com/world/2009/aug/05/inter-services-intelligence-directorate-Pakistan
5. Declan Walsh, *The Nine Lives of Pakistan*, Bloomsbury Publishing, 2010.
6. Rana Banerji, *IDSA Defence Journal* October 2011 special issue on Pakistan: Vol. 5, No. 4.
7. "Reforming the Intelligence Agencies in Pakistan's Transitional Democracy", Carnegie Endowment for International Peace Report, March 6, 2009, p. 2, https://

carnegieendowment.org/2009/03/06/reforming-intelligence-agencies-in-pakistan-s-transitional-democracy-pub-22817. Accessed on July 7, 2020.

8. Mazhar Ali Khan, "The Transgresses", *Dawn*, January 12, 1993, cited in John Kaniyalil "ISI: The Master Manipulater," *Strategic Analysis*, November 1993, p. 993.
9. Hasan-Askari Rizvi, "Civil-Military Relations in contemporary Pakistan", *Survival*, Vol. 40, no. 2 (Summer 1998), p. 100.
10. Zahid Hussain, *Frontline Pakistan: The Struggle with Militant Islam,* Columbia University Press, New York, 2007.
11. Rana Banerji, *IDSA Defence Journal* October 2011 special issue on Pakistan: Vol. 5, No. 4.
12. https://herald.dawn.com/news/1153827
13. See "Text of the Charter of Democracy," *Dawn*, May 16, 2006, https://www.dawn.com/news/192460/text-of-the-charter-of-democracy. Accessed on September 14, 2020.
14. Quoted in Fredric Grare (2009), "Reforming the Intelligence Agencies," n. 3, p. 42.
15. "Towards Peace and Prosperity in Pakistan," Pakistan People's Party Manifesto, 2008, p. 16.
16. https://military-history.fandom.com/wiki/Inter-Services_Intelligence
17. Umber Khairi. "Holy and Unholy Alliances", October 8, 2017, https://www.thenews.com.pk/tns/detail/564149-holy-unholy-alliances
18. Dr. Bidana M. Chengappa, "The ISI role in Domestic politics", *Strategic Analysis*, Vol. XXIII, No. 11, February 2000.
19. Press Trust of India Report, "ISI Funded Political Parties in Pakistan", https://www.rediff.com/news/2002/aug/20pak1.htm
20. Zakir Siddiqui, "The Mehran Bank Scam", *Newsline*, April 1994, pp. 49-52.
21. Dr. Bidana M. Chengappa, n. 18.
22. Jayshree Bajoria, "Islam and Politics in Pakistan", Council on Foreign Relations, April 20, 2011, https://www.cfr.org/backgrounder/islam-and-politics-pakistan
23. Rashid Ahmed, "Descent into Chaos, How the war against Islamic extremism is being lost in Pakistan", *Afghanistan and Central Asia*, London Allan Lane, 2008, p. 506.
24. Chidanand Rajghatta, "PM Imran Khan admits Pakistani Army and ISI trained al-Qaida", *Times of India*, September 24, 2019.
25. "Carnegie Endowment for International Peace Report", 2009, n. 2, p. 25.
26. Shafqat Mahmood, "Covert Operations Fall out", News, March 14, 2003.
27. https://theprint.in/world/pakistans-new-isi-chief-was-accused-of-secretly-helping-imran-khans-party-in-2018-polls/251431/
28. https://www.samaa.tv/news/2021/10/general-faiz-hameed-made-avenfield-case-against-us-maryam-nawaz/
29. Article 4 states that enjoying the protection of the law is the inalienable right of every citizen of Pakistan.
30. Article 8 states that laws inconsistent with, or in derogation of fundamental rights, are null and void, no law that benefits intelligence work can infringe on the constitutional rights of the citizens.

31. Under Article 90, the intelligence agencies are supposed to work within the general ambit of the federal govt executive powers.
32. Sheila Fruman, "Will the Long March to Democracy in Pakistan Finally Succeed?", https://www.usip.org/sites/default/files/will%20the%20long%20march%20to%20democracy%20in%20pakistan%20finally%20succeed.pdf.
33. Hasan Abbas, "Pakistan's Drift into Extremism: Allah, the Army & America's war on Terrorism", p. 156, East Gate book, 2005.
34. https://dailytimes.com.pk/105378/pakistan-reorganisation-of-intelligence-infrastructure/
35. Sajjad Hussain, "Imran Khan visits headquarters of Pak's Spy Agency", June 3, 2020, *Outlook*, The News Scroll https://www.outlookindia.com/newsscroll/imran-khan-visits-headquarters-of-paks-spy-agency/1855239
36. Gul Bhukari, https://www.thequint.com/voices/opinion/pakistani-government-army-internal-power-struggle-ban-on-tehreek-e-labbaik-deep-state-imran-khan-political-engineering
37. Pakistan's new ISI chief and the military's face-saving act https://www.dw.com/en/pakistans-new-isi-chief-and-the-militarys-face-saving-act/a-17948121
38. B. Raman,"Pakistan's inter-services intelligence (ISI)". Paper no. 287, South Asia Analysis Group, August 1, 2001.

Source: ISPR Productions

5. Inter-Services Public Relations (ISPR): A Force to Reckon With

> "*ISPR effectively and institutionally calibrates and disseminates Pakistan's perspective both on the domestic and international stage.*"

Inter-Services Public Relations (ISPR) is the public face of the country's main intelligence organisation, the ISI. This subject is beset with all kinds of conspiracy theories, but there is categorical authenticity in the statement that ISPR has become an important institution in today's age of information revolution. As Joseph Nye put it, "*In today's world, victory is not only about militaries, it is as much determined by whose story wins*".[1] The ISPR is adept at '*creating a winning narrative*' to '*mentally subdue enemy*' in the '*virtual domain warfare*'. This fact was acknowledged publicly by Lt. Gen. Ata Hasnain in a conference at the International Institute for Strategic Studies, London, he stated, "full marks given to Pakistan in the manner in which ISPR not as much as the ISI did an outstanding work for Pakistan, in ensuring detailed alienation of Kashmiri people against Indian Army forces first and then the Indian Nation."[2]

Psychological warfare (PSYWAR) or psychological operations (PSYOP) is the planned tactical use of propaganda, threats, and other non-combat techniques during wars, threats of war, or periods of geopolitical unrest to mislead, intimidate, demoralise, or otherwise influence the thinking or behaviour of an enemy.[3] It is a highly specialised manual for social engineering. Few widely used terms for internet harassment, like "Astroturfing",[4] "Catfishing"[5] "Deep fake"[6] and "Hacking"[7] are used to monitor and influence public opinion.

WHAT IS ISPR?

The inter-services public relations is Pakistan's Army's organic media agency; its function frequently overlaps with those of the ISI, particularly when voices critical of the Army are to be silenced. Referred to as the Army's 'B' Team, its birth is linked with the very creation of ISI. Over the years, it has become a '*joint services information management tool*' for the defence services working under joint services headquarters predominantly controlled by the Army; and wields immense authority to '*manage information flows*' both for domestic audience and for international opinion building; '*publicising the activities and achievements of the Pakistan Army*'. Over the years it has gradually changed its objective to '*social control and social engineering*'; wherein '*protecting and promoting passive acceptance of the military regime*' has become its primary task. Till the late 1990s, ISPR was a small setup and played a very modest role as a media arm of the armed forces. However, in the recent past, it has developed into a well-resourced, well-equipped, well-staffed organization, vicious and brutal in character and attitude.[8]

WHEN WAS IT FORMED?

The Directorate of ISPR was established in 1949 with Army Colonel Shahbaz Khan becoming the first director-general.[9] Founded for two main reasons: First, Pakistan's failure in the Indo-Pak War 1948 was attributed to severe information gaps, lacunae, and perceived military weaknesses. As a result information and intelligence cooperation were necessitated to create greatest effectivity and speed among the Army, Navy, and Air Force. Second, Great

Britain and Russia's "*Great Game manoeuvres and tactics*" in the late nineteenth and early twentieth century necessitated the establishment of a local intelligence agency to provide information and intelligence collection for the Central, South, and West Asia regions.

Reference to such concerns was spelt out in a letter from Sir Francis Moodie, Home secretary during the British Raj, later Governor of Sindh. Engaged in the service of Pakistan after partition, he wrote to a friend in Lucknow—"The facts of the situation are that Pakistan is situated between hostile-a very hostile—India on the one hand and ... an expansionist and unscrupulous Russia (on the other hand). As long as the relations between Pakistan and Britain are good and Pakistan remains in the commonwealth an attack by Russia and also, I am inclined to believe an attack by India on Pakistan brings in the UK and the USA on the Pakistan's side".[10] The creation of ISPR was the necessity of times and over the years it has evolved as the Army's '*public face*', '*image protector and enhancer*'.

WHAT WAS THE INITIAL STRUCTURAL DESIGN LIKE?

The structure of the ISPR was influenced by various other intelligence agencies, like the Iranian SEVAK, MI6, CIA and particularly the IB as the military and civilian professionals from the Indian intelligence organisations formed its backbone during the pre-partition period. Initially, the ISPR's role was linked with the ISI activities, but gradually when information warfare became an important element of statecraft, its scope was streamlined to include media monitoring, surveillance of politicians and even tracking of civil society/social organisation including student groups. It gave warnings and threats if such organisations were coming in the way of the military. Therefore '*promotion of the deep state across various media outlets*' and '*keeping a watch on dissidents*' became its core tasks and its structure was framed according to these needs.

WHAT IS THE ORGANISATIONAL SET-UP?

ISPR can be compared to any government organisation with an enormous social media ecosystem, which acts as an interface between the Pakistan armed forces, civil media and the civic society. It formulates the media policy of the Pakistan Army. The directorate works as the principal voice of Pakistan's

Military, and its director-general serves as the official spokesperson of the armed forces.[11]

As one of the most prestigious directorates of Pakistan armed forces, the pre-dominance of the Army personnel is organic in its organisational structure. As out of 20 director generals (DGs) since its inception, 19 have been Army officers, with the only exception of Commander Maqbool Hussain, who headed the organization from 1952 to 1965. The total numbers have never been made public, but experts estimate around 10,000 officers and staff, which does not include informants or assets.[12]

The Director-General (DG) ISPR, is either a Lieutenant General or Major General, appointed at the behest of the Army Chief. He reports directly to Chairman of Joint Chiefs of Staff Secretariat; Chief of Army Staff, Chief of Air Staff, Commandant of Marines, and the Chief of Naval Staff. Under him, there are four verticals which include, two brigadiers, one Commodore, and one Air Commodore who are designated as directors. Each vertical has a special staff from both the defence services and civilians who are recruited as '*domain specialists*'. Their likely strength is about 55 service officers and about 45 to 50 civilian officers. Apart from these they also hire a lot of young students. Approximately a total of about 400-500 persons having a multitude of skill sets including creative directors, behavioural psychologists, Imams, photographers, audio specialists, speech writers, animation experts, cartoons & meme creators, mimics, musicians and digital library managers work here. The following diagram attempts to show a probable structure of the organisation.

Figure 5.1: DG ISPR

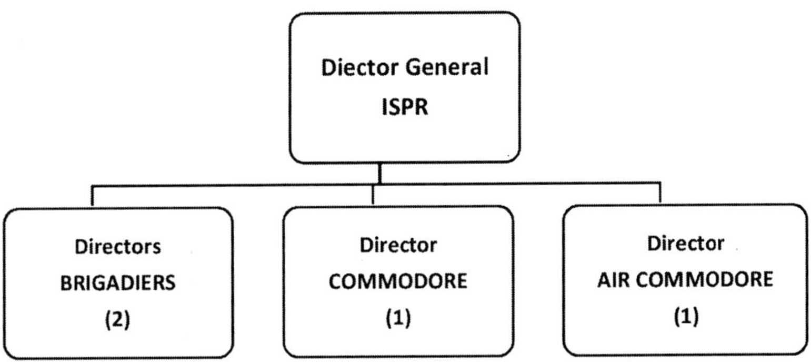

Figure 5.2: Headquarter ISPR

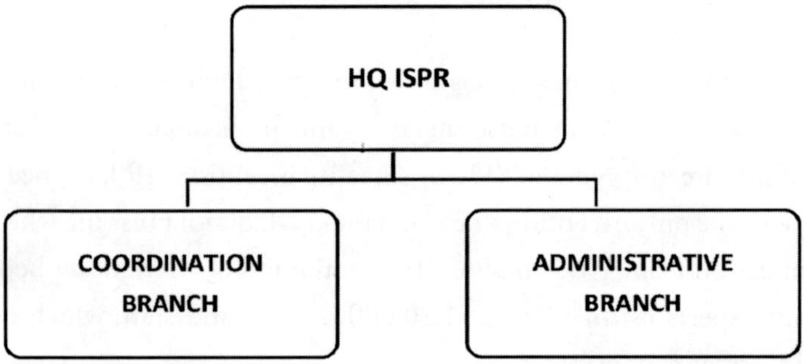

Figure 5.3: ISPR Coordination Branch

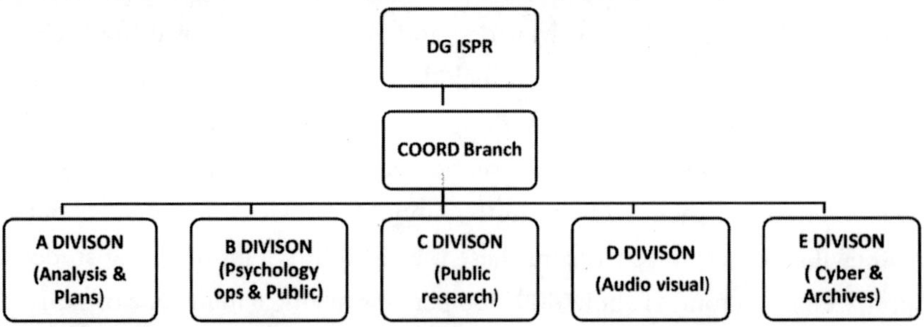

Total Existing Manpower	- 356	Total Existing Officers	- 424
Proposed Manpower	- 536	Proposed Officers	- 695

Figure 5.4: Detailed Organisation of A - Division

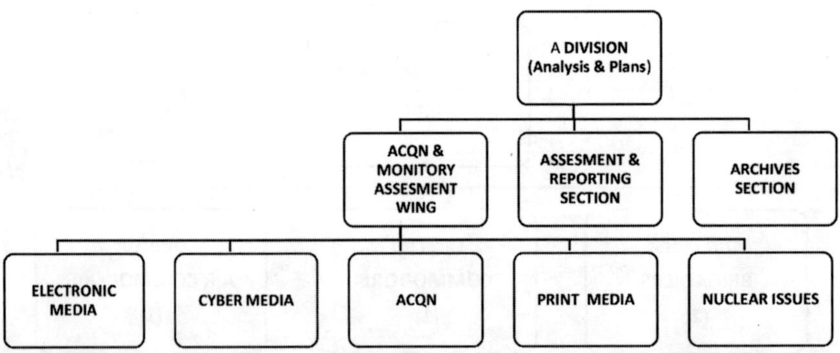

Figure 5.5: Detailed Organisation of B - Division

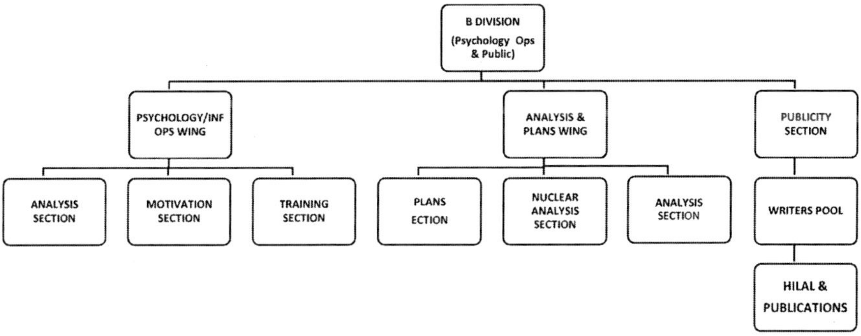

Figure 5.6: Detailed Organisation of C - Division

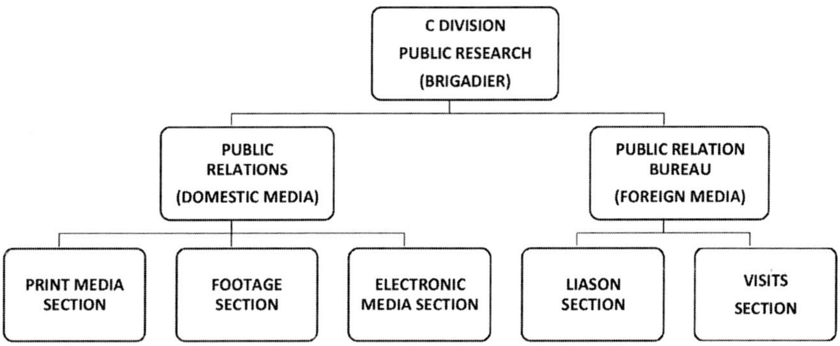

Figure 5.7: Detailed Organisation of D - Division

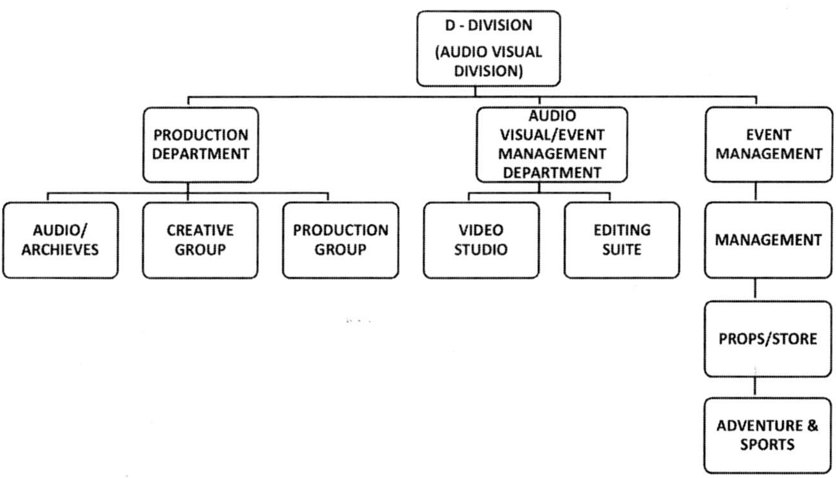

Figure 5.8: Detailed Organisation of E - Division

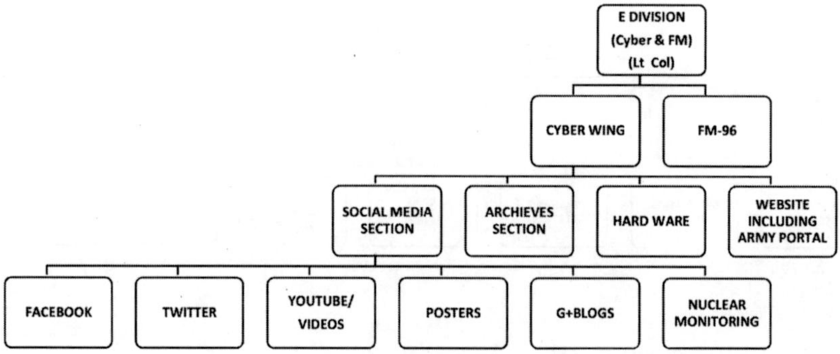

Figure 5.9: ISPR in Pak Army

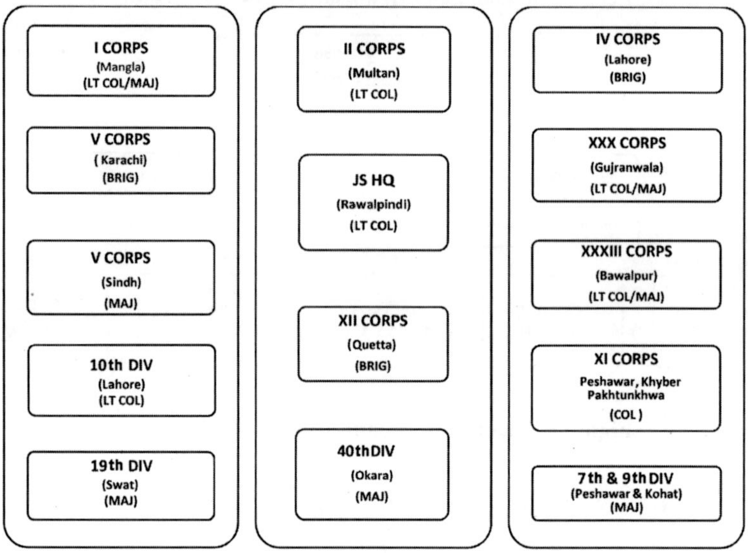

Source: Derived by analysing various web achieves of the ISPR and their regional PRO offices, the numbers are just an approximation based on the analytical research & interviews conducted by the Author.

A number of officers from the ISPR directorate are posted as public relations officers (PRO) in almost all the formations of the Pakistan Army (Figure 5.10). The allocation of PROs are made in accordance to the strategic vitality of the region. For instance, 4 Corps based in Lahore has a Brigadier heading the public relations department along with one Lt Col/TwoMajors/ Captain and the same is true of Corps based in Quetta & Karachi. Other formations like Mangla Corp and Swat Division, have Lt Col/Major rank officers posted accordingly.[13] Officers of Brigadier rank or equivalent are assigned director position, such as director public relations, director productions, whereas the deputy director positions, such as public relations, additional director (Local media), foreign media, and documentaries, are generally held by officers of Colonel rank or below, as shown in the (Figures 5.10, 5.11 and 5.12).

Figure 5.10: Contacts - Web Archives ISPR

S/ No	Appointment	Rank & Name	Contact Information
1.	Director General ISPR	Major General Athar Abbas	Tel Office : 0092-51-9271600 Tel Office : 0092-51-56130041 Fax Office: 0092-51-9271682 Tel Home : 0092-51-9273379 Tel Home : 0092-51-56132209 Cell : 0302-8555741 Email: abbasathar@hotmail.com dg@ispr.gov.pk
2.	Director Production	Brigadier Zulfiqar Ahmed Shaheen	Cell : 0308-5208299
3.	Director Public Relations	Brigadier Muhammad Tariq Jilani	Cell :+92-300-5554763 Email: tariq4c@gmail.com
4.	Deputy Director Public Relations	Col Abdur Rehman Pasha	Cell :+92-323-5113099
5.	Additional Director (Local Media)	Lt Col Attique ur Rehman	Cell : 0321-5376715 Email: attique@ispr.gov.pk
6.	Additional Director (Foreign Media)	Lt Col Baseer Haider	Cell : 0300-5001331 Email: baseer@ispr.gov.pk
7.	Additional Director (Documentaries)	Lt Col Mujtaba Tirmizi	Cell : 0321-5372022 Email: mujtaba@ispr.gov.pk

Source: "CONTACTS' Web Archive ISPR". Inter-Services Public Relations, February 13, 2008. https://web.archive.org/web/20080213140901/.

Figure 5.11: Pakistan Air Force Web Archive ISPR

Pakistan Air Force

Sr. No	Appointment	Rank & Name	Contact Information
1.	Director	Air Commodore Sarfraz Ahmed Khan	Cell : +92-300-8556626
2.	Deputy Director	Wing Commander Tariq	Cell : +92-300-5000231
3.	Deputy Director	Wing Commander Aamir Zaheer	Cell : +92-300-8521299

Source: Inter-Services Public Relations, February 13, 2008. https://web.archive.org/web/20080213140908/.

Figure 5.12: Pakistan Navy Web Archive ISPR

Pak Navy

Sr. No	Appointment	Rank & Name	Contact Information
1.	ADPR - 1	Lt Commander Muhammad Amin	Cell : +92-0302-8998432
2.	PRO	Lt Commander Rizwan	Tel Office : +92-51-20062799

Source: Inter-Services Public Relations, February 13, 2008. https://web.archive.org/web/20080213140918/.

WHAT IS THE ECOSYSTEM OF THE ISPR?

The ISPR ecosystem has evolved over the years to suit the changing needs of the geo-political environment, however, a closer examination reveals, it is likely to resemble a '*three-tier structure*', as illustrated below.

Figure 5.13: ISPR Three-tier Ecosystem

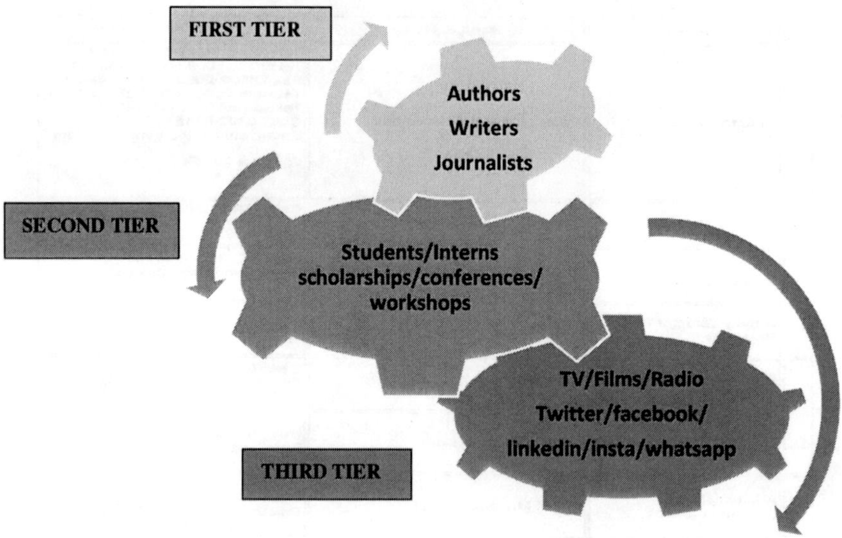

Source: Annotated by the Author.

First Tier: comprises primarily of writers, authors, academicians, and their publications. Their responsibility is to build narratives that portray Army in a positive light. Some Urdu Commentators and writers who have consistently supported the ISPR on numerous occasions are Azaddullah Ghalib, Aslam Beg, Brig Harun Rashid, Ikram Sehgal, Munir Akram, and Jiauudin Kahn, Mohammad Salim Bhat and Kazi Javed Sumera Shaheen, and Pervaiz Iqbal Cheema. Urdu newspapers, like *Ausaf*, *Ummat*, and *Nawai-i-Waqt*, as well as a few English papers like *Daily Pakistan* and *Jamat-e-Islami (JI)* and *Jasarat* newspaper are pro-Army. Since 1948, ISPR's official in-house monthly magazine *Hilal*, been published on a regular basis with a wide readership base across all ages, genders, and literacy levels. The magazine's content appeals to a large audience because it covers both military and non-military topics, not to mention the fact that India is highlighted as a constant security threat in almost every issue.

Second Tier: consists mostly of interns and young researchers, approximately two thousand. As part of its periodic recruitment drive youth competitions, seminars, and talent spotting workshops are conducted at various educational institutions. Every year, about 1,000 interns are taught, with women accounting for over 60 per cent of the total. The incentives are jobs and contracts with Army-owned institutions. Budget is no constraint as the three services, ISI, and the government are its funding agencies. After their internships, students may pursue jobs within or outside of the country, but their commitment to the cause of ISPR may never be broken, hence it is considered a life-long commitment.

Third Tier: encompasses a massive social media external ecosystem with its presence in films/TV/radio/theatres/cinema, productions, video and mobile games. Several media personalities such as Dr Shahid Masood, Arshad Sharif, Sami Ibrahim, Dr Aamir Liaqat and others help indoctrinate pro-military narrative.[14] Milbus, or the military industry, also produces pro-Army movies and television shows. Their sponsorship of a series of Jamat-ul-Dawa's (JuD)[15] social media seminars in Gujranwala, Sargodha, Multan, Rawalpindi, and Lahore from April 1 to April 16, 2017, was aimed at training volunteers to join efforts in waging a social media war in Kashmir. It operationalised a model of manufacturing one lakh content of the workshop each day and released it into the public domain to deceive Kashmiris via WhatsApp, Facebook, Twitter and other social media platforms. Any government organisation would have found this a challenging assignment.

The '*ISPR is a cog in the wheel of the Pak Army*' and has played a key role in consolidating the command of the deep state. It has boosted the Army's image through '*propaganda tactics*' and impacted the general public who are blindfolded in accepting the virtual picture, rather than the real one.

WHAT IS ITS WORKING MECHANISM?

A thorough examination is essential to understand ISPR's functioning. An effective '*social media manipulation*' is carried out by employing platforms such as TV, radio, cinema and print, both online and offline, to '*influence the cognitive domain*'. Through its '*Social Media Control Centre*', '*monitoring and controlling of all local print-audio-visual media*' takes place. Believing in the adage that 'lies spread quicker than truth', and "a lie if repeated a thousand times become truth", this centre builds the national narratives by imposing a coherence and sequencing of events in a way that the targeted audience is convinced. Narrative can be defined as the style and manner in which a story or an argument is told or the way in which a set of incidents, facts or ideas are described.[16] Hence, their role in '*ideologically brainwashing*' impressionable young minds and turning them into unscrupulous perpetrators of violence, leads to the willing and unquestioningly following of the commands of even the terrorist leadership.[17]

This propaganda machinery is based on a lie, deceit and deception, as referred to by the US President Donald Trump's in his tweet on January 1, 2018, where he used these particular words and mentioned, they i.e., Pakistan has been fooling them. What is to be understood is that ISPR is not only fooling the world; but their own people as well. The media may not be successful much of the time in telling people what to think but it is stunningly successful in telling its readers, what to think about? states Bernard Cohen.[18] "In war, narrative is much more than just a story. 'Narrative' may sound like a fancy literary word, but it is actually the foundation of all strategy, upon which all else-policy, rhetoric and action-is built," believes Michael Vlahos.[19]

The Army took a proactive approach in leveraging the rapid expansion and growth of the information revolution, investing substantially in the public relations directorate. This was especially evident in the year 2012, under DG ISPR, Lt. Gen. Aseem Bajwa, who is believed to be responsible for directorate's complete overall transformation and expansion with his well-established team of '*social media warriors*'.[20] The ISPR undertook a greater political role publicising activities against dissenting politicians, objective intellectuals and other activists through systematic harassment, disinformation campaigns, fictitious trials, kidnappings, torture, and assassination.[21]

ISPR's functions are carried on by a strong workforce of over 25,000 full-time personnel, and an additional 30,000 informants with responsibilities like '*countering alternative and contrarian view points in all languages*'. By the late 1970s, it began working with academics and publishing houses to urge them to write favourably about the military and Pakistan. The Cynthia Ritchie[22] case was motivated by the need to improve Pakistan's image and publicise the establishment's point of view overseas. Its '*effective strategising of social media game plan*' includes '*honey-trapping*' foreign diplomats, defence officers, and journalists at international conferences. The rapid expansion of social media has accelerated the ISPR's operating mechanism.

Data on Pak social media reveals that media participation has grown rapidly because of the increased use of smartphones, high-speed mobile internet, improvement in software tools and the availability of all these at affordable prices, courtesy China. Detailed data on social media penetration in Pakistani society is given in the following (Figures 5.14-5.17). Facebook is the most popular with a user base of 34.59 million, majority in the age group from 18-24 years. WhatsApp has approximately 9.30 million users in Pakistan as of 2021.[23] Instagram[24] has 9.47 million users in Pakistan and 6.7 million people are maintaining LinkedIn profiles.

Figure 5.14: Total Social Media Users

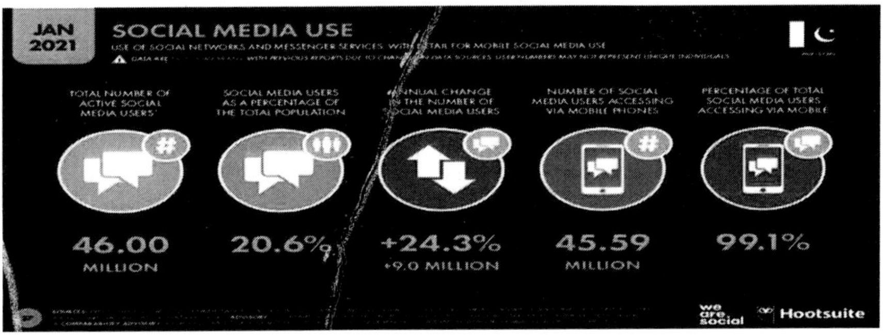

According to the World Bank Report, overall Pakistan's population in 2021 is 226.9 million.[25] Out of which 46 million (20.6 per cent) of the total population are active members of social media with around 45.59 million (99.1 per cent) users accessing via mobiles phones. Between January 2020 and January 2021, the number of social media users in Pakistan increased by 9.0 million (+24.3 per cent).

Figure 5.15: Total Mobile Users, Internet Users and Active Media Users

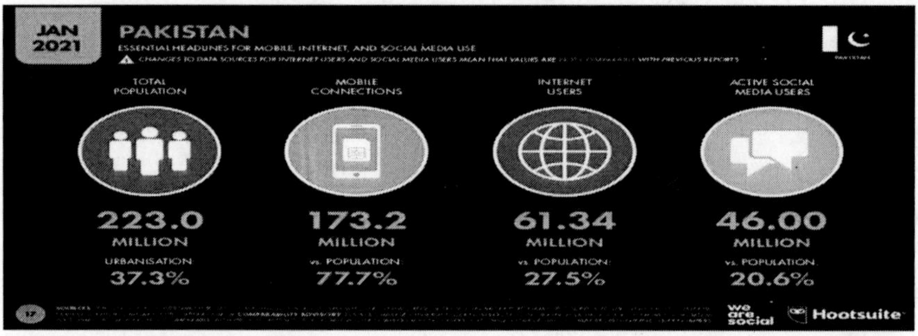

Source: https://datareportal.com/reports/digital-2021-pakistan?rq=pakistan

Out of the total population, around 82 million (37.3 per cent) live in urban areas.[26] 173.2 million people (77.7 per cent) of the total population have mobile connections. And about 61.34 million are internet users (27.5 per cent of the total population). Active users account of social media are with 46 million people (20.6 per cent of the total population) which is reasonably a very active proportion of media users (Figure 5.15).

Figure 5.16: Different Perspectives: Internet Adoption

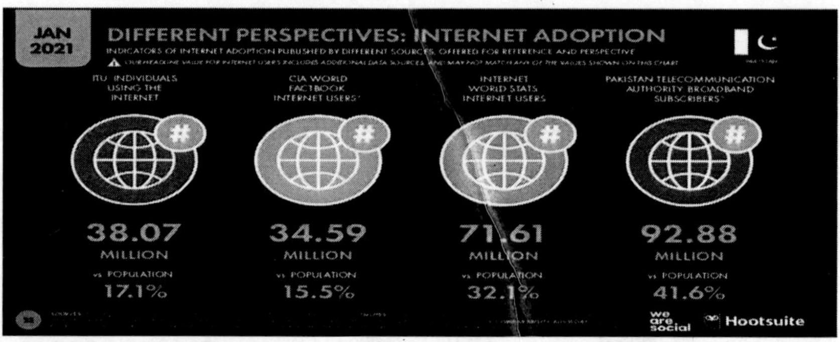

Source: https://datareportal.com/reports/digital-2021-pakistan?rq=pakistan

Various agencies have reported varying numbers on internet adoption in Pakistan. According to the International Telecommunication Union (ITU), the total number of people utilising the internet in January 2021 was 38.07 million (7 per cent) of the entire population of the country. As per the CIA's World Factbook, Pakistan has 34.59 million internet users (15.5 per cent) of the country's total population. According to World Stats, Pakistan has 71.61

million internet users (32.2 per cent) of the country's total population. Data from the Pakistan Telecommunication Authority shows that the country has about 92.88 million (41.6 per cent) of total population broadband subscribers.

Figure 5.17: Social Media Audience Profile

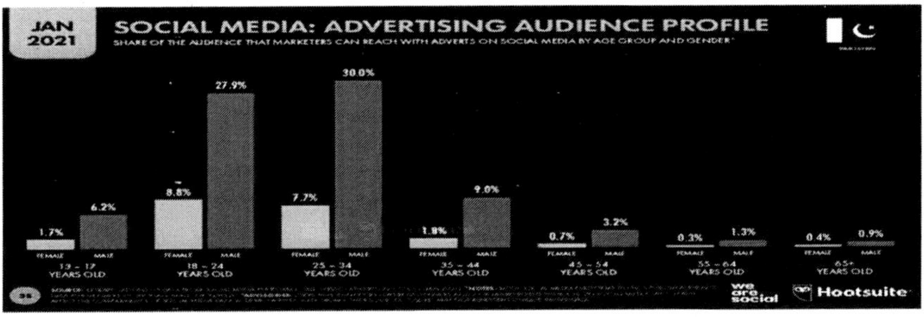

Source: https://datareportal.com/reports/digital-2021-pakistan?rq=pakistan

As an overview, the 25-34 age group seems to dominate most social media platforms. People in the age group of 65+ are the least users of social media. The one common trend present in all age groups is that males are more prominent users of social media than females. The age group of 13-17 years are using (7.9 per cent) and the age group of 18-24 years use around (35.7 per cent), the next is 25-34 age group (37.7 per cent), age group 35-44, the cumulative percentage is (10.8 per cent), the next age group 45-55 years is (3.9 per cent), 55-64 years age group is (1.6 per cent), 65+ only (1.3 per cent) are using social media.

Such an explosive growth in social media has led to the emergence of a new venue of intelligence and surveillance known as '*Social Media Intelligence*' (SOCMINT).[27] As a result, some media and private channels have established strong links with the Intelligence agencies and some are heavily censored. The ISPR media cell's ability to generate, influence, and then convert perceptions into conviction is its power, believing it has the right to define what is good or bad for society. A case to prove this point, following the horrific killing of Ahmadis in Lahore massacre on 28 May 2010, a number of significant media figures started building on the narrative that this minority Muslim community would be "*definitely massacred*" as '*kafirs*'. On the 16th of June 2010, Mubasher

Lucman, host of Point Blank on Pakistan's Urdu Channel Express News, gathered three well-known Muslim academics to explain to the viewers why Ahmadis were not Muslims. Ahmadis were declared "dajjal" (anti-Christ), liars, worse than Kafirs/murtads by a panel of experts. The clerics came to the conclusion that "murtads are deserving of death." During a commercial break, the host said that he absolutely agreed with this and that they are truly "worthy of slaying."[28] Hence, the pro-Army media channels have created a situation which rationalises the way the Ahmadiya's are treated and endorsed by the clerics too.

In recent years, Social media has grown increasingly unpredictable, chaotic and anarchic to the point that the "*breaking news syndrome*" and "*commercialization of electronic media*" have effectively compromised the genuine content of the news. This new found power is also being exploited by ISPR, which has no accountability and sets its own agenda, even if it means weakening national institutions mistakenly or intentionally. It is estimated that it controls around 367 daily or weekly publications, 81 TV channels, 24 news channels, 134 FM radio stations, and a slew of domestic and international news organisations.[29]

According to the World Press Freedom Index 2020, The Reporters Sans Frontiers (RSF), Pakistani social media had become a priority target for the country's 'deep state' and its influence has increased dramatically since Imran Khan became Prime Minister in 2018.[30] A recent Report of the European Commission noted, there had been a '*serious deterioration of media freedom in Pakistan, a trend that began in the lead-up to the general election in 2018 with national security widely used as a 'pretext for cracking down on freedom of expression*'.[31] Few cases to prove this trend are discussed. Mir Shakil-ur-Rahman, or MSR as he is popularly called, the Jang-Geo Editor-in-Chief was taken in custody of the National Accountability Bureau (NAB) since March 12, 2020, for a property transaction that took place 34 years ago. The Lahore High court released him on bail after eight months, observing that the case was "made with discrimination" and was "not appropriate".[32]

Another example, a live Geo News interview of former President Asif Zardari by well-known journalist Hamid Mir was cut short after just a few minutes without any explanation (2019). Similarly, another live interview with Maryam Nawaz, daughter of Nawaz Sharif, on Hum News was '*stopped forcefully*' a few minutes into transmission. The signals of three other Pakistani TV news channels, Abb Takk TV, 24 News and Capital TV, were suddenly suspended from cable TV services on July 8, 2019, for several days as these channels were giving her coverage. Journalists like Talat Hussain, Najam Sethi, Nusrat Javedand Murtaza Solangi were forced out of their jobs and some like Taha Siddiqi and Gul Bukhari were lucky to have found refuge abroad. Few like Sajid Hussain, who has been living in asylum in Sweden for his reporting on Balochistan, have turned up dead.[33]

A key part of its operating mechanism is the establishment of a '*doctored military culture*,' as depicted through commemorative rites such as the Youm-e-Shuhada (YeS),[34] and Youm-e-Difa (YeD).[35] The annual Youm-e-Shuhada (YeS) function (April 30), started in 2010 but was discontinued after 2015, focused on martyrs from Federally Administered Tribal Areas of Pakistan (FATA) and the older Youm-e-Difa (YeD) commemoration (September 6), observed after the 1965 war. Its role is displayed effectively and systematically in '*manipulating the emotions of military personnel's martyred families*' with '*carefully crafted narratives of grief and mourning.*' Army officers meticulously observe martyrs' families' preparation during rehearsals, "*to exhibit exactly the correct emotion and some acting*," while skilfully manipulating camera work to determine what should be presented. It has become customary for the Army Chief to deliver a "State of the Nation" speech, highlighting the heroism and sacrifices made in the face of the enemy.

While a mother's sacrifice is typically revered because it is considered 'pure, even asexual,' a shaheed's wife's participation is prohibited because the 'show of romantic love is deemed 'tricky' and might have 'un-Islamic connotations'. The sentiments of women to their lost sons differed from those of dads, who found it easier to find peace in public acknowledgement of their sacrifice. The master narrative, which aims to mould and control residents' perceptions of the military and its purpose, is defined by these rituals, which are televised across the country.[36] Hence an avoidable death is turned meaningful by the military which functions as a modern kinship group rewarding its subjects with pay, pensions, and other benefits including land grants. Such inducements act as bargaining chips that permit continued membership in the kinship group. This appeal of militarism remains a powerful political act, used to challenge its subjects. It can also be displayed as a heady mix of grief and ceremony for the larger nation when needed.[37] Such display of dramatics and manufactured emotions carried out in these ceremonies display ISPR's narrative, acting as a '*manufacturing machinery*' churning minds of the soldiers filled with their content. Hence, influencing and controlling the mindsets of the people has become the most cost-effective and non-lethal medium employed by Pakistan's military media wing both on the public and the adversary. Undoubtedly, the DG ISPR's as seen in Figure 5.18 take the credit for guiding narrative building practice to perfection.

Figure 5.18: Ex Directors & Director Generals of ISPR (1949-2021)

Colonel
Shabaz Khan
May 1949 - Jul 1952

Commander
Maqbool Hussain
Aug 1952 - Oct 1965

Colonel
Z A Suleri
Nov 1965 - Aug 1966

Lieutenant Colonel
Masud Ahmed
Sep 1966 - Feb 1967

Brigadier A R
Siddiqui
Mar 1967 - Nov 1973

Brigadier Fazal ur
Rehman
Dec 1973 - Mar 1977

Brigadier T H Siddiqui
Apr 1977 - Jul 1985

Brigadier Siddiq Salik
Aug 1985 - Aug 1988

Major General Riaz Ullah
Dec 1988 - Sep 1991

Major General Jahangir Nasrullah
Oct 1991 - Apr 1993

Major General Khalid Bashir
May 1993 - Jul 1994

Brigadier S M A Iqbal
Aug 1994 - Feb 1995

Major General Saleem Ullah
Mar 1995 - Aug 1998

Brigadier Ghazanfar Ali
Sep 1998 - Oct 1998

Major General Rashid Qureshi
Nov 1998 - May 2003

Major General Shaukat Sultan
Jun 2003 - Feb 2007

Major General Waheed Arshad
Feb 2007 - Jan 2008

Major General Athar Abbas
Jan 2008 - Jun 2012

Lieutenant General Asim Saleem Bajwa
Jun 2012 - Dec 2016

Major General Asif Ghafoor
Dec 2016 - Jan 2020

Major General Babar Iftikhar
Feb 2020 -

Source: https://ispr.gov.pk/director-detail.php

WHAT ARE THE TOOLS OF SOCIAL MEDIA NETWORKS?

Three power centres exercise jurisdiction over the media: the ISPR, the government, and the Pakistan Electronic Media Regulatory Authority (PEMRA). Through its Media Control Centre, the ISPR monitors all local print-audio-visual media. PEMRA has the authority to impose reasonable restrictions in the interest of Pakistan's religion, integrity, and national security, as defined by Article 19 of the Constitution.[38] The following is an in-depth assessment of the instruments of social media networks:

Twitter

The first officer to project ISPR in Twitter mode is undoubtedly Lt. Gen. Asim Salim Bajwa (2012-2016), also known as the '*Army's Media Tsar*'. He was instrumental in transforming the organisation into a gigantic and high profile institution with increased resources and authority.[39] His hallmarks include the '*digital troll armies*', the '*hashtags*', the '*branding of then Army Chief Gen. Raheel Sharif*, by idolising his role in eradicating militancy through Operation Zarb-e-Azb. With three million Twitter followers, he became the new constant in social media combat.[40] It wouldn't be unfair to allude to him as the '*Twitter General*.' He wielded such power that in 2016, posters surfaced in Karachi and Islamabad demanding the Army Chief's term extension. Because of his high-profile role, when Gen. Qamar Javed Bajwa took over as COAS, he removed him and replaced him with a Major General rank officer rather than a Lt General, possibly to restrain its powers.

Under the next DG ISPR, Major General Asif Gafoor (2016-20), enhanced coverage of the COAS continued, including themes relating to the Pakistan Army's revisionist attitude on Kashmir and Afghanistan were pushed a step further; his near dominance over Pakistan's elected government could be seen by the jump in his Twitter followers. The official Twitter handle of the Pakistan government was overtaken by the DG ISPR account. The Twitter handle of the official government of Pakistan (@pid_gov) had 1.5 million followers,[41] while the official page of DG ISPR (@OfficialDGISPR) has 4.2 million followers.[42] This speaks volumes about the clout and public engagement of the ISPR primacy over and above the Pakistan government. These tweets demonstrate Army's keen involvement in domestic political concerns and foreign policy matters, which should fall under the jurisdiction of the elected government if there was a true democracy, but in Pakistan, '*Uniformed democracy rules the roost*'.

Under the '*Cyber propaganda war against India*', ISPR has been publicly advocating violence in Jammu and Kashmir. It has always been playing the victim card, accusing Indian armed forces of targeting the civilians in PoK. Hashtags like #GobackModi, #ChaosInIndia, #Islamophobia and #ShameonModi.[43] Twitter handles are also misused when the names of the '*account are changed*'. For instance, @pak_fauj changed its name to @SayyidaMona who is an Omani Royalty named Mona bint Fahd al Said. It started posting anti-India tweets about the ties between India and the Gulf. All these tweets showed ISPR's role.[44]

The ISPR makes every effort to publicise COAS's involvement in critical infrastructure projects and his resolve to see the project through. For instance, tweets regarding major infrastructure projects such as the China Pakistan Economic Corridor (CPEC), and other connectivity projects in Balochistan highlights the Pakistani Army pledged support to such projects in spite of there being ample evidence that many of these projects had developed major problems highlighted in the tweets below:[45]

Figure 5.19: Twitter account of Asim Bajwa ISPR

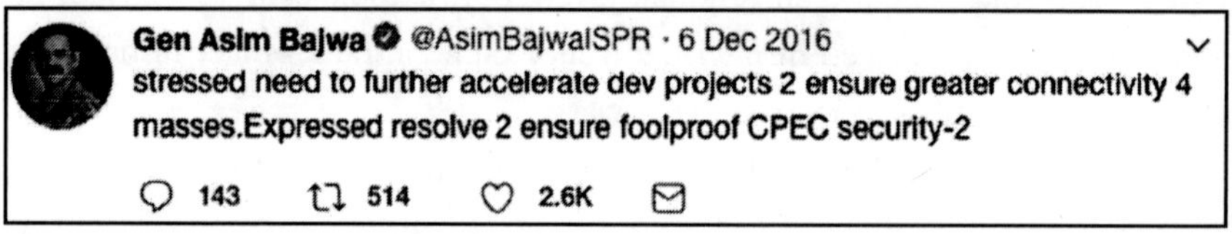
Gen Asim Bajwa @AsimBajwaISPR · 6 Dec 2016
stressed need to further accelerate dev projects 2 ensure greater connectivity 4 masses.Expressed resolve 2 ensure foolproof CPEC security-2
143 514 2.6K

Because of the Army's strong support, politicians have no room to deal with China on their own terms. In fact, the DG ISPR gives the Army Chief an '*exceptional amount of power over the civilian domain, political system, and security system.*' By constantly tweeting meetings with ordinary folks, tribal leaders, politicians, and international leaders, the chief's '*image as a statesman*' and '*de facto ruler*' is bolstered.

Major General Asif Ghafoor will be remembered for his emphasis on '*Fifth Generation Warfare*',[46] his numerous press conferences, tweets, idea and popularity of the Bajwa Doctrine, all contributed to a '*political-ideological and geostrategic narrative*'. ISPR Army includes tens of thousands of trolls who are identified as patriots, Muslims, pro-Army, pro-Kashmir, and PTI supporters. These trolls strike in swarms and act like bullies, using WhatsApp to coordinate their attacks. Each troll with a hierarchy of contacts offers them daily instructions on what content is to be distributed. Satire, parody, deceptive content, imposter content, created content, altered content, and threatening content are all employed. This is how ISPR has hijacked Pakistani discourse with its troll Army, which employs a network of dodgy Twitter, Facebook, and Instagram accounts, many of which are frequently put down.

It creates a narrative of an Army that is accustomed to ignoring, disregarding and influencing civil government rules, by portraying politicians in an unfavourable light. Its twitter expositions are leading to a two-fold effect, ensuring zero criticism and predominance of the Army in the domestic and foreign domain thereby helping in the deep state continuum. This is certainly not good for a healthy democratic society, a glaring example of its dominance could be seen in the audacious tweets concerning the Panama papers case and Dawn Leaks I and II, where the confrontation between the ISPR and the civilian government came out openly in their tweets. In the case of Panama papers, massive leak of around 11.5 million documents with some unaccounted money abroad, named Pakistan Prime Minister Nawaz Sharif in money laundering case. A Joint Investigative Team (JIT) was deputed by the COAS which was constituted of mainly Army officers, along with the support of the compliant judicial system convicted and forced Nawaz Sharif to resign.[47] Many believe, it was the presence of the Army officers on the JIT that particularly led to Nawaz Sharif being convicted of a Petty crime.[48]

Dawn Leaks case[49] again brought out the supremacy of the ISPR as through its tweets it admonished and outrightly rejected the elected government's notification on this case. It all started when a newspaper report titled "Exclusive: Act against militants or face international isolation, civilians tell military" on October 6, 2016.[50] Referring to the leaked minutes of the meeting between the (DG) ISI, Lt. Gen. Rizwan Akhtar, PM Nawaz Sharif, CM of Punjab & PM's brother, Mr Shahbaz Sharif, and the National Security Advisor (NSA), Naseer Janjua. What was noteworthy in this meeting was the assertive tone decision of the PM on two pertinent issues; First, there should be no interference of the intelligence agencies if any law enforcement agencies banned any militant groups; Second, restart the trial of the Mumbai attacks and conclude the report on Pathankot investigation. These two decisions communicated to the ISI were leaked and published as a report by Cyril Almedia, assistant editor of a reputed newspaper DAWN. The COAS termed this leak as a national security issue.[51]

What followed was the forced resignation of the minister of information and broadcasting Mr Pervez Rasheed; constitution of a commission by the government headed by the retired high court judge to investigate the controversial report. Since its contents were leaked as well as aired on news channels, Zafar Abbas and Cyril Almeida were referred to the All-Pakistan Newspapers Society (APNS) for necessary disciplinary action.[52] The (DG) ISPR rejected the government notification in a single and very terse tweet as shown below:

Figure 5.20: DG ISPR Tweet of April 29, 2017: Rejection of Government Notification

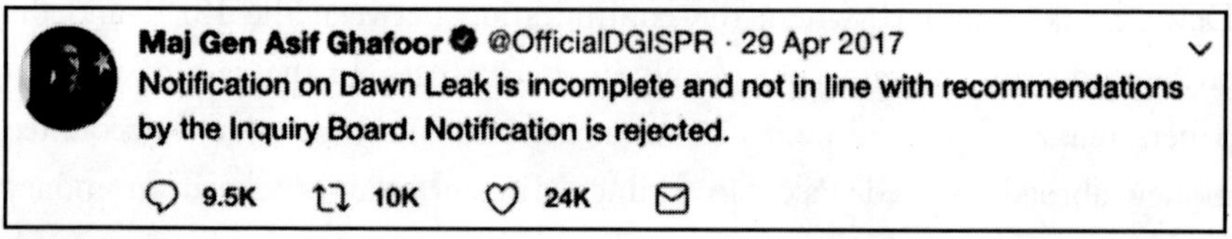
Maj Gen Asif Ghafoor @OfficialDGISPR · 29 Apr 2017
Notification on Dawn Leak is incomplete and not in line with recommendations by the Inquiry Board. Notification is rejected.
9.5K 10K 24K

Another tweet reflecting the coercive deep state role in the internal security matter was with regard to the Islamabad protest marches (November 8-27, 2017) and dharna led by the Tehreek Labaikya Rasool Allah (TLY), Tehreeki-Khatm-i-Nabuwwat and the Sunni Tehreek Pakistan (ST), at the Faizabad interchange which connects the twin cities of Islamabad and Rawalpindi.[53] The dharna was against the Election Act 2017, which had changed the final oath stating the finality of the Prophethood of Mohammad (Khatm-e-Nabuwwat). When the protestors refused to vacate despite the government amending the same, the Islamabad High Court issued orders to the protestors to end their agitation, asking the local laws enforcement agencies to use force, but it was of no use.[54] Finally, the DG ISPR steeped in on November 25, 2017, by giving an advisory tweet of the COAS to the Prime Minister to handle this crisis situation peacefully, as reflected in the Tweet below:

Figure 5.21: Twitter Account of Official DGISPR

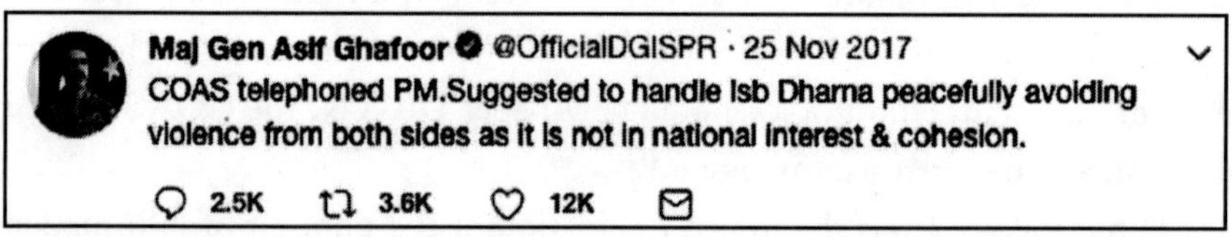
Maj Gen Asif Ghafoor @OfficialDGISPR · 25 Nov 2017
COAS telephoned PM.Suggested to handle Isb Dharna peacefully avoiding violence from both sides as it is not in national interest & cohesion.
2.5K 3.6K 12K

The COAS took charge and without using force, he politically and tactfully handled the situation with the satisfaction of the leader of the protestors.

Khadim Rizvi thanked the Army Chief for his intervention and "special efforts".[55] This episode validates the civilian government's inability to handle crisis situations and the Army's/ISPR's strength has the '*sole protector of the internal security, though without any constitutional authority*'.

Another case, Dawn Leaks II, gives sufficient evidence to demonstrate ISPR as the "*true guardian of Pakistan Twitter social media.*" Former Prime Minister Nawaz Sharif admitted in an interview with Cyril Almedia on May 12, 2018, that the country cannot be run with two or three parallel governments, referring to the prevalence of the Army and ISI nexus, i.e., deep state, as well as his statements on the active prevalence of militant organisations in Pakistan and question about allowing non-state actors to cross borders, killing of 150 people in Mumbai attacks raised questions, the DGISPR immediately tweeted that Nawaz Sharif's statements were misleading.

The Dawn leak case is sufficient testimony to the fact that even a sitting Prime Minister, Shaheed Khaqan Abbasi was summoned by the National Security Council meeting to evaluate the ramifications of this interview, dubbed as the Dawn Leaks II. Cyril Almedia was placed on the exit control list and detained on treason charges.[56] The following tweets simply serve to highlight the COAS's tremendous power in summoning a PM to the Army HQ and forcing the government to arrest the journalist.

Figure 5.22: Twitter Account of Official DGISPR

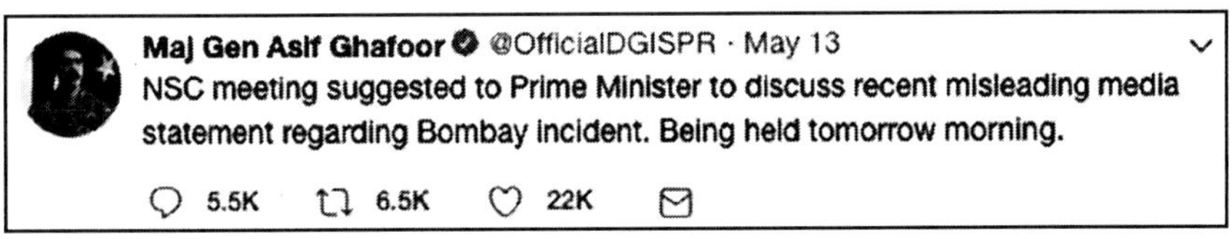

Another example of the ISPR's harshness and judiciary-military confrontation emerged when for the first time in Pakistan's history, the Army Chief was found guilty of high treason and condemned to death under Article 6 of the Constitution. The Army stood with him, as evidenced by the ISPR tweet, which stated that the court's verdict was received with great sadness and anguish by the rank and file of the Pakistan Army. They slammed the court's verdict as hastily reached; "*considering his service to Pakistan, Musharraf cannot be*

a traitor," said ISPR.[57] On December 19, 2019, Pakistan Army spokesman, DG ISPR, Maj Gen Asif Ghafoor, stated in a brief press conference that "*today's verdict transgresses humanity, religion, culture, and any other values.*"[58]

Figure 5.23: ISPR Press Release Statement

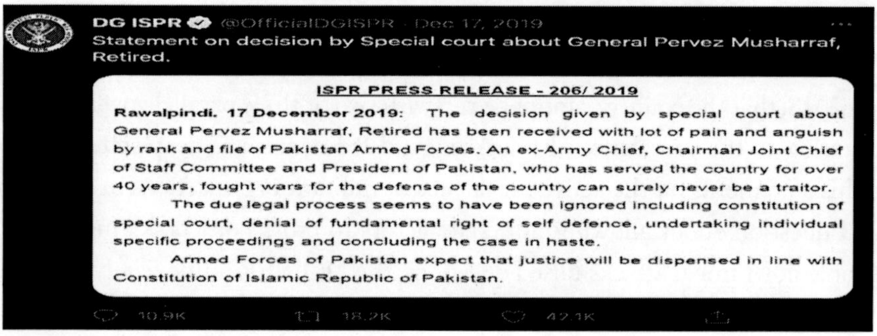

DG ISPR @OfficialDGISPR · Dec 17, 2019

Statement on decision by Special court about General Pervez Musharraf, Retired.

ISPR PRESS RELEASE - 206/ 2019

Rawalpindi. 17 December 2019: The decision given by special court about General Pervez Musharraf, Retired has been received with lot of pain and anguish by rank and file of Pakistan Armed Forces. An ex-Army Chief, Chairman Joint Chief of Staff Committee and President of Pakistan, who has served the country for over 40 years, fought wars for the defense of the country can surely never be a traitor.

The due legal process seems to have been ignored including constitution of special court, denial of fundamental right of self defence, undertaking individual specific proceedings and concluding the case in haste.

Armed Forces of Pakistan expect that justice will be dispensed in line with Constitution of Islamic Republic of Pakistan.

10.9K 18.2K 42.1K

Source: DG ISPR (@OfficialDGISPR) December 17, 2019.

"Due legal process appears to have been ignored," according to the ISPR press release shown above (Figure 5.23). Such tweets only illustrate the Army's media wing's "*total disrespect for the civilian-elected administration,*" boosting the populist narrative of the Army as the country's vanguard.

Asif Ghafoor was removed because he became too high profile & big for his boots, now aspiring to become DG, ISI, which was not liked by his peer group officers and also, perhaps, Gen Bajwa, who replaced him with Maj General Babar Iftikhar, who took overs from 1st February 2020. Brig A R Siddiqi, a former ISPR Chief, wrote in his book "Military in Pakistan: Image and Reality" that self-promotion generals have become the ISPR's perception management's scourge. Military power has become synonymous with the country's national image.

FACEBOOK

Pakistani network especially in relation to Facebook is "*big and long-lasting network*" with the oldest page dating back to 2011, reports Ben Nimmo, an analyst and senior fellow for Information Defence at the Atlantic Council's DFRLab.[59] Since then, ISPR has increasingly utilised Facebook profiles as a '*watchdog*' to prevent anti-Pakistan Army messages and encourage aggressive anti-India posts. To corroborate the allegation, five bloggers who blogged about minorities' oppression and pushed for human rights were silenced by the Army and ISPR in January 2017, and they vanished within a week. Individuals like Salman Haider, Waqas Goraya, Aasim Saeed, Ahmed Raza Naseer, and Samar Abba had Facebook profiles, as did groups like Mochi and Group, Citizens for Secular Democracy, and Civil Progressive Alliance Pakistan (CPAP). Military-controlled networks such as ARY and Bolt TV mounted a large-scale television and social media campaign depicting them as anti-Pakistani and anti-Islam before their disappearance. They were all freed three weeks later from confinement, where they had been tortured, and were ordered not to publish or speak out against the Army or pursue legal action. Many youngsters have terminated their Facebook accounts as a result of the tragedy, and some have fled Pakistan for fear of their lives.

The ISPR has '*manipulated social media*', including news channels, by muting speeches, censoring, or even shutting down broadcasts. Leaders like Mahmood Achakzai, Mohsin Dawar, and Akhtar Mengal, for example, have been constant in requesting greater rights for their provinces and communities, yet they were either not displayed or parts of their speech were muted while speaking to the vast crowd. This has made a mockery of the concept of editorial freedom and reduced the coverage of private news channels to the level of a state broadcaster by censoring the speeches of its critics; the official machinery is nullifying the inclusive progress towards greater integration. This is a short-sighted and self-defeating approach that does more harm than good.[60] In an age that requires transparency and leveraging the rapid flow of information, Pakistan appears to be swimming against the tide.

On April 1, 2019, a Facebook investigation under Nathaniel Gleicher, Head of Cyber Security Policy revealed that it had taken down 103 pages, that included 24 pages across Facebook and Instagram, 57 Facebook accounts, 7 groups and 15 Instagram accounts that inflamed tensions with India, pushed Pakistan's claims over Kashmir and praised the (Pakistan) Army, frequent posts about local and political news of the Indian government, political leaders and military, all were operated by the employees of the military's Inter-Services Public Relations (ISPR) department.[61]

The head of ISPR, Major General Asif Ghafoor, went a step further in demonising India with extreme rhetoric to stigmatise India and the Indian armed forces as shown in Figure 5.24.[62]

Figure 5.24: Twitter Account of official DGISPR

Source: The Print, April 3, 2019, https://theprint.in/defence/pakistan-army-pages-pulled-down-by-facebook-called-indian-security-forces-monkey/215996/

Facebook took down such pages as they had used fake accounts to misrepresent themselves, Pakistan-based Facebook pages posed as Kashmiri activists to push anti-India rhetoric posted in Urdu and English, the pages boasted a combined total of more than three million followers by the time they were exposed and pulled by Facebook.[63]

According to Facebook, around 2.8 million accounts followed these pages and may have been influenced by the content.[64] One such post praising Ghafoor is shown below.

Figure 5.25: Facebook Page praising DGISPR

Source: Medium.

The government's control over the internet sector has been proven by the passage of The Citizens Protection (against online Harm) Rules 2020, which will delete any inflammatory anti-state, anti-Army, anti-judiciary, vulgar, and hateful information, including barring speeches of former Prime Minister Nawaz Sharif.[65] Senator Mushahid Ullah Khan, human rights organisations, and digital enterprises have all accused the government of violating citizens' fundamental rights.

RADIO STATIONS/FM

ISPR runs many radio channels without license. Two main frequencies under it are FM 89.04 (largest FM radio network) and FM 96.00, with a reach in more than 55 cities. Pakistan Electronic Media Regulatory Authority (PEMRA) has never issued a radio frequency to the Army but they run through 'Radio Pakistan'.Illegal radio channels run by ISPR are now a well-established fact, even pointed out by Asma Jehangir, a human rights activist, president of the Supreme Court's Bar Association, who had started a debate in Pakistan as early as 2016, where she appealed the Supreme court and PEMRA to disclose the number of FM channels that come under the ISPR.[66] Matiullah Jan, a Pakistani journalist also raised concerns about ISPR's illegal radio network in the year 2018, but it remained deaf ears of the authorities. According to an estimate, there are 203 estimated FM frequencies working in Pakistan out of which only 160 have a commercial license from PEMRA and 43 frequencies still working without any license including some religious channels with high rate of influence. Some FM stations, particularly in Jammu and Kashmir and Punjab, have been set up solely for the aim of '*spreading psychological warfare*'. At least 15 round-the-clock-are FM stations hurl the most venomous insults at India.[67]

Pakistan's disinformation propaganda through radio stations has been documented in post-doctoral research titled, 'Radio Kashmir: In Times of Peace and War, conducted by Rajesh Bhat. He analysed fifteen FM Pakistani channels detected in various areas of Indian Jammu and Kashmir and Punjab", operating as '*Pakistan's psychological warriors*', "These channels while broadcasting news on Jammu and Kashmir reflected alleged atrocities committed by Indian security forces on Kashmiris and justified bandh calls given by Hurriyat leaders besides condemning restrictions in Kashmir. His study found some pro-militant radio stations which are active on the opposite side of the border, making various allegations and appeals to seduce and sway the Kashmiri people against India. Although the transmission stations are on the other side of the LOC, the signals penetrate borders to impact listeners in the immediate vicinity.[68] Local Pakistani radio stations such as Radio Buraq FM 104-105 MHz, Radio Swat Network 100 FM, and Voice of Kashmir 95.8 were audible in the Kashmir region, according to the study, increasing locals hostility and animosity against India. Earlier, *The ISI had built more radio stations, especially around the Indo-Pak border,* as part of '*Operation Tupac*,'[69] *to overwhelm airwaves with hostile rants.* This is an ongoing operation.

His study disclosed how Radio Pakistan meticulously planned coverage in Jaipur, Kanpur, Bikaner, Ambala, Saharanpur, Meerut, Aligarh, Farrukhabad, and portions of Nepal to arouse anti-India sentiment in some populations. It further mentioned how 'Radio Pakistan' and 'Azad Kashmir Radio' served as a '*conduit between infiltrators and their masters*', allowing them to communicate with one another. The messages were largely written in Gojri, Pahari, Urdu, and Punjabi, which are spoken on both sides of the LoC and in Pakistan's Punjab region. The majority of Pakistani radio stations broadcasting in J&K and Punjab dedicate a significant amount of time to '*religious programming*'.

FM 101 Sialkot, Mast FM 103 Gujranwala, Radio Buraq Sialkot, Voice of Kashmir 95.8, Radio Swat Network 100 FM, and Radio Buraq FM 104-105 MHz, Peshawar, are clearly heard spewing vitriol against India in the Jammu division. The transmissions of these '*radio stations are intermingled with Bollywood and Punjabi music in order to brainwash J&K listeners, who mistake them for Indian stations*'. For the past decade, full-fledged radio stations have been operating in Pakistan's occupied Kashmir's Mirpur, Muzaffarabad, Kotli, Trarkhal, Rawalakote, and Haveli areas, as well as Sialkot, Gujranwala, Lahore, Faisalabad, and Peshawar. People living in India's border districts are being wooed by Azad Kashmir Radio in Muzaffarabad and Trarkhal, as well as Sada-e-Hurriyat-e-Kashmir.[70]

PRINT AND TELEVISION

The goal of self-censorship on both print and television media journalists has been undertaken by the ISPR. Those critical of the Army are targeted and coercive measures are taken, as in the case of Salim Shehzad, Hamid Mir, Cyril Ahmedia, and Taha Siddiqui.

Since the abrogation of Article 370, ISPR has increasingly voiced their anti-India narratives in its broadcasts in the Jammu and Kashmir region, where it has been particularly prominent, proactive, and consistent. This compelled the Indian Government to warn the cable operators in the region from broadcasting channels from Pakistan, Iran, Turkey and Malaysia.[71] Pakistani channels like Zakir Naik's Peace TV, Madni Channel, Noor TV, Hadi TV, Hidayat, Ahli-bait TV, Duniya News, Saudi Al-Sunnah Al-Nabawiyah, Dawn News and a few more Arabic and Pakistani news channels which were advocated to be spreading fake news have been banned.[72]

In the year 1990's ISPR established its footprints as a '*production house*' as a '*weapon of mass influence*' with the production of its first two family dramas '*khajoor Main Atka*' and '*Sunehray Din*' based on the life of an Army officer. Between 1994 and 2004 it produced six more military-oriented dramas.[73] The year 2015 marked a shift in its media policy from dramas to documentaries and songs, most of them relating to patriotism, Army's role in nation-building, Kashmir issue, Army operations in Waziristan have been encapsulated in around 21 documentaries and 60 songs.[74]

Dramas made a comeback with '*Ehd-e-Wafa*,' television series started in 2019, an attempt to promote anti-India propaganda while masquerading as a patriotic performance. The show portrays four friends—a politician, a journalist, a bureaucrat and an Army captain and delineates them celebrating the victories of Balakot airstrike, Pulwama attack, the Kargil War and the capturing of Wing Commander Abhinandan Varthamam.[75] The defeat of India and her portrayal as an arch-nemesis of Pakistan is clearly visible in the show foretold by the ISPR. A small glimpse of its home production is shown below.

Figure 5.26: ISPR Productions

Source: https://ispr.gov.pk

NEWSPAPERS, ARTICLES AND BOOKS

Most of the national and vernacular publications like journals, books, magazines, news papers come under the ISPR's scanner. This was noticeable during the abrogation of Article 370 (August 5, 2019),[76] when newspapers like *Dawn* and *Geo* carried full releases from the ISPR, half of them were baseless.[77] Such disinformation propaganda campaigns were carried out through various fake news websites during the abrogation, showing pictures of different war scenes, with violence and losses allegedly accredited to the Indian Army. Some websites were only tasked to make paper clips and mould present news in some other context. While tracing their IP addresses they were located in Islamabad, Rawalpindi, Dubai and Saudi Arabia.[78]

Figure 5.27: Fake Photos

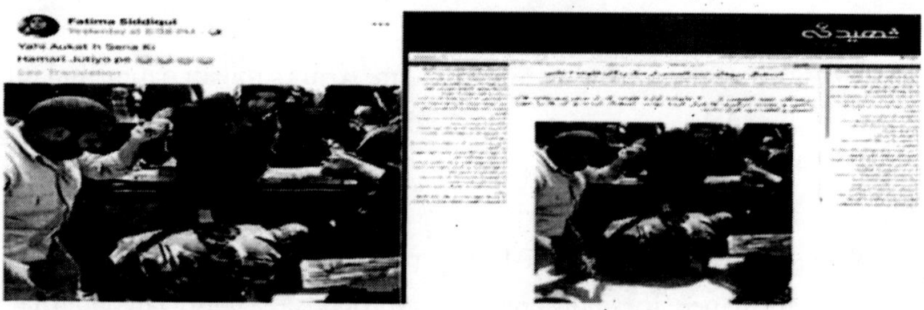

The account used a picture of a girl, originally from Iraq, posting as a Kashmiri, to insult the security personnel of Jammu and Kashmir

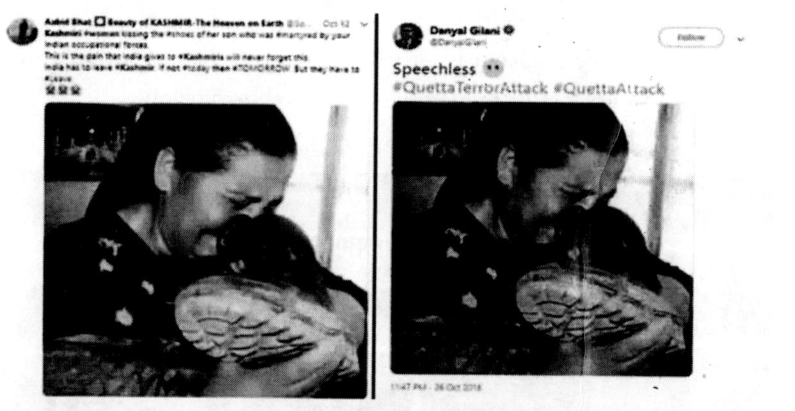

Mother of a August 2016 Quetta bomb blast claimed that woman morning the loss of her son who was killed by Indian Security Officials

Source: http://www.indiandefencereview.com/spotlights/disinformation-propaganda-pakistans-newest-weapon-on-kashmir/

ISPR modus operandi also involves '*creation of camouflage groups*' on countless WhatsApp, Facebook, Snapchat applications with a fake name. Innocent people are attracted through these channels, later the groups admin starts feeding people's minds with poisonous details. The creation of fake data which is violent in nature is circulated by their '*media warriors*' in major worldwide groups, using manufactured data, edited photos and videos as shown below:

Figure 5.28: Fake ID's

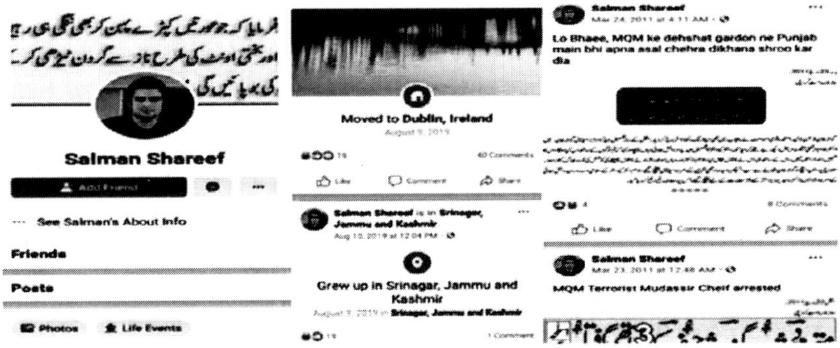

Fake IDs running from Pakistan propagating disinformation

Pakistani Army media wing (ISPR) busy in broadcasting Hindus as terrorists using Bollywood images from out of context

Source: http://www.indiandefencereview.com/spotlights/disinformation-propaganda-pakistans-newest-weapon-on-kashmir/

Figure 5.29: Morphed Photo & Virable Fake Datas

- **Hoardings & Flashboards:** Pakistani establishment got exposed badly when her representative shown pellet embedded girl's image in UN. In reality, that image was from Palestine shot by British photographer. Creating and circulating such pellet images are taking in millions of reach across Pakistan & worldwide where simple images are edited software's like Corel, pixelpro and many others.

Pakistan's permanent representative to United Nations, Maleeha Lodhi showing a photograph of a girl from Gaza, injured in Israeli air strike

Virable fake datas

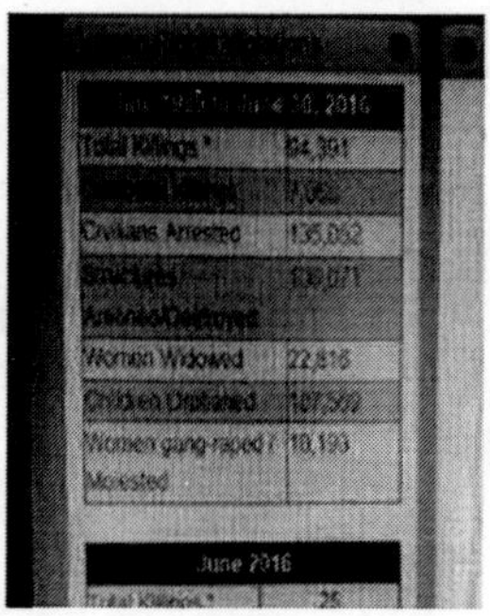

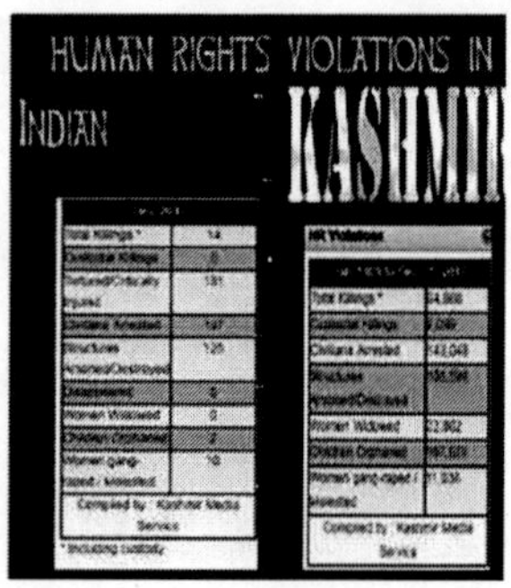

Source: http://www.indiandefencereview.com/spotlights/disinformation-propaganda-pakistans-newest-weapon-on-kashmir/

Army's official in-house publications, like the *Green Book*, *Hilal* Magazine and Defence Journals essentially are driven by '*propagandist mind games*,' where Kashmir is inadvertently highlighted in almost every publication. The monthly magazine *Hilal*, has five versions, namely Hilal English, Hilal Urdu, Hilal for Her, Hilal for Kids and Hilal for Kids Urdu, the magazine has a wide readership across age, gender and literacy levels.[79] Their distribution is managed in eleven cities across the country, with the maximum presence in Punjab. All the issues of these magazines highlight the military achievements & involvement in various activities in politics, foreign policy, and social-religious domain and reiterate India as a threat. This '*communication strategy*' intends to promote '*alternate and counter narratives*' with an emotional appeal.[80]

Figure 5.30: Hilal Magazines

Hilal English Magazine

Hilal for Her

Hilal Urdu Magazine

Hilal Kids (English)

Hilal Kids (Urdu)

THE PLIGHT OF PALESTINIAN & KASHMIRI CHILDREN

While the humans experience so much in this world that life seems to be just a little. With only a difference that we have a choice to become whatever we want and whatever religion we follow, we all suffer at the hands of whatever occurs, be it a natural disaster or manmade tragedy. The natural disaster doesn't discriminate between Muslim and non-Muslim or whatever, but the manmade tragedy targets specific community and nation or followers of a specific faith.

Only those nations can stop such tragedies and face such disasters who stand steadfast, headstrong and rock solid against it and protect themselves to live on.

We haven't been recovered yet from the Covid-19 disaster, its continuing toll is so heavy worldwide that we the children are compelled to think that life is nothing in face of such calamitous occurrences. It is more than a year now that we are stock within our homes; our schooling has stopped and our extracurricular activities are only homebound. Doesn't life amidst the spreading epidemic seem so indeterminate?

At the same time though we have found a lot many things as blessings in disguise; we have learnt many positive lessons from it. A calamity faced with unity and discipline can be averted. Deaths at massive level may occur but life goes on and only those may survive who adopt preventive measures, take precautionary steps and follow standard operating procedures (SOPs) well in time and with togetherness.

The holy month of Ramadan brought to us a happy difference as we enjoyed fasting, *sehr* and *iftar*. Eid is our most sacred and traditional event that brings us joy and happiness, smiles and relatives, give charity to the needy and help the poor and deserving. *Chand Raat*, the first moon night of the Islamic month of *Shawal*, is traditionally celebrated with great enthusiasm and religious fervor.

Coinciding with Eid, we heard very disturbing news – from Palestine; the children, women and elders there were being targeted, many had been killed or injured, buildings and residential apartments razed to ground. The news reports, images and videos on TV channels and social media were horribly scary. It looked as if the world for the children of Palestinian Muslims has been made worthless. This was so shocking and so upsetting that my siblings and I couldn't sleep properly for many days. Despite, the world at large and the Muslim populations around the globe were protesting against the unashamed aggression by Israelis, the belligerence and barbarism continued unabated. Question is whether life is so uncertain for the Palestinian children and their families?

And same goes for the children of Indian Illegally Occupied Jammu and Kashmir. The

...lice and paramilitary, Hindu fanatics of RSS and ...JP, that too amidst the heavy toll inflicted by ...ovid-19. They haven't been able to go to school ...r almost two years now. Many young students ...ve been arrested and put in lockups and ...tention camps. There is curfew for indefinite ...riod and therefore the sufferings unending. The ...ng suspended water and food supplies have ...ade the life in the occupied valley a hell. Is the ...orld for children and people of Kashmir not ...orth living? Is there no end to the long dark night ...llen on them?

I am afraid the Indians and Israelis have ...osen the wrong target. Targeting children and ...e killings of women and the elderly is an act of ...wardice and timidity at its peak. It is also an ...dication of the fear and scare, dread and ...epidation these nations have in their hearts ...out the Muslims' likely renaissance. History is ...itness to the fact that when the cruel aggressors ...oop so low to resort to killing children for fear of ...surgence, then they get perished sooner than ...ter.

join hands together and act in unison to save th... humanity from suffering, without interfering ... others affairs. The killings of innocent Palestinia... and Kashmiri children must stop. This needs ... end now. Stop it.

THE BURNING PALESTINE!

O' my burning Palestine!
It is unbearable and painful to see,
The falling homes and debris,
On the broken paths and ruined streets.

The sky over you remains mourned,
To see the holy land this way torn.
The walls of sacred mosque are faded
With bombshell fire on them that shaded.

Wait a second! It is a soldier there!
A small-young child hurling a stone here.

Source: www.hilal.gov.pk

Some issues of the Hilal children magazine have used articles and photos to spread misleading narratives, such as the article referred to above (Figure 5.30), which claims that "*food and water are not provided to the children of Indian Kashmir during the lockdown.*" Such writings are not authentic, but are published in their official magazine, indicating the insidious ISPR role. Such psychological hold on the children is also seen with respect to their schools textbooks and curriculum. Communal perception of India permeates in young minds when images of a Hindu baniya (trading class) is deliberately built up in a pejorative manner. To reinforce the propaganda, a Hindu is portrayed as an untrustworthy *Kafir.*[81]

Criticising Pakistan's Tehreek-e-Insaaf (PTI) administration's decision to review the school textbook curriculum by the religious leaders, Pervez Hoodbhoy, an Islamabad-based scientist and author commented that "*Pakistan has been put in reverse gear by inviting mullahs to monitor biology textbooks,*" Initially, Saudi Arabia and the Gulf Cooperation Council countries were regarded to be the most conservative in the world, whilst Pakistan was thought to be one of the most open and relaxed. The circumstances have shifted. Pakistan is not simply in reverse gear; it is determined to reverse as soon as possible. The future generations of the PTI curriculum modifications would be jumbled, confused, and uninformed.[82]

MOBILE GAMES

ISPR has become a role model for '*weaponising social media by employing mobiles as a weapon rather than a gadget*'. Mobile games like The Glorious resolve, a Pak-Indo Army Game, and Yalghaar, a Delta IGI Force Glorious Mission, portray the "*Patriotism of The Armed Forces*".[83] The game's start-up screen begins with an intense ISPR briefing, with live-action clips of soldiers. When you play for the first time, you are asked what rank you'd like to choose; General, Colonel, etc., and then you are given a character to play. Such mobile games not only popularise the Army but playing them, again and again, inculcates a certain kind of viewpoint.

Figure 5.31: Mobile Games Cover Page

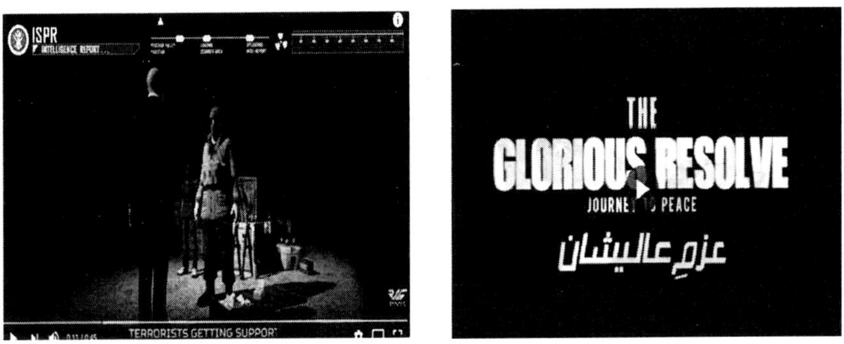

Source: https://play.google.com/store/apps/details?id=com.rockvillegames.thegreatarmy&hl=

YOUTH INTERNSHIPS PROGRAMME AND SCHOLARSHIPS

ISPR has offered internships since 2005, however, they were not publicised at the time. In 2018, for the first time, an internship notice (NO.PR-237/2018) was posted on the ISPR website.[84] Their primary job is social media outreach, which includes fabricating articles to counter anti-Army narratives. Programmes curriculum includes lessons on '*narrative warfare*' '*military advocacy and strategic public relations*' and '*cyber propaganda.*'

The method includes a detailed listing of social media handles of influential Indians, positive narrative building on Pak leaders, soldiers and bureaucrats. For instance, Major General Ghafoor tweeted a picture of the wreck of a trainer aircraft, that didn't participate in the Balakot operation, citing Pakistan had shot down the Indian aircraft during Balakot incursion. He also claimed the Pakistan Air Force had shot down two Indian Air Force jets. These kinds of propaganda were being uploaded by ISPR every day and interns were being trained to do so.[85] The teenagers are instructed by the ISPR that they are fighting a '*narrative war with India and that they are as vital as soldiers*'. Young interns are encouraged to flood social media with phoney photographs of Indian soldiers killed in shooting even before Pakistan violates the ceasefire across the Line of Control.[86]

Various competitions are organised almost every month, including employment opportunities and contracts with well-known enterprises. "*On Twitter and Facebook, the most followed and retweeted tweets get the award.*" The intern wins the award when some influential social media handler across the globe endorses or questions the fake narrative against India, sent out by ISPR. It is estimated that more than 100,000 interns have participated in these competitions. The COAS address at the ISPR headquarters in Rawalpindi for the annual internship programme has made this a prestigious event.[87] More such interactions take place with the university students across the country and visits to military institutes, such as the Pakistan Military Academy (PMA), as a way to encourage the youth, for instance around 250 students visited PMA under the 2017 internship programme.[88]

The educational affiliations of the interns vary from National Defence University/Islamabad to COMSAT Institute information technology/Abbottabad. Refined job titles, such as '*media specialists*', '*psychological operations*', '*media propaganda*' or '*media analyst*', are deliberately used by ISPR to camouflage the real nature of work, including digital espionage (in other words, honey-trapping).[89] Around 98 personnel of the Indian Armed Forces are believed to have been honey-trapped between 2015 and 2018.[90]

Young interns like Gharidah Farooqi,[91] Sharza Shakeel,[92] Ysa Chandna, Hina Shaik and Sarsar Uzaiir[93] have been trained and recruited for similar online espionage activities, besides helping in popularising a pro-military stance. Mahmood Adeel, a Pakistani blogger labelled the interns as the '*future troll Army*' as the underlying motivations of the ISPR in hiring youngsters in such huge numbers, visits and interactions between the COAS and university students is a way to influence the youth.[94]

Figure 5.32: ISPR Annual Internship Program Photo

Youth undergoing annual internship program at Inter-Services Public Relations (ISPR) pose for a photograph with Chief of Army Staff (COAS) General Qamar Javed Bajwa and DG ISPR Major General Asif Ghafoor.—ISPR handout photo

Figure 5.33: ISPR Interns interacting with COAS, Gen Bajwa

Source: http://new-pakistan.com/2019/08/02/isprs-future-troll-army/

Using the country's young educated and tech-savvy youth as a low-cost strategic tool for cyber propaganda and online espionage is their way to train and indoctrinate the country's young brains. This programme adds value to their portfolio enriching their job options within ISPR and beyond. Poor job market and high unemployment levels attract the youth to join the internship programmes as the rewards include lucrative offers and contracts with fauji foundation (run by the retired Army officer as a welfare organisation) counted amongst South East Asia's most diversified business conglomerates.

Youth Scholarships have been patronised by the Pakistan Army especially towards the youth of Jammu and Kashmir for over two decades. It was in 2004 that for the first time, 100 such scholarships were offered to students from 'India-occupied Jammu and Kashmir'.[95] In February 2020, Pakistan announced 1,600 academic scholarships for students of J&K in colleges across Pakistan including Pak Occupied Jammu and Kashmir (POJK), but especially coming six months after the abrogation of Article 370 was red-flagged by the security agencies. A large number of Kashmiri students estimated to be around 700 enrol in universities, the majority of whom pursue an MBBS degree. Additional degrees such as BSC Veterinary, BA Economics, and MBA were added in response to the All-Party Hurriyat Conference's request (APHC). Notably, these students are usually granted a full scholarship and housing, as well as other benefits.[96] Pakistan has been using Kashmiri students' academic aspirations to facilitate their radicalisation and motivate them to engage in anti-India activities—at worst, joining terrorism; given the political and security complications that await them once they return to India, the possibility of generating/accentuating a cycle of grievances/alienation emerges. These scholarships are linked to the All-Party Hurriyat Conference with perhaps, the possibility of inciting terrorism in Kashmir, which is seen as part of Pakistan's larger psychological campaign against India.[97]

WHAT IS VIRTUAL SOCIETAL WARFARE?

ISPR has made the term '*hybrid war*' fashionable in the media, replicating the Gerasimov Doctrine, which is defined as "*the function of mobile, mixed-type units of forces acting in a single intelligence-information area.*" The hawkish ISPR not only engages in '*information warfare manoeuvres*' such as '*denial and deception*', but it has also weaponised its authority to launch a '*full-frontal cyber-enabled information offensive*'. This high-profile institution has huge resources and clout, making it the victor in virtual social warfare on both a domestic and international scale.

In terms of functionality, the ISPR's tweets are mostly intended for the local home audience, but they also impact the international media by tweeting about the external environment. Both ISI and ISPR work together to generate resources for the *'Image Domain of Virtual Societal Warfare,' for instance* 'honey traps' are carried out by ISI, but profiles are generally done by ISPR. As a social media hegemon, it has complete *'perception control,'* portraying the COAS as a figure with unparalleled powers over national security, internal, and foreign affairs.

As a result, the ISPR has been successful in influencing social media sources to follow its policy guidelines. To take this further, the deliberate mockery of Pakistan's armed forces will be considered a criminal and punishable offence, according to a new criminal law (Amendment Bill) bill introduced by the Tehreek-e-Insaaf Amjad Ali Khan, which was passed by the National Assembly Standing Committee on Interior in April 2021. This bill proposes a two-year prison sentence and a fine of Rs 500,000 or both for the heinous crime of mocking the Pakistan Army.

Although the ISPR social media network appears to be directing the country's media policy, its operations must be understood in the context of the military's philosophy and doctrine. Hence, *'propagandist overtures'*, *'mind games,'* *'promoting alternate and counter-narratives with an emotional appeal'*, *'building false narratives especially vis-à-vis India'* will remain. It has weaponised its mandate to wage a full-frontal cyber-enabled information offensive, correctly echoed in the statement—"If there is a Pakistani inter-services directorate as lethal as the Inter-Services Intelligence, it is, undoubtedly, the Inter-Services Public Relations."[98]

NOTES

1. Nye, Joseph S. 2014. "The Information Revolution and Soft Power". *Current History* 113 (759): 19-22, https://dash.harvard.edu/bitstream/handle/1/11738398/Nye-InformationRevolution.pdf
2. http://mobile.twitter.com/atahasnain53/status/1111925220997255269?lang=en
3. Robert Longley, "An introduction to Psychological Warfare", October 22, 2019, https://www.thoughtco.com/psychological-warfare-definition-4151867
4. This means a group of internet forum posters with a paid agenda pose as random citizens and attach themselves to an issue, be it political or commercial.
5. Named after a 2010 documentary film called "CATFISH" in which a person is led astray by the creation of fake persons.

6. The use of "a form of artificial intelligence called deep learning" to make manufactured images, audio, and/or video that appear real.
7. The gaining of unauthorized access to data in a system or computer.
8. Seminar Report, "Pakistan: The Changing Security Dimension", CLAWS, February 7, 2020, https://www.claws.in/event/07-02-pakistan-the-changing-security-dimension
9. Jump up to: a b c d e f g h i j k l Adache, PhD, Col. John (2014). *The Military and Public Relations*. Author House Publications., Bloomington, Indiana. Retrieved on November 18, 2014.
10. Narendra Singh Sarila, The shadow of the Great Game, the Untold Story of India's Partition, p. 325, HarperCollins Publishers, Noida, India 2005.
11. Adache, PnD, Col. John (2014) The military and Public relations, Bloomington, Indiana (US).
12. Pike, John (25 July 2002). "Directorate for Inter-Services Intelligence". Federation of American Scientists. Archived from the original *on* 15 May 2008. Retrieved on December 13, 2008.
13. The rank structure given is not sacrosanct, it could vary with the important role of the formation and the sensitivity of the situation.
14. How many radiostations, journalists work for you? Asma Jahangir asks ISPR, Daily Pakistan Global. Retrieved on December 22, 2017.
15. *Jamat-ud-Dawa (JuD)* is a banned political arm of the terrorist organisation lashkar-e-Taiba (LeT) banned by UN SC Resolution 1267 on December 10, 2008.
16. Jess Kroll, "The difference between a Narrative and a narrative and a story", *Pen and the Pad*, March 23, 2017, http://penandthepad.com/difference-between-narrative-story-10038404
17. Ann-Sophi Hemmingsen and Karim Ingrid Castro, "The trouble with Counter-Narratives", Danish Institute for International Studies, https://pure.diis.dk/ws/files/784884/DIIS_RP2017_1.pdf
18. https://www.sciencedirect.com/topics/social-sciences/agenda-setting-theory
19. Michael Vlahos, "The Long War: A self-defeating Prophecy", *Asia Times*, September 9, 2006.
20. Ayesha Siddiqa, "Pakistan Military won't Take Budget Cuts Easily, even for Covid. So This Man has been Hired", The Print, April 30, 2020 http: The print.in/opinion/Pakistan-military-wont-take covid-budget-cuts-hired-ex-dg-ispr/411641/, accessed on May 20, 2021.
21. Iftikhar H. Malik, *State and Civil Society in Pakistan: Politics of Authority, Ideology, and Ethnicity* (New York: St. Martin's Press, 1997), p. 104.
22. CynthieRitche shot up to fame when she became noticeable on social media publicizing Pakistan's good image and ridiculing dissenting voices and opinion, during tenure of DG ISPR, Maj. Gen Asif Ghafoor.
23. https://www.statista.com/forecasts/1144756/whatsapp-users-in-pakistan
24. https://www.statista.com/forecasts/1138739/instagram-users-in-pakistan
25. https://data.worldbank.org/indicator/SP.POP.TOTL?locations=PK
26. https://worldpopulationreview.com/countries/pakistan-population
27. Ibid., p. 168.

28. Imran Jattala, "A call to kill Ahmadi Muslims in Pakistan … again", *Examiner*, June 17, 2010, http://www. examiner.com/islam-in-los-angeles/a-call-to-kill-ahmadi-muslims-pakistan-again, accessed on January 26, 2011.
29. Seminar Report, "Pakistan: The Changing Security Dimension", CLAWS, February 7, 2020, https://www.claws.in/event/07-02-pakistan-the-changing-security-dimension
30. "World Press Freedom Index 2020", The Reporters Sans Frontiers (RSF).
31. https://www.tribuneindia.com/news/comment/pak-deep-states-war-on-media-80023
32. Sohail Khan, "Truth Finally triumphs:Mir-Shakir-ur-Rahman gets bail after eight months", November 10, 2020, International The News, https://www.thenews.com.pk/print/741637-truth-finally-triumphs-mir-shakil-ur-rahman- Newsgets-bail-after-8-months.
33. https://www.tribuneindia.com/news/comment/pak-deep-states-war-on-media-80023
34. The annual Youm-e-Shuhada (YeS) function (April 30), which started in 2010 but was discontinued after 2015, which focused on martyrs from FATA.
35. This YeD; Defense Day, a national military commemorative ceremony was started to commemorate the 1965 war martyrs observed on September 6.
36. Maria Rashid, dying to serve, *militarism, affect, and the politics of sacrifice in the Pakistan army,* Stanford University Press, 2020, p. 30,
37. Rana Banerji, "How narratives of sacrifice is of supreme import for the Pakistan Army", June 7, 2020, *Indian Express*, https://indianexpress.com/article/books-and-literature/rashid-ali-malik-new-book-pakistan-army-6445898/, accessed on June 7, 2020.
38. Article 19 of the Constitution of Pakistan, 1973, every citizen shall have the right to freedom of speech, freedom of expression and freedom of the Press, subject to any 'reasonable restriction', imposed by law in the interest of the glory of Islam or the integrity, security or defence of Pakistan or any part thereof, friendly relations with foreign states, public order, or in relation to contempt of court or incitement to offence.
39. ISPRs role, *Dawn*, February 4, 2020, https://www,dawn.com/news/1532397, accessed on May 19, 2021.
40. https://theprint.in/opinion/i-asim-bajwa-quit-but-head-cheese-pizza-economic-corridor/522630/.
41. Official Twitter page of Government of Pakistan (@pid_gov). Followers as on October 31, 2020.
42. Official Twitter page of DG ISPR (@OfficialDGISPR). Followers as on October 31, 2020.
43. (https://ciso.economictimes.indiatimes.com/news/pakistan-ups-cyber-warfare-against-india-on-twitter/71586601
44. https://www.dnaindia.com/india/report-pakistani-twitter-account-posing-as-omani-princess-shares-anti-india-material-old-tweets-show-ispr-s-role-2822148)
45. Khurram Husain, 2016. "2016: The Year Of The CPEC". DAWN.COM. https://www.dawn.com/news/1305582.
46. Fifth generation warfare refers to the use of misinformation and other non-kinetic means such as fake news and propaganda, which is leveraged well.

47. Inam Sehrise, 2012. *Judges and Generals of Pakistan,* Volume 1. Grosvenor House Publishing, Grosvenor.
48. Inter-Services Public Relations 2017. "ISPR Press Release 216/217". https://www.ispr.gov.pk.press-release-details.php?id=3937.
49. Azhar Ahmed, 2017, "What Are the Dawn Leaks'? A look Into Pakistan's Headline-Making News Scandal-ARYNEWS". ARYNEWS, http://arynews.tv/en/what-are-the-dawn-leaks-a-look-into-pakistan-infamous-news-scandal/.
50. Cyril Almedia, 2016, "Exclusive: Act Against Militants or Face International Isolation, Civilians Tell Military", DAWN.COM. http://www.dawn.com/news/1288350/exclusive-act-against-militants-or-face-international-isolation-civilians-tell-military.
51. "Corps Commanders View Leak from High-Level Meetings as Breach of National Security: ISPR". 2016. DAWN.COM. http://www.dawn.com/news/1289976.
52. Sardar Sikander, 2017. "Army Rejects PM Office Statement On Dawn Leaks Report", *The Express Tribune.* https://tribune.com.pk/story/1396876/pakistan-armyrejects-govt-notification-dawn-leaks/.
53. "How The Islamabad Protests Happened". 2017. DAWN.COM. https://www.dawn.com/news/1372800.
54. Samaa Digital, 2017. "Faizabad Dharna: Govt And Protesters Signed An Agreement". Samaa TV. https://www.samaa.tv/news/2017/11/faizabad-dharna-govt-protesters-reached-agreement/.
55. "Text of Agreement Signed with Protesters". 2017. Thenews.com.Pk. https://www.thenews.com.pk/latest/249475-religious-parties-reach-agreement-with-govt-to-end-faizabad-sit-in.
56. Kamran Haider, 2018. "Pak Journalist Whose Reports Angered Army To Be Arrested For Treason". NDTV.Com. https://www.ndtv.com/world-news/cyril-almeida-dawn-journalist-ofpakistan-to-be-arrested-on-charges-of-leaking-sensitive-information-1921731.
57. www.arabnews.pk, node, Pakistan.
58. ISPR blasts detailed verdict in Musharraf treason case, deems ...www.dawn.com, news.
59. https://twitter.com/benimmo/status/1112657758724259841.
60. *Dawn*, "No right to censor", Editorial, October 20, 2020. https://www.dawn.com/news/1586034.
61. Nathaniel Gleicher, Head of Cybersecurity Policy, Facebook, Removing Coordinated Inauthentic Behavior and Spam From India and Pakistan, https://about.fb.com/news/2019/04/cib-and-spam-from-india-pakistan/, accessed on April 4, 2020.
62. https://theprint.in/defence/pakistan-army-pages-pulled-down-by-facebook-called-indian-security-forces-monkey/215996/?amp
63. BEN NIMMO and Kanishk Karan, "Pakistan-based Facebook pages posed as Kashmiri activists to push anti-India rhetoric", April 3, 2019, https://theprint.in/author/ben-nimmo./, accessed on April 3, 2021.
64. Ibid., https://theprint.in/defence/pakistan-army-pages-pulled-down-by-facebook-called-indian-security-forces-monkey/215996/?amp

65. DW.COM, "Pakistan seeks to 'control digital media' amid anti-government protests", https://www.dw.com/en/pakistan-seeks-to-control-digital-media-amid-anti-government-protests/a-55422291
66. https://www.dawn.com/news/1271957) Nasir Iqbal, "How may FM stations under ISPR, Asma asks SC", *Dawn*, Pakistan, July 20, 2016.
67. https://www.tribuneindia.com/news/archive/j-k/pakistan's-psychological-war-on-through-15-fm-stations-686928, Dinesh Manhotra, "Pakistan Psychological war on through 15 FM stations", *The Tribune*, November 21, 2018.
68. Ibid.
69. Op Tupac is alleged code name of the ongoing military, and intelligence activities supporting anti-Indian activities in Kashmir, Punjab and North East. It is active since 1980's and run by the ISI. It was started by Gen Zia-Ul-Haq
70. Ibid.
71. https://www.indiatoday.in/india/story/centre-bans-content-from-muslim-nations-on-television-in-j-k-1620329-2019-11-18.
72. https://www.opindia.com/2019/08/govt-orders-complete-blackout-of-non-permitted-channels-including-zakir-naiks-peace-tv-and-pakistani-channels-in-kashmir-valley/.
73. The list of dramas is as follows: *Mujahid* (1994); *Ujalay se Pahlay* (1996); *Alpha, Bravo, Charlie* (1997); *Wilco* (2008); *Jaan Hatheli Par* (2012); *Faseel-e-Jaan se Aagaiy* (2014).
74. Divya Malhotra, "Inter-Services Public relations (ISPR), Assessment of the Pakistan Military's Discreet Propaganda Factory Post-1990, MP", Institute for defence Studies and Analysis, *Journal of Defence Studies*, Vol. No. 4, October-December, p. 38
75. https://theprint.in/opinion/letter-from-pakistan/a-pakistani-official-politician-army-man-reporter-walk-into-a-tv-show-only-one-is-a-hero/393347/.
76. Article 370- Indian constitution gave special status to Jammu and Kashmir, a region located in the northern part of Indian subcontinent which was administered by India as a state from 1954 to 31 October 2019, conferring it with the power to have a separate constitution, a state flag and autonomy over the internal matters.
77. http://www.indiandefencereview.com/spotlights/disinformation-propaganda-pakistans-newest-weapon-on-kashmir/
78. Ibid.
79. https://www.hilal.gov.pk/hilal-english
80. Green Book 2020, National Defence University, Kakul (Abbottabad), 6 February 2020, p. 73, https://ndu.edu.pk/downloads/green book-2020-final-06-feb-2020.pdf, accessed on December 2020.
81. Pakistan Project report, "Second edition, Wither Pakistan? Growing Instability and implications for India", IDSA, New Delhi 2010.
82. Pervez Hoodbhoy, "Mullahs are supervising biology books. Imran Khan govt has put Pakistan in reverse gear", June 20, 2021, https://theprint.in/opinion/mullahs-are-supervising-biology-books-imran-khan-govt-has-put-pakistan-in-reverse-gear/681165/, accessed on June 20, 2021.

83. https://play.google.com/store/apps/details?id=com.rockvillegames.thegreatarmy&hl=en&gl=US
84. ISPR, "General Qamar Javed Bajwa, Chief of Army Staff (COAS), visited Inter Services Public Relations Directorate (ISPR) Today", Press Release No. PR-237/2018-ISPR, August 6, 2018, n. 71.
85. Ibid.
86. "Pakistan ISPR recruits Youth for cyber Propoganda War on India", *The Economic Times*, January 3, 2020, https://www.newindianexpress.com/nation/2020/jan/03/pakistan%E2%80%8Bs-ispr-recruits-youth-for-cyber-propaganda-war-on-india-2084489.html, accessed on April 21, 2021.
87. ISPR, "General Qamar Javed Bajwa, Chief of Army Staff (COAS), interacted with Youth undergoing Annual Internship Program at ISPR", http://www.ispr.gov.pk/press-release-detail-php?id+4845, accessed on May 9, 2021.
88. Geo News, 9 August 2017, http://. geo.tv/amp/153014-250-students-visits-pma-under-internship-program-ispr
89. Divya Malhotra, "Inter-Services Public Relations (ISPR): Assessment of the Pakistan Military's Discreet Propaganda Factory Post-1990", *Journal of Defence Studies*, Volume 14, Number 4, October-December 2020.
90. Syed Ata Hasnain, "Civil Society in Jammu and Kashmir: Democracy verses Terrorism', London: International Institute for Strategic Studies, March 28, 2019, https://www.iiss.org/event/2019/03/democracy-versus-terrorism accessed on May 9, 2021.
91. She became in TV anchor in ISPR's affiliated TV channel like ARY News or BOL News.
92. She mentioned in her job description 'Psychological operation'.
93. Sardar Uzaiir, "Great Experience and some Òld memories of my Life", Steemit, 2018, https://steemit.com/pictures/@sardaruzaiir/great-experience-andsome-old-memories-of-my-life, accessed on December 8, 2020.
94. "250 students visited PMA under Internship Programme", Geo News, August 9, 2017, http://www.geo.tv/amp/153014-250-students-visit-pma-under-internship-program-ispr, accessed on May 9, 2021.
95. "100 scholarships for IHK students okayed", *The Dawn*, June 2, 2005, http://www.dawn.com/news/141772/100-scholrships-for-ihk-students-okayed, accessed on May 9, 2021.
96. Basharat Masood (2020), "Explained: How Pakistan offers professional courses to Kashmiri students", *Indian Express*, July 22, 2020,https://indianexpress.com/article/explained/syed-ali-shah-gilani-pakistan-medical-education-kahmiri-students-hurriyat-6491266, accessed on May 9, 2021.
97. Tejaswi Shukla, Issue Brief, Nov 2020, No. 256 CLAWS.inhttps://www.claws.in/publication/pakistans-academic-scholarships-to-jks-youth-a-charade/Pakistans
98. Pukhraj Singh, "Gerasimov of South Asia, Pakistan's ISPR's Asif Gafoor", *Deccan Herald*, April 2, 2019, https://www.deccanherald.com/opinion/main-article/gerasimov-of-south-asia-726631.html.

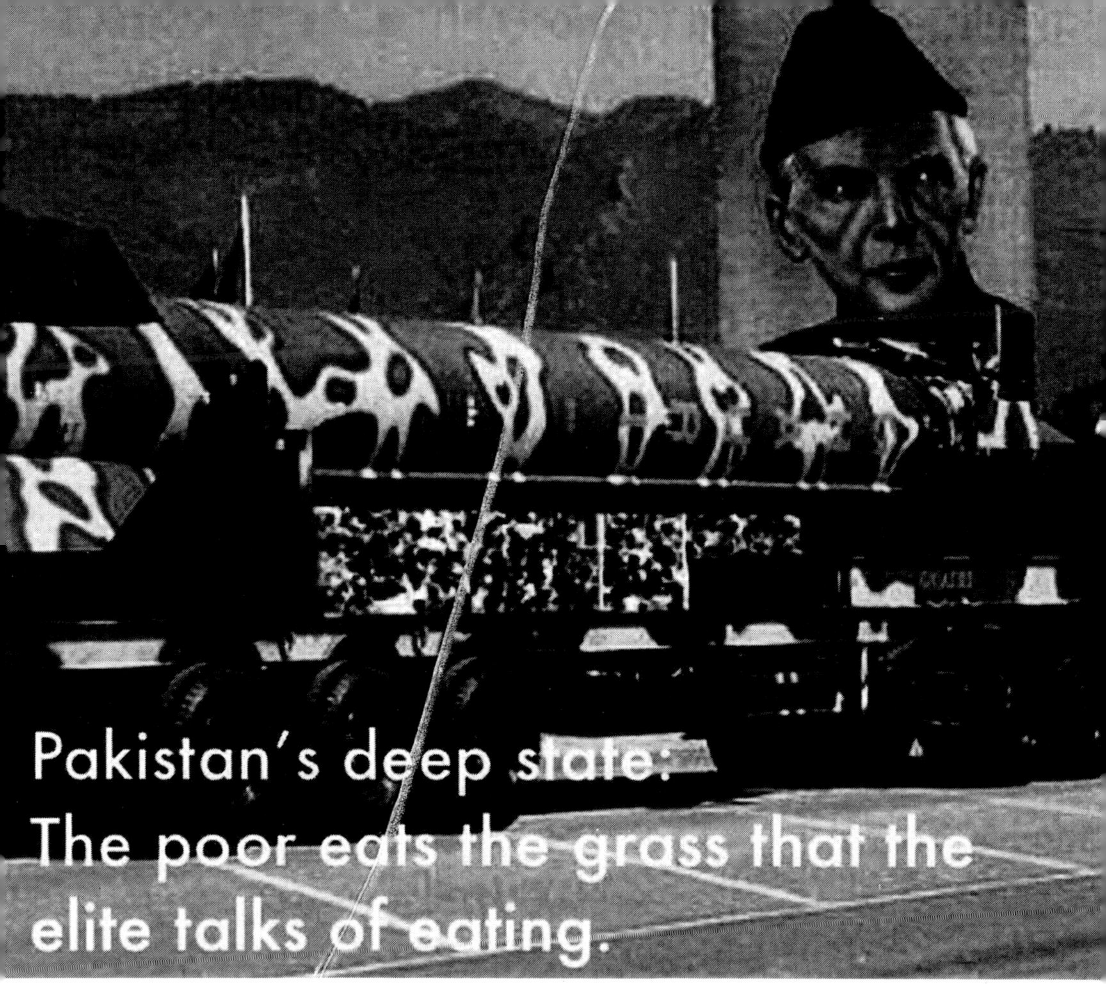

Source: https://www.globalvillagespace.com/pakistans-missile-and-nuclear-technology-the-flawless-deterrence-to-indias-anti-satellite-missile-test/

6. Implications for India

> *"The deep state continuum has far-reaching repercussions for India on geo-strategic, geo-political, geo-economic and socio-cultural fronts."*

Not only Pakistan, but South Asia as a whole is affected from the deep state continuum, which hampers the peace, stability and development of the region. Despite physical proximity, common history, socio-cultural linkages of a quarter of the world's population, and roughly 3.5 per cent of the planet's land surface area with the highest population density, South Asia remains one of the least connected regions. Intra-regional trade accounts for less than 5 per cent of overall international trade, the lowest in the world, while investment accounts for less than 1 per cent of total global investment in the region, restricting the regions economic growth. With a third of the world's poor, the region faces numerous economic and environmental concerns which have been aggravated with the COVID-19 Pandemic.

India and the rest of South Asia will surely benefit from a stable, democratic Pakistan. A significant security threat is posed by the inherent flaws in its overall securitisation policies; India's concerns as a threat; the government's ambivalence toward the phenomenon of Islamic radicalism; around 30,000 to 40,000 terrorists or militants operational; proliferation of narco-terrorism; small arms and nuclear weapons. As a result, understanding the ramifications for India is essential.

GEO-STRATEGIC

With intrusions into the Indian subcontinent, Pakistan benefits from its geo-strategic location lying in the underbelly of Central Asian Republics, adjacent to West Asia. It has been able to pull out a "rescue act" when it has been besieged. Beginning in the 1950s, it got military aid from the United States, and after the 1965 US embargo, it started receiving military aid from China. These countries viewed Pakistan as a '*frontline state*,' a '*strategic asset*,' and were unwilling to intervene in the country's expansion of 'terrorist organisations.'

Proxy wars, insurgencies, and terrorism have been inextricably linked to Pakistan's "*Fabian Strategy*" since 1947, with disastrous consequences for India. It has been able to constrain India by presenting the impression that the proxy war is out of its control and that it is a victim of such terror attacks. So far, it has been able to avoid large-scale conflict by gradually increasing the intensity from low to high and then lowering it to avoid spiralling out of control. This has resulted in a lengthy struggle in which moral and ethical rules that ordinarily govern conflict have been thrown out the window and dovetailed no less than an act of war.[1]

Pakistan-based terror infrastructure poses a threat not just to India and South Asia, but also to the US, its allies and quite possibly even China in the future. This reality is far bigger than any strategic utility Pakistan might offer to these countries in the shortrun.[2] In the name of promoting geo-strategic interests, it has been providing '*safe haven spaces for the radical terror outfits*', authenticating Brahma Chellaney's statement, "*water is flowing from India to Pakistan and terrorism is flowing from Pakistan to India.*"[3] For the deep state, a policy mix of '*terror and talks*' is the strategy for India. The US State Department's Country Report on Terrorism, September 21, 2021, states—Pakistan has "continued to serve as a safe haven for certain regionally focused terrorist groups," and has "allowed groups targeting Afghanistan ... as well as groups targeting India ... to operate from its territory". The Report has identified Pakistan as a base of operations and/or target for numerous armed, non-state militant groups, some of which have existed since the 1980s.[4] Out of 67 active terrorist groups in the world, Pakistan is home to at least 12 groups, including five of them being India-centric, like Lashkar-e-Taiba (LeT) and Jaish-e-Mohammad (JeM).

Since 1947, Jammu and Kashmir has been used by Pak for launching and planning terror across India in the name of giving support to the local populace. There exists a pool of modules that can be instructed to commit acts of terror just about anywhere in India. For example, during the 2001 attack on the Indian parliament, Afzal Guru, an overground worker located in J&K, provided logistical support. Linkages amongst Lashkar-e-Taiba (LeT), Students Islamic Movement of India (SIMI) and Indian Mujahideen (IM) transit through Kashmir. Pak continues to sponsor terrorist groups in the Indian state of Jammu and Kashmir, funding, training and arming them in their war of attrition against India. "There are at least 42 terrorist training camps in Pakistani Occupied Kashmir (POK) alone."[5] India retorted strongly at United Nations General Assembly recently, when Pakistan Prime Minister Imran Khan raked up Kashmir in his speech and offered a skewed narrative to damage India's benign image. India countered by exposing the hard reality, Pakistan acts like 'firefighter' but is actually the 'arsonist'.[6] Lashkar Chief Hafiz Sayeed, after his release from ten months house arrest reiterated, "*full-scale armed jihad will begin soon in Kashmir after American forces withdraw from Afghanistan.*"[7]

ISI and the Army has expanded to make a '*pan India-Jihad structure*' wherein it can reach anywhere, be it Mumbai, Guwahati, Delhi, Hyderabad, Jaipur, Bangalore, with support to the insurgent groups, like the United

Liberation Front of Assam (ULFA), Northeast insurgents groups and separatist organisations. Pak support to these groups is with the aim of making insurgency self-sustaining, as Kautilya had articulated, '*a war abetted by an external power and executed by local people is the most dangerous war to combat*'. This is the biggest challenge with Left Wing Extremism (LWE). The ISI and the non-state actors have managed to create an environment of insecurity in India. National festivals like Republic day parades, Independence Day celebrations and Gandhi Jayanti all remain under the shadow of terror threat. An additional layer of security is added each year which inadvertently means an encroachment on public freedom and their shrinking spaces.

Pakistan will continue to raise the nuclear bogey and has even deployed TNWs at operational levels intended to deter India as a recuse to bridge the conventional asymmetry. According to public sources, Pakistan already has dozens, if not more than 150 nuclear warheads.[8] Such weapons would put India in grave danger, pushing regional tensions to unprecedented heights, especially given China's crucial support in Islamabad's nuclear and ballistic-missile programmes. Furthermore, the possibility that it may hand over individual weapons to terrorist groups for detonation anywhere in the world would make a new 9/11 incomparably more deadly.[9]

There are severe implication for India as the deep state has supported, funded and trained anti-India insurgent and terrorist groups, since the 1970s. Today in Kashmir the local flavour of terrorists activities is being encouraged by protecting and raising the Resistance Force (TRF), an offshoot of Pak-based terror outfit LeT, resorted to selective killings of non-Kashmiris and the minorities in the Kashmir valley in sheer frustration, after the abrogation of Article 370. The prominence and rise of the political clout of terrorism is credited to the deep state's '*unique patronage*' and '*support for their political ascension and development*' by catering to their educational, social, administrative, and economic demands. Aiding this is American funding of more than $33 billion since 2002, including $14 billion to combat terrorism and insurgents in the region.[10] The location of multiple militant camps inside Pakistan has been exposed by FBI satellite imagery, with Jihadists confessing to being schooled to fight and foment insurgency in India, as acknowledged by Pakistani government officials. In a 2012 interview with the BBC, Pakistani President Asif Ali Zardari confessed that previous governments "*deliberately developed and nurtured militants as a policy to achieve some short-*

term tactical objectives".[11] In another interview aired by private TV channel in 2018, Gen Musharraf acknowledged that terrorists were trained in Pakistan. "*We trained Taliban and sent them to fight against Russia. Taliban; Haqqani, Osama bin Laden and Zawahiri were our heroes then.*"[12] During his official visit to the United States in July 2019, Prime Minister Imran Khan admitted the presence of 30,000-40,000 armed terrorists in his country. "*All key Taliban leaders were born and raised in Pakistan*," Pakistani Interior Minister Sheikh Rashid (2021) claimed in an interview on the Hum News show. We trained them as part of our 'service,' and many more may be studying.[13]

A high level of Pak's interconnectedness and dependency remains with the Taliban and terrorist organisations. For example, terrorist organisations such as Jaish-e-Mohammad (JeM) have their headquarter in Bahawalpur, which is within a short distance from the Pakistan Army's 31 corps headquarters. Simply put, Pakistan cannot afford to alienate a well-armed and well-trained Punjab-based militant organisation.[14]

Pakistan's nexus with fundamentalist organisations is well established, like Jamaat-e-Islami and its offshoots; the Tablighi Jamaat and Markaz Dawa-al Irshad; volunteers from non-state actors like Sipah-Sahaba, Lashkar-e-Jhangvi, and Hafiz Syed's Jaish-e-Mohammad are trained in their military camps. Dr Yunis Khushi, noted that the ISIS terrorist group is paying something around Rs 50,000 to 60,000 per month to every warrior, which is a hefty amount for an unemployed youth.[15]

Figure 6.1: ISIS Posters

(a): ISIS will chalking and posters displayed in Karachi

(b): ISIS Recruits in Baluchistan Province of Pakistan on the right, the picture shows atomic blast by Pakistan in Chaghi, Baluchistan on May 28, 1998

Source: https://www.hilarispublisher.com/open-access/isis-in-pakistan-a-critical-analysis-of-factors-and-implications-of-isisrecruitments-and-concept-of-jihadbilnikah-2151-6200-1000276.pdf

ISI's significant covert support to the Taliban, employing it as a proxy force is not hidden. With the completion of US and NATO troops withdrawal and Taliban's return, Pak has successfully achieved its strategic objectives in Afghanistan. A case in point is the intelligence agencies and the Army supporting the ISIS terrorist networks in various districts in Pakistan as well as inside Afghanistan, Central Asia, and Russia.

Today the new weapons for carrying our cross-border terror skirmishes are drones. For instance, ahead of Indian Independence Day, on August 8, 2021, the Punjab Police recovered a tiffin box dropped by a drone from Pak with an improvised explosive device (IED) from a village in Amritsar, near the border.[16] IB (International Border) and the LoC continue to face instability with such acts. Without fear of legal retaliation or reprimand, such an organisation would continue to thrive and launch brazen attacks against India. When the Pak-government and the institutions feel that these actors are out of control and are about to take action against them, they mobilise people in the name of religion in order to get mass support and get rid of governmental operations.[17] Such terrorist organisations play a crucial role in mobilising the locals to fight against India and publicising the cause of Kashmir.

The upsurge of terrorism undermines economic growth and stability. The *economics of terrorism* speaks that terrorist attacks may cause short-term disturbance to the economic system; the people may decide to postpone their economic activity due to such events. This kind of behaviour impacts the future of public consumption and investment.[18] The 26/11 Mumbai attack disrupted human life in the city and posed uncertainty in financial markets, for a long time. The cost of sustained tension with Pak is an external check on India's rise, as also proved by the respondents to the questionnaire conducted by the author. Around 94 per cent of the respondents felt that the deep state will continue to regard India as an existential threat and 60 per cent felt it will affect India's rise to a super power status.[19]

Pak is the testing ground for Islamic radicalism and a hotspot of terrorism, which is spreading to other South Asian countries, including Afghanistan, Bangladesh, Nepal and Myanmar as the '*military extensions of the Pakistan Army*'. Following September 9/11, when international soldiers in Afghanistan were viewed as an illegitimate occupying force, the demand for jihad resurfaced, and Pakistan became the epicentre of terror.[20]

Close links with the ISIS can be seen in the recruitments drive for ISIS which have been going on in Pakistan since 2012, but the government has been denying its presence. Many people from Lahore, Islamabad, Karachi and Sialkot have been arrested for their association with these networks. Men have been recruited as jihadis and women as jihadi wives to provide for the sexual needs of fighters fighting in Syria and Iraq.[21] Many women are brain washed to accepting the concept of Jihad-Bil-Nikah.[22] The most secret and law-enforcement agencies have behaved like silent bystander to the activities of ISIS which has become an unofficial channel of providing soldiers to provide the Saudi demands for fighters to fight on behalf of Saudi armies in Yemen and Syria. In 2017, the Wahhabi deadly terrorist organisation, Islamic State of Iraq and al-Sham (ISIS, also known as IS and ISIL) had exposed its presence in Pakistan after the killing 45 citizens.[23]

The Pakistan Army's jihadist commitment appears to be more than a tactical tool; it appears to be a paradigm through which the institution understands and attempts to alter the world. In the same line of thinking, Admiral Mike Mullen, outgoing Chairman of the United States' Joint Chiefs of Staff, submitted a written testimony asserting that "*extremist organisations serving as proxies of the government of Pakistan are attacking Afghan troops and civilians as well as U.S. soldiers.*" He alleged that the Haqqani network, the most powerful of the Taliban's constituent forces, was in fact strategic arm of Pakistan's Inter-Services Intelligence agency (ISI).[24] Taliban victory enabled by ISI has also empowered the Islamists inside Pak and its claim of defending Islam in Kashmir.

The new modus operandi of terrorism after the abrogation of Article 370, is to indoctrinate and train local Kashmiri youth in militancy by inviting them through proper visa channels, rather than having them take the risk of crossing the border illegally. Such facts were laid bare when a newspaper article quoted an Indian Army spokesperson statement, "at least 40 youths travelled on visas to Pakistan for studying purposes but were sent back as terrorists, 27 came back with weapons and have been killed in encounters. Rest is still across the border, and a few of them are in touch with their families."[25] On September 18, 2021, an attempt of infiltration by seven Pakistani terrorists, including a 19-year-old Lashkar-e-Taiba's incendiary, at LOC[26] proved yet again that Pakistan has been '*fostering terrorism*' at the expense of the world peace.

Figure 6.2: Photo of the ISIS Letter

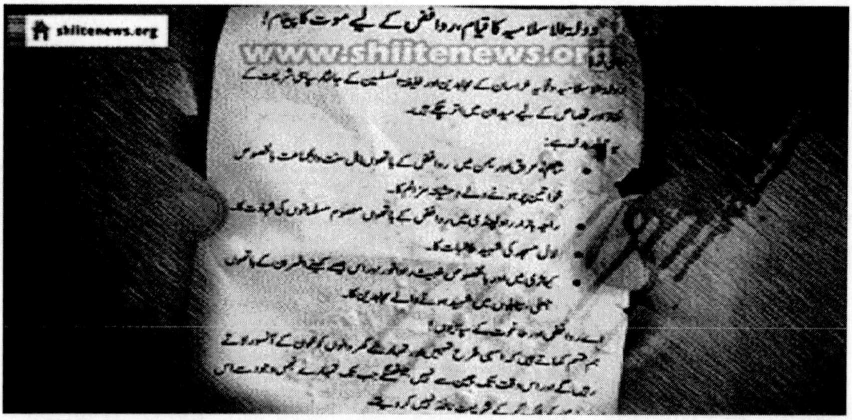

Letter dropped by ISIS at the scene of bus attack at Safoora Goth, Karachi. The pamphlet say: ISIS has come into the field to implement Sharia and to take revenge of the Sunnis murdered in Syria, Iraq and Yemen, murder of innocent Sunnies in Raja Bazar Rawalpindi, murdered in fake police encounters by bartered police officials like off the elements which are responsible for all the above acts. We will make your family members cry out blood tears from their eyes. (Photo taken from Shia News website)

Source: Yunnis Khusi, "ISIS in Pakistan", *Social Science Journal*, June 26, 2017.

GEO-ECONOMICS

Geo-political considerations, rather than economics, drive policymaking in Pakistan. Despite sharing a long border of 3,323 km, a natural land and sea route for trade, the trade is abysmally low. "*Economic considerations have always been deemed secondary in Pakistan's policy priorities, important only to the extent of finding resources for greater goals such as securing Kashmir, facing the 'Indian threat' or reviving Islam's lost glory.*"[27] This status quo in Pakistan benefits both civilian and military elite, who have cartelised important industries such as automobiles, fertilisers, and sugar. Their gains come from anti-competitive import barriers and large, distorting subsidies. The deep state apparatus is in charge of a significant chunk of the economy and does not want to relinquish its control.

The direct bilateral trade between India and Pakistan is around $2.6 billion, the potential could exceed $37 billion which can be mutually beneficial given the geographical interdependency of industry and raw materials on both sides. It is a known fact that while gypsum, cement and rock salt provides an edge to Pakistan. In the sugar, cotton yarn and pharmaceuticals, India has a definite edge and can meet Islamabad's requirements easily and competitively. While SAARC has remained stunted due to the region defeating politics, SAFTA arrangements have carried on in a limited way.[28] The intra-regional trade has performed abysmally low, as bilateral movements of goods is throttled between India and Pakistan. Over the period, the region has emerged as one of the fastest-growing in the world with an average rate of GDP increase estimated at above 7 per cent, which can help reduce poverty and unemployment, but the incessant rivalry in India-Pak relations has kept the regions development at bay.

Few economists believe that Islamabad's decision to suspend trade with New Delhi would hit Pakistan more in comparison to India, due to latter's low dependence on exports to its neighbour. Bilateral trade relations, took a new low when Prime Minister Imran Khan decided to suspend trade relations in response to India's move to end special status for Jammu and Kashmir. India revoked Pakistan's most-favoured-nation (MFN) status following the Pulwama terrorist attack that killed about 40 Central Reserve Police Force (CRPF) personnel in February 2019 and imposed up to 200 per cent duty on import of Pakistani goods.[29] These Trade ban measures since 2019 have severe implications for the economies of both countries with negative repercussions as follows:

- There are significant costs of non-cooperation adding to the debt servicing costs of both countries. For Pakistan, the costs of non-cooperation are estimated to be $2.67 billion per annum (about 6.7 per cent of its total imports) which it can save if it sources only 25 per cent of its current import's basket from India. Savings from such imports can reduce Pakistan's cost of debt servicing by almost 50 per cent. For India, the cost of non-cooperation is estimated to be a significant $24.55 billion, which could save India 26.5 per cent of its debt servicing cost.[30]
- The impact on Pakistan's domestic industry will be greater than on India's. Although raw materials, and pharmaceutical sectors account for about 82 per cent of India's exports to Pakistan, imports from Pakistan are substantially lower but nevertheless important for Indian industry.
- Both countries suffer as a result of the trade war, as they are forced to pay higher costs for products that could be imported at a lower cost. For

example, onion costs are higher in India, as compare to Pakistan; similarly, tomato prices in Pakistan are skyrocketing than in India. Negative repercussions are felt on employment, as any form of barrier to trade can reduce the average level of wages in an economy.

- The suspension of cross-LoC trade has had an impact on people's livelihoods in Kashmir, as well as on people-to-people engagement, which is critical for building trust.
- The informal economy on the other hand is booming. The amount of informal commerce between India and Pakistan is estimated to be close to $4.71 billion, which is about twice the value of formal trade between the two nations prior to the trade ban.[31]
- Anti-India sentiment runs deep in Pakistan's deep state policymakers, but it does not help its struggling economy. As Khurram Husain, a Pakistani business journalist states, anti-India sentiment is rooted in geo-politics, nothing else. "*It grows and diminishes with the requirements of Pakistan's foreign policy. Goods from India are always cheaper than from anywhere else.*"[32]

Regional cooperation through SAARC has not been able to leverage the drivers for economic growth in member countries. It is evident from the fact that countries here are better integrated with those outside compared to own neighbours. The economic integration of South Asia could deliver large benefits to its poor population with potential to include high-market integration, better transport, improved energy, wider information and communication technology and people-to-people connectivity, more investment in infrastructure development, and this may help in reducing common vulnerabilities and risks. Attempts at regional economic integration with adaption of trade liberalisation on preferential basis by strengthening SAARC economic cooperation through South Asian Free Trade Area (SAFTA) or South Asian Preferential Trading Agreement (SAPTA signed on April 11, 1993), have been held hostage by Pakistan's insistence that the Kashmir dispute is resolved before any movement on the trade front. SAFTA negotiations have continued, but at a slower pace.[33]

Pakistan's fragile economic situation has slid deeper into crisis since Imran Khan took over in 2018, GDP growth fell from 5.6 per cent to -0.4 per cent. The country is in debt to the tune of nearly $114 billion (€96.85 billion)—more than 85 per cent of its gross domestic product.[34] Aggravated further by the third wave of Coronavirus pandemic. Pakistan cannot afford hostility with India, experts say. "*Even limited trade with India will certainly help Pakistan's sluggish economy.*"[35] But economic factors, have always been regarded as secondary to its strategic interests. The fact of the matter remains that deep state controls a significant portion of the economy, and would not lose control of the key industries.

Lessons should be drawn from US-China economic relations. Despite having two opposing political systems and hostile diplomatic relations, their commercial relationship remains intact. In 2020 China was the largest US goods trading partner (total trade at $659.5 billion), the third largest US export market (at $120.3 billion) and the largest source of US imports (at $539.2 billion). China is the second largest foreign holder of US treasury securities (at $1.05 trillion as of October 2020).[36] Informal economic diplomacy between India and Pak should be ongoing and hopefully yield good results. Restarting the trade will also help in fighting poverty in the region.[37] Geo-economics should not be merely a declaration of intent, but should be seriously examined.

GEO-POLITICAL

The diplomatic relations have been sporadic rather than consistent. Whenever the political establishment in both the countries attempts to talk about peace or progress, a terrorist assault or assassination destabilises the process, exposing the deep state's power and influence over and above its own elected government. The renewal of 2003 India-Pak cease-fire agreement in 2021 is an example of military diplomacy gaining precedence, but such instances are very few.

The power and influence that Pak sponsored non-state actors wield with the deep state collaboration stymies any peace moves. Prime Minister Atal Bihari Vajpayee travelled to Lahore on a friendship bus on February 19, 1999 and two days later signed the Lahore Declaration—a bilateral agreement reaffirming faith in the Simla Agreement in letter and spirit and implementing confidence-building measures to improve the security environment.

This peace move was disrupted due to the Pak Army incursions into the Indian territory of Kargil led by Gen Musharraf, on May 3, 1999 and the battle lasted until July 26, with Indian victory and territorial status quo. The same year Indian Airline IC 814 was hijacked by Taliban with the tacit support of the ISI.

The next Indian Prime Minister Manmohan Singh too, sought peace with his Pakistani counterpart President Pervez Musharraf under the Agra Summit 2021, expecting the Pakistani military to approve it. But all he got was a series of terror attacks by Pakistan-based Indian Mujahideen (IM) and Pakistani Taliban, and November 2008 Mumbai terror attack, which occurred just days after Pakistani President Asif Ali Zardari made the remarkable statement that Pakistan, like India, was willing to adopt a "no first use" policy for its nuclear weapons. In December 2015, Indian Prime Minister Modi made a surprise visit to Lahore on his way back from Kabul to wish his then-counterpart on his daughter's wedding. A week later, the Jaish-e-Mohammad (JeM) attacked the Pathankot airfield in Punjab. Fortunately, Indian soldiers were able to avert a high-impact attack that would have led to the destruction of Indian Air Force assets and obliterated the city.[38] Such terror incidents have derailed peace initiatives and instead led to heightened tensions between the two countries.

A few deductions can be drawn from such occurrences. *First*, the deep state opposes reconciliation between the two countries, and incites terror incidents as they understand that, in the aftermath of a terrorist incident, the Indian government will be unable to conduct bilateral negotiations due to domestic pressure, resulting in persistent hostility. *Second*, it is in the corporate interest of the praetorian military to see India as threatening 'other', to be able to access state resources and remain atop the power pyramid.[39] *Third*, Kashmir is still the unfinished business of partition in their eyes. Stephen Schwartz argues that Afghanistan is not the only state where Pak supports terrorist groups, it even supports terrorists in Kashmir. Pakistan's leaders have repeatedly courted religious nationalism to advance their personal agendas. "*The historic alliance between Islamists and Pakistan's military has the potential to frustrate anti-terrorist operations, radicalise key segments of the Islamic world, and bring India and Pakistan to the brink of war yet again*," Haqqani warns.[40] General Musharraf too admitted that his Army trained militant groups to fight India in Kashmir. Speculations that the fauji foundation has contributed more than 5,000 retired

Army soldiers and officers in the Army of the ISIS terrorist groups. Major Agha Amin (Retd.), a Lahore-based Defense analyst, revealed that Pakistani fighters went to Syria and Iraq with the support of the Army and government.[41] *Fourth*, domestic polity thrives on anti-India narrative.

Fifth, a major setback has been for regional organisations like SAARC, founded in 1985 with the goal of strengthening regional cooperation, has suffered the weight of the India-Pakistan rivalry, with the deep state perhaps bearing primary responsibility. The goal of strengthening regional cooperation is stalled due to the region's defeatist politics. *Sixth*, a major problem lies in the fact that Islamabad has declined to take any meaningful action against terrorist groups operating against India from its soil, and it has not abandoned its cross-border terrorism assistance and sponsorship plan. India has insisted that "*Talks and Terror*" cannot continue, and this is where the line is drawn. It's unclear how the two will reconcile their diplomatic and security concerns. In an interview with a German publication as the US withdrawal is underway, Afghanistan's president, Hamid Karzai, stated, Pakistan wants Afghanistan to break off relations with India, and wants to exert strategic influence in Afghanistan through the Taliban.[42] India's march to superpower status and even its participation in the United Nations as a permanent member is in disarray as also suggested by the results of the questionaire.[43]

The South Asia's regional security picture predicts conflict relations rather than connectedness. Moreover, despite the restoration of a cease-fire agreement along the Line of Control, there are no signs that either side will make the types of concessions on the Kashmir conflict that would be required for a lasting peace.[44]

SOCIAL-CULTURAL

The impact of the Indo-Pak strained relation has also been felt on the social-cultural dimension. Issues like humanitarian crisis, medical aid, religious tourism, sporting activities such as cricket, hockey, kabaddi, etc., and disaster crisis management should be encouraged as they have the potential to overcome political divides.

Though positives with regard to religious tourism have riders like security concerns, but religious connections between the two nations has been there for long, though limited, and at times none at all. A few years after the Indo-Pak war of 1971, a Protocol on Visits to Religious Shrines, to facilitate citizens of each country to travel to shrines and holy sites in the other country was signed. In 1988, the Cultural Cooperation Agreement,[45] was signed which seeks to "promote linkages in the field of art, culture … mass media and sports," following it up with a Memorandum of Understanding (MoU) on Cultural Cooperation in 2012. In the past, visits by Pakistani (zaireen) pilgrims were banned due to a dispute over the alleged Indian spy Kulbhushan Jadhav, who remains in Pakistan's captivity to this day. The decision to promote religious tourism was the important take away from PM Narendra Modi's meeting with his then counterpart Nawaz Sharif in a bilateral meeting in Russia's Ufa in 2015.[46]

Sports like cricket is closely followed in both countries, but it too has been impacted by the strained relations, as a result matches which take on a warlike tone have been amiss. Cricket diplomacy too, has a history as shaky as the two countries' political relations. It has, at the very least, been able to establish a mirror of peace that is frequently shaken by the ripples of armed war. Such mirrors of peace via "cricket for peace project," was witnessed when former Pakistani President General Zia-ul-Haq travelled to India in February 1987 to observe a test match between the two teams. Given that Pakistan's current Prime Minister is a former cricketer, the diplomatic matches held between the two teams in order to enhance the relations have been abysmally low.

The military establishment policies have a bearing on the cultural relations as well, despite the fact that several cultural linkages run deep into history and are closely knitted. Be it the fashion industry or entertainment industry. Both countries populations are exposed to each other's fashion through serials and movies; marketplaces such as Dubai cater to this desire. Popular Indian designers such as Rohit Bal and Sabyasachi are in high demand in Pakistan, while the Indian market favours Sana Safinaz, Maria B and Faraz Manan designs.

Figure 6.3: Poster of Indian Film

Many in Pakistan grew up watching movies starring Bollywood star Shah Rukh Khan

The two countries share, exchange, and appreciate each other's cultural pursuits with respect to the cinema industry, bollywood has a sizable fan base in Pakistan, and Indians prefer Pakistani soap operas to their own. For instance, songs from Coke Studio Pakistan, a Pakistani entertainment programme, are frequently played in Delhi restaurants. Zindagi, a Zee entertainment channel that aired soap operas, was favourably accepted by Indian television audiences. Bollywood remains the primary choice of the movie goer in Pak and the loss of Indian movies has impacted its film industry so much that they are not able to produce and distribute enough movies to fill theatres every week.[47]

Such tense relations have also affected the '*organic cultural link*' between India and Pakistan, especially following the Uri attack in Indian-administered Kashmir in September 2016, which killed 19 Indian troops, was attributed to elements within Pakistan, which stirred up anti-Pakistan sentiment across the country. Spilling also into the film industry, the Pakistani actors working in India were told to leave the country and vice versa.

History is replete with examples wherein both countries have been consistently using Bollywood as a pressure valve during political turmoil. Going back to the 1965 Indo-Pakistani war, Pakistan had enforced a 40-year ban on Indian cinema, which led to deterioration of the industry and the closure or conversion of numerous theatres across Pakistan into retail malls or wedding halls. Following India's decision to withdraw Article 370, Pakistan imposed a blanket ban on all cultural contacts with India, including barring Indian programmes from Pakistani screens.[48] The All-India Cine Workers Association (AICWA) too reacted quickly, calling for an indefinite ban on Pakistani artists, diplomats, and bilateral connections with the country and its people.

BBC's Ilyas Khan and Shumaila Jaffrey stated Bollywood ban may hurt Pakistan more than India. Pakistan's Supreme Court went even further, ruling that no Indian programs could be shown on Pakistani television. The restriction extended to Indian advertisements, soap operas, and films. According to entertainment journalist Hassan Zaidi, Indian films generate almost 70 per cent of the revenue in the Pakistani film business. "This prohibition just cannot be sustained," he stated. "The local film industry cannot exist without Bollywood."[49] Despite the fact that these tit-for-tat bans are more symbolic than effective in the digital age, Bollywood is likely to remain a powerful bridge of connection despite current tensions, but such bans do highlight the shrinking space for cultural exchange between the two countries in the current political climate.

Figure 6.4: Indian Film Posters in Pakistan

Pakistani's film industry profits massively from Bollywood

In times of crisis situation, both India and Pakistan embrace a stronger sense of nationalism, a narrow exclusive patriotism which threatens to sever cultural links. Propaganda is more likely to escalate psychological barriers to collaboration, and prolonged tensions or crises are more likely to consolidate these perspectives. When governments take increasingly antagonistic views against each other, it is the cultural collaborations and exchanges at the people-to-people level which are critical in mobilising Indians and Pakistanis to collectively combat hate, hyperbole, and divisive politics, though doing so may become increasingly difficult. The real question is whether cultural diplomacy can survive in such an environment? Even if peace activists, human rights organisations, peaceniks, journalists, academicians, businessmen and the comman masses all lobby for better India-Pakistan relations, the deep state is likely to play spoilsport time and time again, as its own survival becomes shaky if the relationship remains peaceful for an extended period of time.

INCREASE OF MILITARY BUDGET

India is continuously engaged with ongoing friction and border tensions on two fronts, Pakistan and China. This is contributing to the spike in military purchases. India is the world's third-largest military spender in 2020, behind only the US and China. It spent $72.9 billion on its military, accounting for 3.7 per cent of global military spending, its spending has climbed by 2.1 per cent since 2019. Due to the ongoing military confrontation in early May 2020 with China in eastern Ladakh, India had to make numerous emergency arms purchases.

According to the SIPRI report, it must maintain a force of roughly 15 lakh soldiers due to the two active and unresolved borders with China and Pakistan.[50] While India spent 2.9 per cent of its GDP on the military, Russia and Pakistan spent 4.3 per cent and 4 per cent of their GDP on defence forces, respectively. Despite spending a higher percentage of GDP on defence, Pakistan's total military spending is $10.3 billion, putting it in 23rd place on the list of countries.[51] Apart from fighting militancy, Pakistan's defence spending is Indian centric given the animosity between the two nuclear-armed neighbours.[52] The budget document shows that the defence outlay for 2020-21 would be Rs 1,289 billion as compared to Rs 1,152 billion earmarked for the ongoing fiscal year. The increase, however, is 5 per cent if compared with the revised spending of Rs 1,227 billion in 2019-20.

Part of the excess defence spending has been attributed to the continued tensions between the two countries which have been spiralling downwards ever since the Pulwama attack in the Indian part of Jammu and Kashmir in

February 2019. As long as tensions in India-Pak and India-China relations remain, the two front war scenario will keep the defence expenditure on the upward path.

SOCIAL MEDIA

Anti-India narratives and the portrayal of Pakistan as a peaceful country are likely to continue to flood Pakistani social media sites such as Twitter, Facebook, Instagram, and even LinkedIn. All such networks are controlled by individuals who work for the Pakistan Army's ISPR branch.[53]

One example of a post that demonised India by using "*extreme rhetoric to stigmatise the Indian armed forces*" is the alleged quote from Ghafoor targeting Indian forces saying, "*We will shut these monkeys*" as shown below in Figure 6.5.

Figure 6.5: DGISPR Instagram Post

Source: Post by Instagram account @armythebest123, referencing MG Ghafoor calling the Indian Army "monkeys." (Source: @armythebest123 / archive)

Such inflaming narratives about India continue with the blessings of the deep state. To cite another example. After a suicide attacker from Indian-administered Kashmir, (Pulwama) killed 40 Indian policemen on February 14, 2019, a Pakistan-based Islamist group claimed responsibility. Pakistan's social media was outspoken in their derision for India. Accusing Pakistan, India launched air strikes into its territory on February 26, Pakistan denied responsibility, and the following day shot down an Indian fighter and captured the pilot. Such sentiments on instagram post is shown in Figure 6.6.

Figure 6.6: Instagram Painters Palette

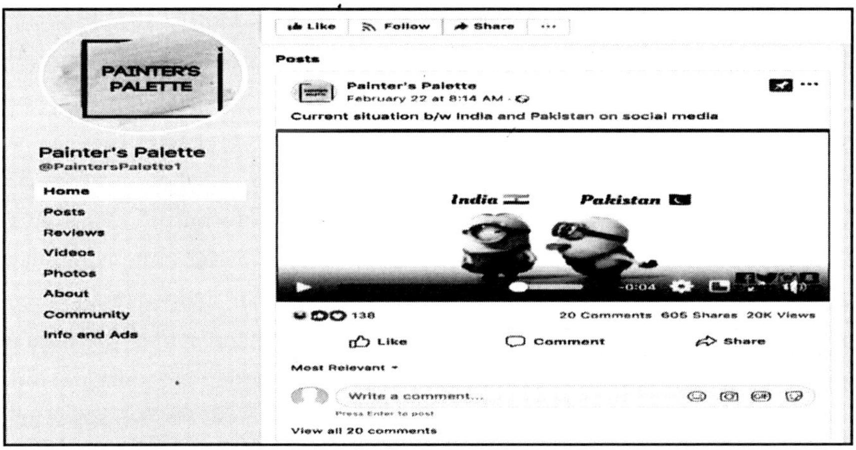

Post by Painter's Palette characterising the online conflict from a distinctly one-sided viewpoint. (Source: Painter's Palette/archive)

This post portrays Pakistan's strategic narratives, display their Army's strength, and India as an evil and weak enemy. Because of its size, antiquity, and context, the network is notable. Most crucially, amid the February showdown between South Asia's nuclear powers, they were vociferous amplifiers of Pakistan's narrative which was divided, combative, and polemic, escalating in regional tensions between the two nuclear powers.[54] The ISPR conducted information warfare manoeuvres like denial and deception, putting the Indian machinery in reactive mode, especially after the capture of a fighter pilot in Balakot strikes, ISPR has been weaponising its mandate further to wage a full-frontal cyber-enabled information offensive.

China's hand is also visible as it helps Pak in this propaganda and uses Fake ID's to sell propaganda.[55] With many successful iterations over the years, these exercises simulated massive mobilisations, augmented by net-centric warfare, stopping short at the tactical nuclear weapons threshold. Azm-e-Nau (a new beginning) further chiselled Pak's home-brewed philosophy of '*hybrid war*'—fusing together many conventional and unconventional elements of conflict, power and diplomacy. This is something the Indian security may need to be wary of, as our domestic political environment is ripe for exploitation.[56] The Indian Government finally took action on December 2021, The Information and Broadcasting Ministry blocked 20 YouTube channels and two websites after receiving intelligence inputs. Fifteen channels are owned by Naya Pakistan group, while the others include 'The Naked Truth', '48 News' and 'Junaid Halim Official'. The Total user base is estimated to be 3.5 million, their content related to India has had 500 million views. Fake news related to farmer protests, Kashmir, and other anti-Indian content were their feeds. After a month, on January 21, 2022, the Ministry again issued order to ban 35 more YouTube channels on the online social media platform.[57]

These channels had more than 130 crore views with 1.2 crore combined subscribers strength. They were all based in Pakistan and were involved in spreading anti-India fake news in a coordinated manner over the digital medium. Two websites, two twitter accounts, two Instagram accounts and one Facebook account were also blocked. It identified two networks, namely Apni Duniya Network which was operating 14 YouTube channels, and Talha Films Network operating 13 YouTube channels. These channels propagated contents to encourage separatism, divide India on religious lines and create animosity among the various sections of the Indian society.[58]

CONCLUSION

It is a commonly accepted fact that the Pakistani military's hardline stance towards India remains at the root of strained relations, and this is in the *'corporate interest of the praetorian military'*. With India seen as a threat, easy access to state resources helps in remaining atop the power pyramid. It is in India interests that democracy succeeds in Pakistan so that the dividend of 'democratic peace' can be harvested in South Asia. Direct contacts with the military would not only undermine civilians but also empower the Army, further skewing civil-military relations in Pakistan.[59]

Pak's perceptions and policies are conditioned by an insecurity complex vis-à-vis India and its self-importance as an Islamic nuclear state. It has refused to accept India's natural preponderance in South Asia and regards it as a hegemonic state seeking to impose its will on smaller states. It also sees Indian predominance as Hindu predominance refusing to accept its diversity and democratic credentials especially with respect to Kashmir. Repeated Indian assurances and peace moves have failed to convince that India has long reconciled to Pak sovereign status and would not pose any physical threat to it unless provoked. Pak should realise that using various means like, alliance with external powers, acquisition of strategic weapons, tarnishing India image through propaganda, spreading violence in Kashmir, Punjab, Northeast and consistent use of terrorism as an instrument of its foreign policy has led to a creation of hydra-headed monster which in times to come will perhaps engulf its own creator.

The key to peace and prosperity lies in the military returning to the barracks and the civilian administration assuming the responsibility of governance. Its never-ending pursuit for parity should not determine its relations with India; rather, it should straighten out its own house and rise above the label of a failing state. It is in India's best interests to assist Pakistan in becoming a robust and stable democracy that is at peace with itself and its neighbours.

Pakistan former Ambassador Shahid M. Amin, Pakistani Foreign Service (1999) eloquently summarises the path Pakistan needs to take, in his words:

> "*It is high time that the country became ruthlessly realistic about its limitations and priorities. First and foremost, Pakistan's survival must precede everything else, including our attachment to the Kashmir cause. Secondly, It has to be understood that our economy is our weakest point and has to be given priority over any other consideration.*"[60]

Unfortunately even after 75 years, the lesson has not been learnt, as Pakistan continues to remain insecure vis-à-vis India and this belief has weakened it even more. The way forward would include, unmasking of the deep state, the diaspora recognising their role as an active and participatory citizens, stress on human development, staunch belief in rule of law & constitutional democracy, practised by at least three to four terms of successive democratic regimes.

NOTE

1. Narender Kumar, "Inexorable proxy war by Pakistan, Need for Change in Strategic Perspective", Manekshaw Paper, No 52, 2014.
2. Pranab Dhal Samanta, "View: Pakistan is a threat not just to India, but to the US, its allies and even China", September 30, 2019, *The Economic Times*, https://economictimes.indiatimes.com/news/politics-and-nation/view-pakistan-is-a-threat-not-just-to-india-but-to-the-us-its-allies-and-even-china/, accessed on June 10, 2021.
3. Hovering threats are the result of our oblivious strategic ineptitude. Sixth Maharaja Ranjit Singh lecture delivered by Brahna Chellaney, on March 30, 2013.

4. US Congressional report 2021 on Pak terrorist groups, September 23, 2021, https://crsreports.congress.gov. For a detailed report see Appendix 5.
5. https://www.sj-r.com/opinion/20161017/letter-pakistan-responsible-for-terrorism-in-india
6. *The Hindustan Times*, September 25, 2021, https://www.hindustantimes.com/india-news/pakistan-acts-like-a-firefighter-but-is-actually-the-arsonist-india-s-strong-retort-at-unga-101632537853094.htm, accessed on September 27, 2021.
7. Shishir Gupta, "Pakistan's New Game Plan: capture Kabul, Cripple Kashmir" *Hindustan Times*, August 8, 2013.
8. https://www.defensenews.com/global/2019/06/16/heres-how-many-nuclear-warheads-exist-and-which-countries-own-them/
9. https://www.washingtonpost.com/opinions/2021/08/23/john-bolton-taliban-takeover-pakistan-extremists/
10. September 28, 2021, Arthur Herman, The Hill.com, https://thehill.com/opinion/national-security/573686-its-time-to-pull-the-plug-on-our-toxic-relationship-with-pakistan, Arthur Herman, opinion contributor—09/28/21.
11. See also "Pakistan—Terrorist groups", South Asia Terrorism Portal and "Pakistan's militant Islamic groups", BBC News, January 13, 2012.
12. https://www.thehindu.com/news/international/south-asia/pakistan-supported-trained-terror-groups-like-lashkaretaiba-pervez-musharraf/article7813284.
13. https://www.hindustantimes.com/world-news/pakistan-minister-says-top-taliban-leaders-born-and-trained-in-pak-101630559079232.html.
14. https://www.telegraphindia.com/opinion/why-pakistan-s-deep-state-needs-jaish-e-mohammad-and-masood-azhar/cid/1686425.
15. Yunis Khushi "ISIS in Pakistan: A Critical Analysis of Factors and Implications of ISIS Recruitments and Concept of Jihad-Bil-Nikah", *Arts and Social Sciences Journal*, https://www.hilarispublisher.com/open-access/isis-in-pakistan-a-critical-analysis-of-factors-and-implications-of-isisrecruitments-and-concept-of-jihadbilnikah-2151-6200-1000276.pdf.
16. Punjab on high alert after tiffin box bomb 'dropped by drone from Pak' found in Amritsar, recovered from Dalekevillage under Lopoke police station in Amritsar Sunday.
17. *Imperial Journal of Interdisciplinary Research* (IJIR) Vol 3, Issue 4, http://www.onlinejournal.in, http://www.onlinejournal.in/IJIRV3I4/267.pdf, accessed on March 3, 2021.
18. https://www.tandfonline.com/doi/full/10.1080/1331677X.2019.1638284
19. For detailed questionnaire refer Appendix 4.
20. Surinder K Sharma and Anshuman Behera, n. 5.
21. Yunis KhushiI, "SIS in Pakistan: A Critical Analysis of Factors and Implications of ISIS Recruitments and Concept of Jihad-Bil-Nikah Arts", *Social Science Journal*, Volume 8, Issue 3, 1000276, June 26, 2017, pp. 1-13.
22. Women get divorce from their Pakistani husbands, to marry a Mujahid of ISIS for a certain period, come back give birth to the child of Mujahid, and then remarry their former husband. Some decide to continue that marriage for rest of their lives.

23. Ibid.
24. https://www.npr.org/sections/thetwo-way/2011/09/22/140710972/pakistans-proxies-are-attacking-afghans-and-americans-mullen-says.
25. August 1, 2021, https://www.firstpost.com/india/no-govt-jobs-security-clearance-or-passports-for-anti-national-elements-in-jk-says-report-9854991.html.
26. Name of the boy is Ali Babar Patra, belonging to Lashkar-e-Taiba, son of late Mohammad Latif resident of Onkara, Punjab district, Pakistan, https://economictimes.indiatimes.com/news/defence/pakistani-terrorist-who-surrendered-in-uri-belongs-to-lashkar-e-toiba-indian-army/videoshow/86583002.cms.
27. https://theprint.in/opinion/pakistan-linking-trade-and-kashmir-issue-shows-leaders-still-dont-understand-geo-economics/636843/.
28. Amb Anil Trigunayat, "India and Pakistan: Trading without trade-offs", April 5, 2021. https://www.financialexpress.com/defence/india-and-pakistan-trading-without-trade-offs/2227030/. Accessed on May 25, 2021.
29. https://economictimes.indiatimes.com/news/economy/foreign-trade/suspension-of-trade-relations-with-india-will-hit-pakistan-more-badly-experts/articleshow/70575700.cms?utm_source=contentofinterest&utm_medium=text&utm_campaign=cppst.
30. An unpublished report by the Ministry of Commerce and Industry (2018) estimates the cost of Non-cooperation for both India and Pakistan.
31. Policy Brief, "India & Pakistan, Regional prosperity in South Asia, opportunities and constraints in economic and environmental dimensions", *The Chao track*, February 2020, pp. 34-46.
32. https://www.dw.com/en/india-pakistan-kashmir-tensions-trade/a-57102900.
33. https://theprint.in/opinion/pakistan-linking-trade-and-kashmir-issue-shows-leaders-still-dont-understand-geo-economics/636843/.
34. Sushant Sareen, "COVID-19 and Pakistan: The Economic Fallout", Observer Research Foundation, Occasional Paper, June 4, 2020.
35. https://www.dw.com/en/india-pakistan-kashmir-tensions-trade/a-57102900.
36. "Congressional Research Services", In focus, https://www.census.gov/foreign-trade/balance/c5700.html#202.
37. Milan Mansha, "Backdoor diplomacy with India ongoing, may bear fruit", *Dawn,* February 4, 2022.
38. Pranab Dhal Samanta, "Pakistan is a threat not just to India, but to the US, its allies and even China", September 30, 2019. https://economictimes.indiatimes.com/news/politics-and-nation/view-pakistan-is-a-threat-not-just-to-india-but-to-the-us-its-allies-and-even-china/articleshow/71381703.cms?utm_source=contentofinterest&utm_medium=text&utm_campaign=cppst, accessed on May 25, 2021.
39. https://idsa.in/system/files/jds_5_1_aahmed.pdf.
40. https://carnegieendowment.org/files/haqqani_testimony_07-2005.pdf.
41. The army, Agha Amin said, allowed General Hamid Gul to take former Pakistani soldiers to Iraq and Syria. In 2014, a three member Daesh delegation reached Pakistan from Syria. The delegation was headed by Zubair Al Kuwaiti and included Uzbek Commander Fahim Ansari and Sheikh Yusuf.

42. "Pakistan wants Afghanistan to break off relations with India says former Afghan President", *Foreign Affairs*, May 24, 2021, http//www.raksha-anirveda.com, accessed on May 24, 2021.
43. The questionnaire conducted by the author revealed at least 60 per cent respondents felt, Pakistan deep state is a roadblock for India rise to super power status. For a detailed questionnaire refer Appendix 2.
44. https://foreignpolicy.com/2021/04/05/pakistans-geoeconomic-delusions/.
45. Ministry of External Affairs, Bilateral/Multilateral documents, Protocols on visits to religious shrines, September 14, 1974, https://mea.gov.in/bilateraldocuments.htm?dtl/6199/Protocol+on+visits+to+Religious+Shrines.
46. Dr. Jyoti M. Pathania, "Religious Tourism: An Informal Confidence Building Measure in the Indo-Pak Lexicon?", January 15, 2019, https://www.claws.in/religious-tourism-an-informal-confidence-building-measure-in-the-indo-pak-lexicon/, accessed on May 25, 2021.
47. Zaidi, Mazhar 2019,"Why can't Pakistan afford to ban Indian Movies", *The New York Times* July 1, 2019. http://www.nytimes.com/2019/07/01/opinion/India-pakistan-movie ban.html.
48. RushaliSaha, "The shrinking space between cultural diplomacy between India and Pakistan", February 24, 2020. https://southasianvoices.org/the-shrinking-space-for-cultural-diplomacy-between-india-and-pakistan/.
49. "Bollywood ban may hurt Pakistan more than India", BBC NEW, March 3, 2019, https://www.bbc.com/news/world-asia-47479747.
50. Trends in world military expenditure, 2020 – SIPRI.
51. https://timesofindia.indiatimes.com/india/india-is-the-worlds-3rd-largest-spender-on-its-military-but-/articleshow/82305528.cms.
52. Kamran Yousaf, "Defence budget up by 11.9% amid tensions with India", *The Express Tribune*, June 12, 2020, https://tribune.com.pk/story/2241435/1-defence-budget-11-9-amid-tensions-india.
53. Khurram Husain, "Facebook removes fake accounts linked to India and Pakistan", April 2, 2019, https://www.dawn.com/news/1473284. Accessed on October 5, 2019.
54. https://theprint.in/opinion/pakistan-based-facebook-pages-posed-as-kashmiri-activists-to-push-anti-india-rhetoric/216204/.
55. Francesca Marino, "How Pakistan and China are using 'Fake ID's' to sell propaganda", *The Quint*, April 5, 2021.
56. https://theprint.in/opinion/an-adversary-india-has-paid-little-attention-to-pakistan-armys-public-relations-wing/215740/.
57. https://www.newindianexpress.com/nation/2022/jan/21/ib-ministry-blocks-pakistan-based-youtube-channels-websites-2409669.html
58. Krishn Kaushik, I&B orders blocking of 35 YouTube channels for anti-India content, *The Indian Express*, January 21, 2022.
59. Ali Ahmed, "India-Pakistan relations: Military Diplomacy vs Strategic Engagement", *Journal of Defence Studies*, Vol. 5, No. 1, January 2011.
60. Shahid M. Amin, "Kargil: The Unanswered Questions II—Time to Shed Illusions," *The Dawn*, July 26, 1999.

Appendices

APPENDIX 1: PROTOCOL ON VISITS TO RELIGIOUS SHRINES, SEPTEMBER 14, 1974

Protocol constituting an agreement between the government of India and the government of the Islamic republic of Pakistan on visit to religious shrines

Islamabad

The Government of INDIA and The Government of PAKISTAN,

TAKING note of the sentiments and devotion of the various communities in the two countries for the historic and sacred shrines in the other

HAVE agreed on the following principles for facilitating visits to such shrines :

1. Such visits from one country to the other shall be allowed without discrimination as to religion or sect. The list of shrines to be visited will be finalised shortly through correspondence. The agreed list may be enlarged from time to time by mutual agreement.
2. Upto 20 parties may be allowed to visit from one country to the other every year. This number may be revised from time to time.
3. Every effort should continue to be made to ensure that places of religious worship mentioned in the agreed list are properly maintained and their sanctity preserved.
4. Such visitors will be given Visitor Category visas.

Sd/-
KEWAL SINGH
Foreign Secretary
Ministry of External Affairs
Government of India

Sd/-
AGHA SHAHI
Foreign Secretary
Ministry of Foreign Affairs
Government of Pakistan

Source: https://mea.gov.in/bilateral-documents.htm?dtl/6199/Protocol+on+visits+to+Religious+Shrines

APPENDIX 2: CULTURAL COOPERATION AGREEMENT BETWEEN INDIA AND PAKISTAN, DECEMBER 31, 1988

CULTURAL COOPERATION AGREEMENT BETWEEN THE GOVERNMENT OF THE REPUBLIC OF INDIA AND THE GOVERNMENT OF THE ISLAMIC REPUBLIC OF PAKISTAN

The Government of the Republic of India and the Government of the Islamic Republic of Pakistan (hereinafter referred to as the Contracting Parties),

INSPIRED by a common desire to establish and develop closer cultural relations, and

DESIROUS of promoting and developing the relations and understanding between India and Pakistan in the realms of art, culture, archaeology, education, mass media and sports,

HAVE AGREED as follows:

ARTICLE 1

The Contracting Parties shall facilitate and encourage cooperation in the fields of art, culture, archaeology, education, mass media of information and sports in order to contribute towards a better knowledge of their respective cultures and activities in these fields.

ARTICLE 2

Each Contracting Party may establish in the territory of the other Cultural Centres in accordance with laws, regulations and general policy of the respective host Government. Prior clearance of the host Government would be obtained before any such centre is established. The details regarding the establishment of such centres shall be settled between the two countries by means of an additional protocol to be negotiated after this Agreement comes into force.

ARTICLE 3

The Contracting Parties shall encourage and facilitate:

(a) reciprocal visits of academicians, education administrators, professors and experts in agreed areas for delivering lectures, study tours and special courses;

(b) reciprocal visits of representatives of educational, literary, artistic, sports and journalists' associations and organizations; and

(c) participation in congresses, conferences, symposia and seminars.

ARTICLE 4

The Contracting Parties shall encourage and facilitate:

(a) exchange in the field of art and culture and in the field of mass media such as documentaries, radio and television;

(b) exchange of materials in the fields of education, sports, archaeology; and

(c) translation and exchange of books, periodicals and other educational, cultural and sports publications, and wherever possible exchange of copies of art objects.

ARTICLE 5

Both Contracting Parties shall endeavour to provide facilities and scholarships to students and research scholars of each other's country to study in its institutions of higher education and research and to participate in practical training programmes.

ARTICLE 6

The Contracting Parties shall examine the diplomas, certificates and university degrees granted by the other Party with a view to arriving at their equivalence.

ARTICLE 7

Each Contracting Party shall endeavour to present different facets of the life and culture of the other Party through the media of radio, television and press by exchange of suitable materials and programmes.

ARTICLE 8

The Contracting Parties shall facilitate :

(a) exchange of artists, poets, writers and musicians;

(b) exchange of art and other exhibitions; and

(c) participation in each other's International Film Festivals.

ARTICLE 9

The Contracting Parties shall encourage visits of sports teams between the two countries and shall facilitate, subject to the national laws and regulations in force, their stay and movements in their respective territories.

ARTICLE 10

The Contracting Parties shall to the extent possible ensure that text-books prescribed for their educational institutions, particularly those relating to History and Geography, do not contain any misrepresentation of facts about each other's country.

ARTICLE 11

For the achievement of the objective of the Agreement, the India-Pakistan Joint Commission will formulate cultural and educational exchange programmes and review the implementation of the Agreement.

ARTICLE 12

This Agreement is subject to ratification. It shall enter into force on the date of exchange of the Instruments of Ratification. It shall remain in force for a period of three years and shall be renewed automatically for each subsequent period of three years unless either Contracting Party gives to the other a six month s' written notice in advance of its intention to terminate it. This Agreement may be modified by mutual consent.

IN WITNESS WHEREOF the undersigned representatives being duly authorised thereto by their respective Governments, have hereto signed this Agreement and have affixed thereto their seals.

DONE at Islamabad on this Tenth day of Pausa 1910 (Saka era) corresponding to the Twenieth day of Jamadi-ul-Awwal 1409 A.H. and to the Thirty-First day of December 1988, in two originals, each in Hindi, Urdu and English languages, all the texts being equally authentic, except in case of doubt when the English text shall prevail.

(K.P.S. Menon) Foreign Secretary	(Humayun Khan) Foreign Secretary
For the Government of the Republic of India	For the Government of the Islamic Republic of Pakistan

Source: Treaty Detail | Ministry of External Affairs, Government of India
https://mea.gov.in

https://mea.gov.in/TreatyDetail.htm?816

APPENDIX 3: LIST OF DIRECTOR GENERALS INTER SERVICES PUBLIC RELATIONS

Ser No	Name with Rank	Period
1	Colonel Shabaz Khan	May 1949 - July 1952
2	Commander Maqbool Hussain	August 1952 - October 1965
3	Colonel Z A Suleri	November 1965 - August 1966
4	Lieutenant Colonel Masud Ahmed	September 1966 - February 1967
5	Brig A R Siddiqui	March 1967 - November 1973
6	Brig Fazal ur Rehman	December 1973 - March 1977
7	Brig T H Siddiqui	April 1977 - July 1985
8	Brig Siddiq Salik	August 1985 - August 1988
9	Maj Gen Riaz Ullah	December 1988 - September 1991
10	Maj Gen Jahangir Nasrullah	October 1991 - April 1993
11	Maj Gen Khalid Bashir	May 1993 - July 1994
12	Brig S M A Iqbal	August 1994 - February 1995
13	Maj Gen Saleem Ullah	March 1995 - August 1998
14	Brig Ghazanfar Ali	September 1998 - October 1998
15	Maj Gen Rashid Qureshi	November 1998 - May 2003
16	Maj Gen Shaukat Sultan Khan	Jun 2003 - February 2007
17	Maj Gen Waheed Arshad	Feb 2007 - January 2008
18	Major General Athar Abbas	January 2008 - June2012
19	Lieutenant General Asim Saleem Bajwa	June 2012 - December 2016
20	Major General Asif Ghafoor	December 2016 – January 2020
21	Major General Babar Iftikhar, HI (M)	January 2020 to present

Source: "Web Archive Ex Directors & DG ISPR." Ex Directors, DG ISPR. Inter Services Public Relations, February 12, 2008." Accessed 3 June, 2021. https://web.archive.org/web/20080212130910/http://www.ispr.gov.pk/General/ex_dgs.htm

APPENDIX 4: QUESTIONNAIRE

1. Is it too far fetched a thought to say that the seeds of military rule in Pakistan were sowed in by their very first President Iskander Mirza, who himself served in the Indian Army as a second lieutenant on July 1920?
2. In your understanding, what does the term "DEEP STATE" signify?
3. In your understanding what is the composition of the Deep State?
4. How deeply are the following factors entangled with or rather form the important constituent of the Deep State?
5. Is the Deep State inextricably intertwined with society?
6. When and which year do you think the narrative of the deep state started in Pakistan?
7. Will the Deep State ever dissolve in Pakistan?
8. How Islamic is the military in Pakistan today under Gen Bajwa's regime? In a scale of 1-10.
9. How the Country's belief in Islamic Ideology today, surpassed THAT existing during Gen Zia's times?
10. In your opinion who controls the nuclear button in Pakistan?
11. The first coup reaffirmed the saying that "Army has a state in Pakistan" is this statement true? or do you feel that right from the very birth of Pakistan, "Army had a state?
12. What makes Pakistan Military so powerful?
13. Will there be another coup in future?
14. How do you rate (scale of 1-5) the CURRENT public perception of the Pakistan Army?
15. Under military rule, is there more constitutional vibrancy, i.e. more amendments and changes to the constitution or less? Please cite an example.
16. Does the military need the backing of the polity for ligitimising its rule?
17. Why can't Pakistan military take genuine democracy LET take roots in Pakistan, just like any other South Asian countries?
18. Do the constitutional debates that take place in the parliament reflect on the changes of Democracy surviving in Pakistan?
19. Chances of true democracy rule in Pakistan?
20. How far do you agree that India factor is a reason for the Deep State?
21. What are the implications of Pakistan's continuation of Deep State for India?
22. Why does the civil society in Pakistan conform to the Deep State policies?

23. Pakistan's ISPR as a success story in the battle of narratives?
24. The country of Pakistan Deep State will impact India's rise to be a superpower?
25. The country of Deep State (Military-ISI/ISPR) will keep playing the India card as an existential threat?
26. Is there a likelihood of the Awaam of Pakistan to rise up and bring in a revolution of sorts to challenge the Deep State?
27. Does the Civil Society in Pakistan also conform to the culture of the Deep State?
28. Pakistan continues to have "Uniformed" democracy-meaning men in uniform are ruling the state and this has been a consistent pattern and now we see a "Couples Coup"

Note: The respondents of the questionnaire comprised the members of the strategic and defence forces as well as university students.

APPENDIX 5: CONGRESSIONAL RESEARCH SERVICE, SEPTEMBER 23, 2021

Congressional Research Service
Informing the legislative debate since 1914

IN FOCUS

Terrorist and Other Militant Groups in Pakistan

U.S. officials have identified Pakistan as a base of operations and/or target for numerous armed, nonstate militant groups, some of which have existed since the 1980s. Notable terrorist and other groups operating in and/or launching attacks on Pakistan are of five broad, but not exclusive types: (1) globally oriented; (2) Afghanistan- oriented; (3) India- and Kashmir-oriented; (4) domestically oriented; and (5) sectarian (anti-Shia). Twelve of the 15 groups listed below are designated as Foreign Terrorist Organizations (FTOs) under U.S. law and most, but not all, are animated by Islamist extremist ideology. Pakistan has suffered considerably from domestic terrorism since 2003, and related fatalities peaked in 2009 (see **Figure 1**). Many observers predict a resurgence of regional terrorism and militancy in the wake of the Afghan Taliban's August 2021 successes.

Figure 1: Terrorism-Related Fatalities in Pakistan, 2000-2020

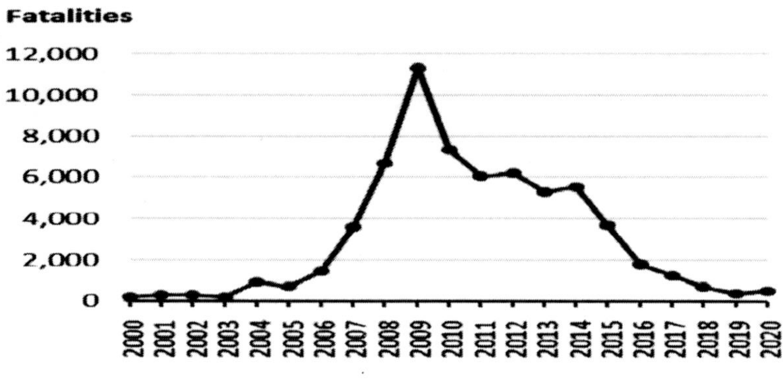

Source: South Asia Terrorism Portal (New Delhi).

According to the U.S. State Department's *Country Reports on Terrorism 2019* (released in June 2020), Pakistan has "continued to serve as a safe haven for certain regionally focused terrorist groups," and has "*allowed* groups targeting Afghanistan ... as well as groups targeting India ... to operate from its territory" (emphasis added). The Department noted "modest steps" taken by Pakistan's government to counter terrorism financing and to "restrain" some India-focused militant groups following an early 2019 terrorist attack in Indian-administered Kashmir. It assessed, however, that "Islamabad has yet to take decisive actions against India- and Afghanistan-focused militants," and that "progress on the most difficult aspects of its 2015 National Action Plan to counter terrorism remains unfulfilled—specifically its pledge to dismantle all terrorist organizations without delay and discrimination." On the topic of "terrorist safe havens," the Department concluded that Pakistan's government and military "acted inconsistently with respect to terrorist safe havens throughout the country. Authorities did not take sufficient action to stop certain terrorist groups and individuals from openly operating in the country."

In 2018, the Paris-based intergovernmental Financial Action Task Force (FATF) returned Pakistan to its "gray list" of countries found to have "strategic deficiencies" in countering money laundering and terrorist financing, where it had been from 2012 to 2015. In 2020, a senior State Department official said, "Completion of the FATF action plan is critical to Pakistan's economic reform efforts ... as well as for demonstrating sustained and irreversible action against all militant groups based in Pakistan without distinction.... [I]f Pakistan were not to meet FATF obligations or were to fail and be blacklisted, that would be devastating for Pakistan's economic reform program and for its ability to attract investors." FATF's "black list" designates "high-risk and non-cooperative jurisdictions." In mid-2021, FATF assessed that Pakistan had completed 26 of 27 recommended "action plan items" and left the country's "gray list" status unchanged.

Globally Oriented Militants

Al-Qaeda (AQ) "core" was established by Osama bin Laden in 1988 in Afghanistan and was designated by the United States as an FTO in 1999. U.S.-led forces expelled AQ from Afghanistan following the group's commission of the September 2001 terrorist attacks on the United States. Since then, AQ has operated primarily from the former Federally Administered Tribal Areas (FATA, now incorporated into Pakistan's Khyber Pakhtunkhwa province; see **Figure 2**) and in the megacity of Karachi, as well as in Afghanistan. It has since 2011 been led by Ayman al-Zawahiri and reportedly maintains supportive ties with many of the groups listed below.

Figure 2: Map of Pakistan

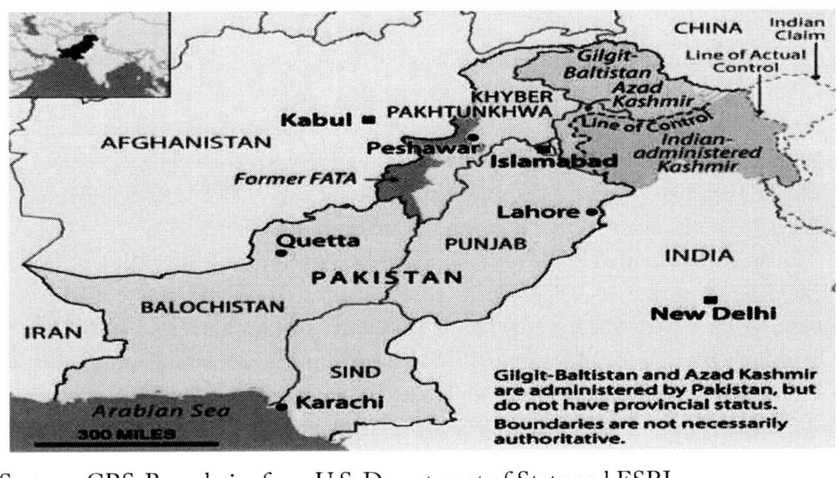

Sources: CRS. Boundaries from U.S. Department of State and ESRI.

Al Qaeda in the Indian Subcontinent (AQIS) was established in 2014 under the leadership of Asim Umar—a now-deceased Indian national and former member of a Kashmiri terrorist group—and was designated as an FTO in 2016. With an estimated several hundred members, AQIS has been implicated in terrorist attacks in Pakistan, including a 2014 attempt to hijack a Pakistan Navy frigate.

Islamic State-Khorasan Province (ISKP or IS-K) is a regional affiliate of the Islamic State of Iraq and Syria (ISIS, ISIL, or the Arabic acronym *Da'esh*) that made inroads in Afghanistan in 2015 and was designated as an FTO in 2016. Its estimated 1,500-2,200 fighters are mostly former members of the Tehrik-i-Taliban Pakistan who are based in Afghanistan but also operate in Pakistan, along with disaffected Afghan Taliban fighters.

Afghanistan-Oriented Militants

The Afghan Taliban emerged in southeastern Afghanistan in the early 1990s, ruled most of that country from 1996- 2001, and were named as Specially Designated Global Terrorists in 2002. Long led by Mullah Omar (who died in 2013) and now led by Haybatullah Akhundzada, during the period 2001 to 2021 its leadership was believed to operate mainly from the Balochistan provincial capital of Quetta, as well as in Karachi and Peshawar. It gained strength as U.S. force levels in Afghanistan decreased significantly after 2014, and retook power in Afghanistan in August 2021.

The Haqqani Network (HQN) was founded in the late 1980s by Jalaluddin Haqqani and designated as an FTO in 2012. Jalaluddin retreated to Pakistan after 2001 and his son Sirajuddin later became the group's leader, also becoming a deputy chief of the Afghan Taliban in 2015 and Afghanistan's acting interior minister in 2021. HQN reportedly has several hundred core members and an estimated 3,000-5,000 armed militants with varying degrees of affiliation, many of whom reportedly operate near the Pakistan-Afghanistan border and have undertaken numerous kidnappings and attacks in Afghanistan. Some U.S. officials have linked HQN to Pakistan's main intelligence service, a charge Pakistan denies.

India- and Kashmir-Oriented Militants

Lashkar-e-Taiba (LET) was formed in the late 1980s in Pakistan and designated as an FTO in 2001. Led by Hafiz Saeed and based in both Pakistan's Punjab province and in Pakistan-administered (Azad) Kashmir, it is more recently fronted by the ostensibly charitable Jamaat-ud-Dawa. LET was responsible for major 2008 attacks in Mumbai, India, as well as numerous other high-profile attacks.

Jaish-e-Mohammed (JEM) was founded in 2000 by Kashmiri militant leader Masood Azhar and was designated as an FTO in 2001. Along with LET, it was responsible for a 2001 attack on the Indian Parliament, among numerous others. Based in both Punjab and in Azad Kashmir, JEM's several hundred armed supporters operate in India, Afghanistan, and Pakistan while seeking annexation of Indian-administered Kashmir into Pakistan. JEM also has openly declared war on the United States.

Harakat-ul Jihad Islami (HUJI) was formed in 1980 in Afghanistan to fight the Soviet Army and was designated as an FTO in 2010. After 1989 it redirected its efforts toward India, although it did supply fighters to the Afghan Taliban. With an unknown strength, HUJI today operates in Afghanistan, Pakistan, Bangladesh, and India, and seeks annexation of Indian-administered Kashmir into Pakistan.

Harakat ul-Mujahidin (HUM) was designated as an FTO in 1997 and operates mainly from Azad Kashmir and from some Pakistani cities. It was responsible for the 1999 hijacking of an Indian airliner, leading to the release from an Indian prison of JEM's future founder; most HUM cadres subsequently defected to that group.

Hizbul Mujahideen (HM) was formed in 1989— reportedly as the militant wing of Pakistan's largest Islamist political party—and designated as an FTO in 2017. It is one of the largest and oldest militant groups operating in Indian- administered Kashmir. HM's cadre of unknown size is composed primarily of ethnic Kashmiris who seek independence for Kashmir or annexation of Indian- administered Kashmir into Pakistan. Although Kashmir- based, HM reportedly has key funding sources in Pakistan.

Domestically Oriented Militants

Tehrik-i-Taliban Pakistan (TTP) was formed in 2007 and designated as an FTO in 2010. It is composed largely of ethnic Pashtun militants who unified under the leadership of now-deceased Baitullah Mehsud, then based in the former South Waziristan FATA agency, with representatives from each of Pakistan's seven former tribal agencies. TTP leadership reportedly fled into the border areas of eastern Afghanistan in response to Pakistani military operations in 2014. Today led by Noor Wali Mehsud, and with suspected links to Al Qaeda, the TTP's estimated 3,000-6,000 members seek to defeat Pakistan's government and establish Sharia law in Khyber Pakhtunkhwa.

Balochistan Liberation Army (BLA), which the State Department named as Specially Designated Global Terrorists in 2019, is an ethnic-based separatist group of up to 1,000 armed militants operating mainly in ethnic Baloch areas of Pakistan.

Jundallah (aka Jaysh al-Adl), designated as an FTO in 2010, is an ethnic Baloch separatist group operating in Pakistan's Balochistan province. It is oriented primarily toward Iran and its ethnic Baloch regions.

Sectarian (Anti-Shia) Militants

Sipah-e-Sahaba Pakistan (SSP), an anti-Shia group established in Punjab in the mid-1980s, is now known as Ahle Sunnat Wal Jamaat. Its 3,000-6,000 members operate mainly in the former FATA, Punjab, Balochistan, and Karachi.

Lashkar-e-Jhangvi (LEJ) is an SSP offshoot designated as an FTO in 2013. With membership in the low hundreds, LEJ operates mainly in the former FATA, Punjab, Balochistan, and Karachi, as well as in Afghanistan. It reportedly has close ties with both Al Qaeda and the TTP.

K. Alan Kronstadt, Specialist in South Asian Affairs IF11934